We normally look at the Armed Forces in light of their equipment and their advanced technology, which have progressed so rapidly. But the Armed Forces is really about people—people who serve our nation and who voluntarily put themselves in harm's way. Col. Jeff O'Leary has captured the stories of some of the heroes many of us have never heard about. The Armed Forces and the people who make up that part of our nation's national strategy are heroes. It's all about people, it's all about lives.

Col. O'Leary's book is also about God and His relationship with these heroes; the One who gives them the "peace that passes all understanding." God makes that peace available to all of us if we only accept His Son as our Savior.

Brave Hearts Under Red Skies will touch your heart and challenge you to be a person of courage, conviction, and consistency in your daily walk as you keep your eyes on Him.

DICK ABEL ★ BRIG. GEN., USAF (RET.)
EXECUTIVE DIRECTOR, MILITARY MINISTRY
CAMPUS CRUSADE FOR CHRIST

Jeff O'Leary gets to the heart of what it means to be in the service of God and country: death and birth, captivity and freedom, suffering and forgiveness, separation and togetherness, war and peace, defeat and victory.

BRUCE L. FISTER ★ LIEUTENANT GEN., USAF (RET.)
EXECUTIVE DIRECTOR
OFFICERS' CHRISTIAN FELLOWSHIP

If anybody needed proof of the old saying, "There are no atheists in foxholes," all they have to do is pick up Jeff O'Leary's book *Brave Hearts Under Red Skies*. He's a thoughtful and sensitive soul. These stories are guaranteed to encourage you.

JERRY NEWCOMBE
AUTHOR AND SENIOR PRODUCER
THE CORAL RIDGE HOUR

Cook Communications Ministries

The Word at Work Around the World

What would you do if you wanted to share God's love with children on the streets of your city? That's the dilemma David C. Cook faced in 1870s Chicago. His answer was to create literature that would capture children's hearts. Out of those humble beginnings grew a ministry that has used literature to disciple generation after generation. More than 125 years later, Cook Communications Ministries is still spreading God's love through the written word.

Cook Communications Ministries is committed to personal discipleship—to seeing people sit at the feet of Jesus and learn His Word, walk in His ways, and minister in His name.

OPPORTUNITIES—AND CRISIS!

God has blessed Cook Communications Ministries. We live in a land of plenty—including plenty of Christian literature! But what about the rest of the world? Jesus commanded, "Go and make disciples of all nations" (Matt. 28:19), and we want to obey this commandment. But how does a publishing organization "go" into all the world? There are five times as many Christians around the world as there are in North America. Christian workers in many of these countries have no more than a New Testament, or perhaps a single shared copy of the Bible, from which to learn and teach.

At Cook Communications Ministries International we are committed to sharing what God has given us with such Christians. Your purchase of books or curriculum products from Cook enables CCMI to provide Bibles and Christian literature to people in more than 150 languages in 65 countries.

Cook Communications Ministries is a not-for-profit ministry. As a self-supporting organization, we cover the expenses of our U.S. ministry as well as our international ministry. This means that 100 percent of donations go to the international programs. The very book you're holding in your hand right now supports this work. CCMI partners with international groups in three ways:

- Our premier International Christian Publishing Institute (ICPI) trains publishing leaders from around the world to develop evangelism and discipleship materials to transform lives in their countries.
- We provide literature for pastors, evangelists, and Christian workers. We provide study helps for pastors and lay leaders in many parts of the world, such as China, India, Cuba, Iran, and Vietnam.
- We reach people at risk—refugees, AIDS victims, street children, and famine victims—with God's Word. CCMI puts literature that shares the Good News into the hands of people at spiritual risk—people who might die before they hear the name of Jesus and are transformed by His love.

WORD POWER—GOD'S POWER

Faith Kidz, RiverOak, Honor, Life Journey, Victor, NextGen . . . every time you buy a book produced by Cook Communications Ministries, you not only meet your personal need, but you're also a part of ministering to José in Colombia, Humberto in Chile, Gousa in India, or Lidiane in Brazil. You help make it possible for a pastor in China, a child in Peru, or a mother in West Africa to have a life-changing book. And because you helped, children and adults around the world will sit at the feet of Jesus and learn His Word and walk in His ways.

Thank you for your partnership in discipling the world. May God bless you with the power of His Word in your life.

For more information about these international ministries visit www.ccmi.org.

BRAVE HEARTS
UNDER RED SKIES

STORIES OF
FAITH
UNDER FIRE

COL. JEFF O'LEARY (RET.)

HONOR
BOOKS

An imprint of
Cook Communications Ministries

Honor Boois is an imprint of
Cook Communications Ministries, Colorado Springs, Colorado 80918
Cook Communications, Paris, Ontario
Kingsway Communications, Eastbourne, England

BRAVE HEARTS UNDER RED SKIES
© 2003 by Jeff O'Leary

This book was published in association with the literary agency of Alive Communications, Inc., 7680 Goddard Street, Suite 200, Colorado Springs, Colorado 80920.

First Printing, 2003
Printed in the United States of America

1 2 3 4 5 6 7 8 9 10 Printing/Year 07 06 05 04 03

Editors: LB Norton; Craig A. Bubeck, Senior Editor
Cover Design:

Library of Congress Cataloging-in-Publication Data

O'Leary, Jeffrey.
  Brave hearts under red skies : stories of faith under fire / Jeff O'Leary.
    p. cm.
  ISBN 0-7814-3812-8
  1. Christian biography--United States. 2. War--Religious aspects--Christianity. I. Title.
  BR1702 .O44 2003
  242--dc21
                                2002154084

*To the memory of those whose sacrifice made
safety our habitation,
freedom our birthright,
and faith our foundation.*

*We thank you.
We honor you.*

We will not forget.

SHARE YOUR STORIES WITH US

If you found this book particularly inspirational, you may realize that you, too, have an inspirational story to share. I would love to hear from you as I begin to work on another inspirational book of faith-filled stories. Our next title in this series will be:

Fire Falls at Night

25 Incredible Stories of Faith

If you have an inspirational account that is uplifting, humorous, encouraging, thought provoking or heartrending, I would love to hear from you.

Information on submitting your story can be found at my Web site: www.jeffoleary.com, or by e-mailing me at jeffreyoleary@jeffoleary.com. You may also write me at:

Jeffrey O'Leary

P.O. Box 6591

Woodbridge, VA 22195

CONTENTS

★
ACKNOWLEDGMENTS

The people in this book are those that I most wish to thank. Your stories of incredible faith in the darkest moments of your lives have served to strengthen me in ways too deep for words. The weeks and months we worked together on each of your stories have been pure joy.

I am grateful to Cook Communications for its excellent support in the persons of my editors, Craig Bubeck and LB Norton, and publicist, Michele Tennesen. I am also very grateful to the cover and interior design team headed by Jeff Barnes. Your work made this book shine.

I am grateful to Lee Hough of Alive Communications. Your wisdom as my literary agent has been so very valuable—but it could not match the value of your friendship.

Finally, I am grateful to my wife, Cindy, and my family. You have given me the courage to pursue this work when another path would have been easier. Your prayers and faith in me have been my treasure.

A WORD BEFORE YOU BEGIN

Unsung heroes—men, women, and, yes, even children—are the main characters of this book. This is not a book about war. Rather it is a book about believers who mixed their faith in God with a large dose of courage while enduring the crucible of war. They were distinctly average and mostly unknown, not wealthy and not beautiful by the world's standards. Yet they left a legacy of hope in the midst of despair, of courage in the midst of war, and faith that God could keep them even as their world fell apart around them.

So where does faith go when the blue skies disappear? When the puffy clouds that lazily drift by are blown away by angry winds and threatening skies, is God still there? When my heart is broken and I sit in grief holding the pieces of my life, does God still care? When all I've trusted seems foolish in the face of my present circumstances, can God bring good out of evil?

This is a book of hope for those who have been touched by suffering. Because the sure and certain promise is this: If God held these in His hands during their darkest hours under the red skies of war, He will surely hold you as well. If He carried them through their valley of grief, will He not carry you as well? If God could meet these in their hours of desperate prayers, will He not be there to shine for you as well?

These stories, from before our nation was born to the present day, are a panoramic view of faith across more than two centuries of American life. Those who came before you also faced the same faith-shaking storms and red skies of war we do today. I wrote this book as a kind of prayer. It was a prayer that no matter what your circumstances, you would find Him present in the sunlight of your joy as well as the darkness of your sorrow.

Sometimes the weight of our sorrow seems great enough to crush out our faith and future. Have your blue skies vanished? Does the coming day look difficult and dark? Then God has never been nearer to you than He is now. I cannot promise that you will find all your answers in this book, but you will find a God big enough to hold all of your questions.

More than this, He is waiting to give you strength that only He can give. He is waiting to give you a "Brave Heart under Red Skies."

RED SKIES IN FLIGHT

*When a flight is proceeding incredibly
well, something was forgotten.*
Robert Livingston, Flying the Aeronca

*The only time an aircraft has too much fuel
on board is when it is on fire.*
Sir Charles Kingsford Smith

*Flexible is much too rigid; in aviation you
have to be fluid.*
Verne Jobst

Never fly the "A" model of anything.
Ed Thompson

*Never fly anything that doesn't have the
paint worn off the rudder pedals.*
Harry Bill

*Keep thy airspeed up, lest the earth come
from below and smite thee.*
William Kershner

*When a prang [crash] seems inevitable,
endeavour to strike the softest, cheapest
object in the vicinity, as slowly and gently
as possible.*
Advice given to RAF pilots during WWII

*The Cub is the safest airplane in the
world; it can just barely kill you.*
Attributed to Max Stanley, Northrop test pilot

*Though I fly through the valley of death I
shall fear no evil, for I am at 80,000 feet
and climbing.*
Sign over the entrance to the SR-71 operating location on
Kadena AB, Okinawa:

*You've never been lost until you've been
lost at Mach 3.*
Paul F. Crickmore

*Never fly in the same cockpit with someone
braver than you.*
Richard Herman Jr., in *Firebreak*

FLAK AT TWELVE O'CLOCK

★

LT. COL. ART SMITH, U.S. AIR FORCE (RET)

*Trust in the LORD with all your heart, and lean not on
your own understanding; in all your ways
acknowledge Him, and He shall direct your paths.*
(Proverbs 3:5, 6, NKJV)

It was Christmas the first time I left the security of my home and family. I was a green B-52 navigator, sent to fly over Vietnamese territory in late December 1968.

We were flying out of Guam and U Tapao Air Base, Thailand, initially in what was termed ArcLight. The weather was always wet; the only question was how much rain were we going to get today. At our daily weather briefings we were always assured that the morning showers would cease by noon.

It was my fifth mission when I realized the deadly significance of what I was doing. I was the lead navigator in a cell of three B-52s headed for a target in South Vietnam. That sortie began much like the previous four missions with a refueling near the Philippines and four hours of flight to the Vietnamese coast. I directed the cell to the initial point (IP), where we began to run our checklists for the bomb run. Just prior to reaching the IP, I contacted our ground site, which was known as "Sky Spot." The ground site served to coordinate our flight and bomb release as we neared our target.

"Sky Spot, Sky Spot, this is Peach Cell inbound."

A few seconds passed, and the radio crackled, "Roger Peach One, authenticate code Alpha Bravo."

I looked up the correct response code and answered, "Roger Sky Spot, Peach One authenticates, Whisky Romeo." A few more seconds passed, and then ground control came back up again.

"Peach One, we paint your beacon at ninety miles at bearing 030 degrees.

"Affirmative, Sky Spot, standing by your instructions."

"Peach One, come to heading 065 degrees.

"065, Peach One."

With one minute to go we connected the bomb release inter-connect switch (BRIC), allowing the weapons to release when we lifted the red-guarded bomb release switches. Thirty seconds to target, we initiated the opening of the bomb bay doors.

"Peach One, come right to 070."

"070, Peach One." The pilot responded and turned the plane gently to the right a few degrees.

We were now ten seconds to bomb release.

"Peach One, I have you correcting to course. Come further right to 072. Stand by my countdown"

"072, Peach One."

"Peach One. Countdown, Ten, nine, eight, seven . . ."

The bombardier pulled the red guards up from over the bomb release switches and awaited the "Hack" command from the ground site.

"Six, five, four, three . . ."

At the count of two, the bombardier would put his hand on the bomb release switch.

The navigator held a pair of sharp-pointed dividers in his left hand near the switch. If for any reason, the bombardier put his hand near the bomb release switch prior to the count of "two," the navigator was authorized to stab the bombardier in the back of his hand. No one wanted 108 conventional bombs to release upon friendly forces because we had gotten a little anxious. This was serious business.

"Two, one, HACK!"

At the HACK command, we dropped our weapons. The two B-52s following in our cell dropped at fifteen-second intervals after our release. As the 81,000 pounds of lead weight dropped from the belly of our plane, the aircraft lurched skyward as though someone had reached down and pulled it upwards at two hundred feet a second. It's quite a feeling when your seat is being pushed up to your chest.

As soon as the pilot gained control of the aircraft, I climbed out of my seat. Sometimes not all of the weapons released, and my job was to crawl back into the bomb bay and determine whether we had any weapons hung up there. That night, all had released, and we could land safely without worrying about a bomb exploding in the aircraft.

As I turned around and began my crawl back into the cockpit, I felt an explosion, and the aircraft shuddered. My heart began to beat pretty firmly, and my adrenaline was pumping. My first four missions had been a cakewalk, but now, for the first time in my combat flying career, I felt my life was truly at risk. I got back into my seat and buckled my belt, waiting for the thuds, booms, and shaking and shuddering of the aircraft to cease.

I was a young lieutenant navigator in my squadron, but I had earned the respect of my peers by my consistent performance. I really enjoyed being a navigator—at least up until now. We finally cleared the flak that had been around us and landed safely at Guam.

Since I had performed well to this point, the operations officer had taken a particular interest in me. He said my chances for good assignments and promotions would be enhanced if I were a pilot. He even offered to help me apply for pilot school and assured me of his help in getting me in.

Sitting in the B-52 that night with the artillery exploding all around me, I thought, "Anything has to be better than sitting in the hole waiting for whatever fate brings." At least as a pilot, I could steer the aircraft and control things. As the navigator, I was at the mercy of uncaring fate—or so I thought.

Besides, I was tired of the months of temporary duty overseas and the long separations from my family. Becoming a pilot would provide new opportunities for leadership and career advancement. I decided that night to put in for pilot training at the first opportunity. The next day I picked up and filled out the paperwork.

I had felt God leading me professionally as early as my college days. But somehow I didn't feel comfortable praying about this new opportunity or consulting my wife about it. I just saw the advantages and went ahead with my plan.

True to his word, the operations officer got me into school, and I was on my way. Life was going to be goooood!

As soon as I passed the solo phase in both the small Cessna T-41 and T-37 jet trainers, I was on to acrobatic maneuvers. I began the day flying with an instructor, demonstrating all the maneuvers I would be evaluated on during my solo ride. Everything went so well that my instructor directed me to fly back to the base to drop him off. I followed his orders and then headed back out to the training area solo. This was it!

I began the procedure by flying a loop. As I came over the top of the loop, the airplane went into a spin. Though I tried the spin recovery twice, the T-37 continued to plummet to the earth. The altimeter passed through five thousand feet, and I thought how ironic it was that I survived combat in Vietnam and now was about to die over an Arizona desert. The emergency manual calls for the pilot to eject at ten thousand feet in uncontrolled situations, but I had lost half of that altitude attempting two recovery maneuvers. At this point it was clear the aircraft was doomed to crash.

I had memorized and practiced the ejection procedure hundreds of times . . . on the ground. In flight, it was a completely different matter. Yet I knew if I didn't do something now I would join a long list of dead student pilots. It was at that moment that I felt the presence of God as never before. I pulled the ejection handles, and moments later I found myself in a chute and then safely on the ground.

When I ejected out of the aircraft I was about fifteen hundred feet above the ground. The last thing I remembered was the canopy exploding above me and flying off the airplane. I don't remember the parachute sequence at all and was on the ground moments later.

As I sat there in a daze, trying to determine whether the whole thing had been a dream, a sharp pain in my hip made me realize that this was no nightmare—it was a very painful reality. As I tried to recover my short-term memory, many facts seemed to be missing. I stood up and managed to fall into cactus, getting stuck in my legs, hands, and in my mouth. I was in such a state of fog and confusion that the longer I was on the ground the more trouble I managed to get into.

The safety and recovery crew picked me up by helicopter, and we returned to the base. After a few days of evaluation, the examining board could find no fault with my handling of the emergency. They gave me the choice to start over in pilot training or to return to the B-52 as a navigator. This time, I prayed for God's guidance in making my decision.

I felt Him leading me to return to my navigator career. While it meant more duty away from my family and many more missions over Vietnam, I felt that I could not refuse God's leading. A week later I returned to my unit. I flew mission after mission, month after month, still in the hole of the aircraft while flak continued to explode around me. But I had felt God leading me, and I had to trust Him now.

Christmas had come again, and here I was back flying in Vietnam. But things were different this time. It was 1972, and President Nixon had called for the resumption of bombing North Vietnam. His goal was to gain the release of the prisoners of war held in and around Hanoi. My crew was assigned to the second wave of B-52 flights that were participating in Linebacker II, which started on December 18. As we approached the Philippines to complete our in-flight refueling, the tankers that were supposed to meet us were delayed. It was mission number 125, a far cry from my number 5, when I thought I was going to be shot out of the sky for the first time.

Prior to taking off that night, we had been recalled to the base to be recertified. There was a heightened sense of alert, and we knew something big was going to happen. It seemed almost surreal as we sat in a large room with a hundred other aviators . . . like a scene from an old war movie. At the front of the stage was a large screen covered with a curtain. When the curtain dropped, the city of Hanoi was revealed as the target.

I think we felt much like the World War II aviators did the first time they targeted cities in Germany. The words we heard were not comforting. Our superiors projected that we might lose upwards of a hundred aircraft. Downtown Hanoi was the most heavily defended area in the world at that time. There wasn't a lot of wisecracking and joking around once that fact was announced.

Now, as we awaited our refueling, reports began to trickle in that the first wave had received serious battle damage from SA-2s (surface-to-air missiles, or SAMS) launched from sites in North Vietnam. We didn't know the number, but a significant number of B-52s had been shot down. We were next, going into the same target area where the SAMs had created havoc just a few hours earlier.

I reflected on my life as we waited for the tankers to arrive. I knew I was doing what I was supposed to be doing, but I wasn't so confident that I was prepared to face the peril before me.

I was blessed to have a godly mother who believed in prayer. She prayed for me every day of my life. I recall as a child that she knelt at the foot of my bed early in the morning praying for me. On the day of my T-37 aircraft accident, my mother woke early with a tremendous burden to pray for my safety. As she prayed, God gave her the assurance that His eye was on her "sparrow." He was going to protect me that day. When I called later to report that I had been in an aircraft accident, mother was concerned, but she wasn't surprised. God had not given her the details of my crisis, but He had assured her He was watching over me.

In my small town, everyone knew Mom as a tremendous woman of God, whether they were a part of her church or not. When I was seven, our house caught on fire one morning, and we didn't discover it until the entire roof was ablaze. The volunteer fire department rolled up, and the chief said, "We'll do the best we can, but I don't think we'll be able to save the house."

My mom asked a neighbor, "Can I borrow your bedroom?"

The neighbor said, "Don't you want to stay and see what happens?"

Mom answered, "I need to talk to the only One who can save the house."

While she prayed, the fire department managed to save the house losing only several rooms on the second floor. Everyone knew that it was because my mother prayed.

I knew my mother was praying for me now.

Sitting in that cockpit that night, I remembered that my parents had taught me that God would give me peace in the middle of the storms of life. And so I cried out to Him. I told Him that I didn't feel His peace, and I needed to hear from Him right now! Immediately a song I had learned as a child came flooding back into my mind: Peace, peace, wonderful peace coming down from the Father above, Sweep over my spirit forever I pray, in fathomless billows of love. I recalled every word of this beautiful song.

I was still frightened. I did not know if I would survive this mission, but I did experience a peace I had never known before. I knew God would provide for my family no matter what happened. It was no longer a Sunday School lesson—it was God reaching down to a frightened man. I was now ready for death as much as I desired life.

"Pilot," the copilot ("co") said over the radio.

"Go ahead."

"We've got a guard transmission; I'm putting it on the radio." Guard was an emergency frequency channel that all aircraft are required to monitor while airborne.

"To all aircraft in this vicinity, beware of heavy artillery in the following area. Stand by for coordinates."

I took down the coordinates and plotted them on the map. They marked the exact location of where we were to strike that night.

"Pilot, nav," I called out. "Those coordinates are bracketing Hanoi."

"Thanks, nav," the crusty pilot chirped back. He was an old major and didn't seem to get too riled up about anything.

The co was about as green as I was in flying the B-52, so he joined in my concern. "Pilot, sir, we need to be careful. We are going to fly right down the middle of the area where they are reporting the heavy artillery."

The co turned his head and looked at the pilot to make sure he had heard and understood.

Now the pilot was put off a little bit, but he still managed to keep his good humor. He pulled his cigar out of his mouth and dryly

replied, "Son, you don't understand. We are the heavy artillery."
And with that, the conversation ended.

But the man who really knew what we were facing hadn't
made any comment during the exchange. He was the electronic
warfare officer—EWO or "E-dub" for short. The E-dub moni-
tored all enemy electronic emissions from aircraft, SAMs, and
antiaircraft artillery (AAA). On a lot of missions stateside, he
would get ribbed for having so little to do. The joke among crew
members was that EWO stood for "extra weight onboard." Prior
to flying in combat, I actively participated in the jokes at the E-
dub's expense. After flying in Linebacker II, I never told another
such joke. In combat, this was the guy who saved your life. Until
we came to bomb release, everyone did what he said on the airplane—everyone, including crusty old pilots.

We crossed into North Vietnam, and it was pitch black in and
outside of the cockpit. My heart was pounding, and my adrenaline went into afterburner when I heard the EWO make the first
call of the night.

"Pilot, E-dub. Looks like we're going to have quite a reception ahead. I'm picking up multiple hits from AAA and SAM
sites at twelve o'clock. Crew, stand by for evasive maneuvers."

"Rog, E-dub," the pilot came back. "Crew, tie everything
down that isn't tied down. We're going to be yanking and banking this beast. Hope you had a light dinner!" Then he laughed.

The radar screen began to reflect the lights of Hanoi as we
neared our approaching appointment with death. I was hoping
death might be a little delayed until we got out of the kill zone.

"Pilot, I've got AAA searching at twelve o'clock. Negative.
It's locked on. Expect flak at twelve o'clock."

"Rog, E-dub. We're going to hold our altitude. I think we're
too high to worry about it, but I'm going to start some gentle
turns to keep them guessing."

The pilot began to turn the aircraft back and forth, almost as
though we were lining up for landing on the runway. That lasted
about two minutes.

"Pilot, I've got a break lock on that AAA. However, I now
have three, no four, check that, I've got five SAMs searching

between ten and two o'clock."

No one responded to the EWO anymore. We just kept doing our jobs. The bombardier and I began to run our bomb run checklists. We were ten minutes out and had a lot to do before we hit the target. The co was watching the horizon for what we called "flying telephone poles"—that was how we described SAMs that were launched at us. Flying at five hundred miles per hour, they had only to nick a plane to bring it down. If it made a full-contact hit, that was all she wrote—fireworks in the sky visible for miles around.

"SAM locked on at ten o'clock. Pilot break right."

The pilot never answered. He just threw that airplane on its right wing the way he'd take a disobedient child over his knees to give him a spanking. We held on to our handles and our maps as the plane almost stood on its side. He moved in this direction about thirty seconds until the E-dub called back.

"Break lock on the SAM at ten."

"Nav," the pilot called, "give me a heading back to course."

I looked at my map and made a few quick calculations. "Rog, pilot. Come left to 195." We were headed in from the north to keep the Vietnamese guessing.

"Hold that, pilot," the E-dub said. "We've got SAM lock at eleven o'clock. Break right."

Back to the same world as the pilot turned us further right off course. By now I had decided that it was time for me to prepare for the worst. I grabbed the ejection handle between my legs and lifted the ring, then squeezed my legs around the solid plastic ring so my hand would need to move only a few inches to grab it and jerk it. From there, I would launch into the atmosphere. I was darned sure I wasn't going to ride down a fatally wounded aircraft if I had my wits about me.

"Pilot," the co squeaked, "I've got a visual on two SAMs at our eleven o'clock."

"Well, boys," the pilot rasped back, "looks like we're in the middle of SAM alley."

"Pilot, break left. I've got a SAM lock at two o'clock."

Great! Now we're bracketed between eleven and two o'clock.

"Pilot," the bombardier called out, "we're about ten minutes to bomb release."

"Rog."

"Nav. Let's run the bomb-release checklist," the bombardier said as he looked over at me, holding onto the table as we made another massive bank to the left. At least this will put us back a little closer to course, I thought.

"Pilot, E-dub. Go to visual acquisition of missile launches. I'm counting at least seven launches of SAMs now between ten and three o'clock."

"Co, keep a sharp eye out now," the pilot said tensely.

"I can see four missiles now coming from two to three o'clock."

The pilot threw the plane into a left bank that had to be close to forty-five degrees. We were hanging onto the table and checklists, trying to configure our equipment for bomb release. And still, I had my eye on that round plastic ring between my legs.

A massive explosion near our aircraft and then another shook the plane momentarily.

"I see two SAMs passing over us. That was too close."

"Pilot, I've got multiple AAA locked up at one and two o'clock, and I have two, no three SAM launches now at eleven o'clock."

"Co, keep a visual on those SAMs. I'm breaking right."

"Got it. I've got four SAM sightings, pilot," the co said loudly.

We heard a series of explosions in the moments that followed, yet we seemed to have escaped those launches without damage.

"Pilot, bombardier. We're two minutes from bomb release. I need you to correct course to a heading of 200 and hold that if we're going to drop on target."

"Okay, crew. Here we go. Co, keep an eye out for SAMs; I'm going to get us on heading, and we're going to pray for two minutes of relief."

The plane came over to heading, and we were straight and level again. Most of the time that is something you relish. Smooth and level flight—eat your lunch, clear off to use the toilet, grab a cup of coffee. Now it was the worst thing we could do, but we had no choice. We had to drop the bombs where they were supposed to go, not where it was safe for us to go.

"Pilot, E-dub. We've got two SAMs locked up on us at eleven o'clock, and I now show two more launches from three o'clock."

"Nav," the bombardier called out as he ran his bomb-release checklist, "I'm connecting the BRIC."

"Rog," I echoed. "Clear to connect."

"Crew," I called out. "Stand by, we are one minute from weapons release."

I knew there were three missiles in flight now, and we were flying straight and level, six miles from the target. I had my hand around the plastic ring and I was gripping it with all my strength, praying the whole time.

"Thirty seconds to target," I advised. "Opening bomb bay doors."

"Rog," the bombardier said by rote. His head was buried in the scope, aiming the crosshairs on a section of downtown Hanoi.

As much as I would have liked to have kept banking and yanking around to avoid the missiles, there were more important things at stake. There were a lot of people who would probably die when these bombs fell. We had POWs in Hanoi, and I didn't want them to be injured because we were trying to protect ourselves. There were also women and children and others who had no part of this war. That was a lot to digest, but I prayed, expecting the worst.

Blam! Boom! Blam! Three explosions occurred nearly simultaneously. The aircraft seemed to slow, shudder, and then regain its airspeed. I looked at the bombardier. He never even looked up from his scope. He lifted the red guarded covers over the bomb-release switches.

"Bomb release." The airplane lifted abruptly again as 81,000 pounds of lead fell out of the bay. As it did, the cockpit went black.

Everything inside—all lights, much of our electrical power—suddenly was gone.

"Co. Nav," the pilot said abruptly. "Check all the circuit breaker panels. Gunner, see if you can look in the bomb bay and see any visible damage from those SAMs. Bombardier, give me a heading."

"Rog, pilot, come left to 050."

"Crew, I see two other B-52s ahead," the pilot informed us. "I'm going to follow them until we get power and lighting restored."

I quietly cheered inside, as I felt we had been given a beacon in the sky to bring us home. We ran our fingers over the circuit breaker panels all over the cockpit, trying to find one that had popped out. The gunner came back a few minutes later from the bomb bay.

"Crew, gunner. Couldn't find any damage in the bomb bay, and all weapons have released."

Suddenly, the co beside me poked me and pointed at a circuit breaker that was popped out. He pushed it in, and the entire cockpit lighting system came to life. I sighed and took a deep breath.

"Pilot, E-dub. I've got a SAM lock at ten o'clock, break right."

"Rog, E-dub."

Unfortunately, now neither I nor the copilot was strapped in, and we were thrown against the right side of the cockpit and onto the floor. Fortunately I had my helmet and gloves on, and that protected me. As the pilot banked and rolled, I held onto the metal grating between the upper and lower cockpit and held my breath.

I didn't even have my ejection ring in my hands. If we were hit, I was unlikely to make it to my seat, get strapped in, and eject in time. All I could do was pray. Isn't that where God often puts us—where there is nothing left for us to do except trust Him?

"Break-lock, pilot," the E-dub said calmly.

"Pilot, come back to heading 045," the bombardier quickly said as I made my way to my seat.

I strapped in and straightened out my maps and began to search for my instruments that had been strewn all over the floor.

As we headed out over the Pacific Ocean to fly back to our

base in Guam, the electronic warfare officer picked up another missile release signal. Our frayed nerves were taxed to the limit again. In short order, we determined that the signal was coming from Hainan Island and was not a threat to our aircraft. The return flight took seven hours. Usually that was the point of the mission when we would trade shifts getting a little shut-eye, but no one slept on the return trip that night. We had counted twenty-two missiles before losing count. And as we approached our home island, the runway lights of Andersen Air Force Base, Guam, never looked so good.

ON FIRE AND BRINGING IT IN

★

MIKE SCRUGGS, U.S. AIR FORCE NAVIGATOR

And the peace of God, which surpasses all understanding, will guard your hearts and minds through Christ Jesus. (Philippians 4:7, NKJV)

Southeast Asia
7 January 1967

Dear folks,

Arrived yesterday at Nakhon Phanom (NKP), Thailand. Everything is neatly military, but the overwhelming impression is hot, dusty-brown, and isolated. The area seems impoverished in both economy and vegetation. NKP is in northeast Thailand near the Mekong River. You can look across and see Laos on the other side.

I have seen some nice sapphires at the Thai Concession at the Base Exchange. I haven't been able to make it to town, but others say there isn't much there. This place doesn't seem to be well defended. Americans are not allowed to bear arms, not even the Air Police. Nakhon Phanom is a Royal Thai air base, and the only people with guns are the Thai army and the CTs (Communist Thais or Com Thais).

So far, my pilot, Jim McCleskey, and I have been living in a big, open barracks. It's pretty miserable. Hope to get better quarters in a week or so. We fly our first combat mission tonight. The time here is exactly twelve hours opposite you EST. Write soon.

Mike

11 January 1967

Dear folks,

I found out I could get a transistor tape recorder or record player here. We are short of light bulbs, batteries, etc., though. It's mostly a seven-day workweek, so there is no time to sit around and gripe. But I can make one general statement: I don't like it and hope to come home early. There is a possibility of my coming home after a certain number of missions, but I haven't got my hopes too high. But pray I'll be home early anyway.

It's too hot to sleep in the daytime and we fly at night, but they've moved us to air-conditioned trailers, so that is good. Enjoy civilization for me.

Love, Mike

14 January 1967

Things have not been too pleasant around here, but I have the day off. Some things I need are medium-size T-shirts, flashlight batteries, and some small penlight batteries.

I tried out some Thai yesterday and got a favorable response. Haven't gotten any mail in a long time. How's the war going? We don't know over here. I sure would like to win and come home.

Have you been using the Karmann-Ghia much? I'd almost forgotten I have a car. May not remember how to drive when I get back. Keep your fingers crossed that I get to come home early.

Love, Mike

26 January 1967

I flew my tenth mission over North Vietnam last night. Ten more and I can come home a month early. Actually, North Vietnam is the safest part of our mission.

I think I have been getting all my mail, but service is fairly bad. I have received only one package so far.

Tell Randy that if he has to be in a war, and has to be in a combat branch, artillery is the best deal. You do the most shooting with the least being shot at.

The weather here is beginning to be unbearably hot. The monsoon rains are supposed to come in March or April. As dusty as this place is, it ought to be a real mud hole.

Love, Mike

7 February 1967

Just spent a bad four hours. Flew escort for a rescue mission that ended in disaster. The downed pilot and three of his rescuers in the helicopter were killed. One eighteen-year-old paramedic miraculously survived. I thank God at least for that.

I am tired of dallying around in this war. If we want an end to it, we're going to have to make the North Vietnamese suffer the consequences of war. We're not really doing that now.

I've been getting lots of letters from relatives and answering them as I have time. Went to chapel again Sunday. It's usually pretty good. Hope you're all going to church too.

Love, Mike

Nakhon Phanom was a small but busy town known mostly for the manufacture and trade of Thai silk. Its most distinguishing feature was a clock tower donated by North Vietnamese dictator Ho Chi Minh. We estimated about two thousand North Vietnamese insurgents in northeast Thailand, which made driving along the roads not entirely safe. They were primarily engaged in political activities and intimidating village chiefs and schoolteachers by maiming or killing them or their family members.

The area around NKP was a slash-and-burn agricultural area with tall trees and sparse foliage, giving the impression of poverty even in the landscape. I found the Thai people very friendly and appreciative of what we were doing and remember the maids weeping the day after two of our crew members were killed.

My pilot, Capt. Jim McCleskey, and I were part of the 607th Air Commando Squadron, a unit that would see a fatality rate of 33 percent by war's end. We flew an A-26k, a revamped model of the old World War II B-26, a twin-prop fighter bomber used principally for night armed reconnaissance during the Vietnam War. The primary objective was to intercept and destroy enemy trucks transporting munitions and supplies from North Vietnam through Laos along the Ho Chi Minh Trail into South Vietnam.

The aircraft was also frequently used to support ground forces in combat and aircraft involved in rescue missions. Although old, the revamped A-26 had the advantage of being able to stay on station much longer than jet aircraft and was considerably more accurate in delivering weapons at night. It had eight .50-caliber machine guns in the nose, eight weapon stations on the wings, and a bomb bay.

It was another hot evening when we reported for duty for our thirty-fifth combat mission. January had disappeared and February was about to do the same. This particular night we were carrying flares on the outside weapon stations, two antipersonnel bombs on the inner stations, and rockets on the four middle positions. In the bomb bay we carried two monstrous thousand-pound bombs.

As we finished our weather briefing I remembered the letter to my folks in my pocket and dropped it in the outgoing mail. I wished I were going along with it.

22 February 1967

Last night was a bad but lucky night. We got hit by a .50-caliber gun and took some near hits by flak. Fortunately the damage was minor and we made it back safely. I sure hope things get better, but they may get worse. I need your prayers.

Went to church on Sunday morning, and Sunday night we roasted two pigs over an open fire. McCleskey and I are flying the dawn patrol tonight and tomorrow. I am getting combat pay, through a quirk of flying into Vietnam every now and then.

Didn't get mail for three days, then I got eight letters, three from you. You might start numbering them so I'll know what I'm getting and missing. The food and conditions of sanitation are poor. Write soon.

Love, Mike

The 607th was part of an Air Commando Wing composed of a wide variety of propeller-driven aircraft used for special missions. Our assigned missions were frequently dangerous, and we had received minor battle damage on two previous occasions. We generally carried two crew members on the A-26k: a pilot and a navigator, seated to the pilot's right in the copilot seat. The navigator performed many copilot, radio, and armament duties as well as navigation and map reading. I had begun to practice landings and takeoffs due to the very real possibility of the pilot being killed or incapacitated on a mission.

Some missions carried a third crew member for special purposes. The A-26k did not have an ejection system like most modern combat aircraft, so we picked up parachutes as well as radios, personal pistols, and other equipment upon reporting to operations that night. Unlike most regular air force units, the Air Commandos allowed crew members some deviation from the standard weapons issue. I carried a light-weight .38-caliber Colt revolver and a Bowie knife. A few in the squadron carried sub-machine guns with folding stocks.

The standard call sign for A-26s at that time was Nimrod, a biblical reference to a mighty hunter. This particular night we were designated Nimrod 37; we followed by thirty minutes another A-26 whose call sign was Nimrod 36. The crew members of Nimrod 36 were both good friends of mine whom I shared an apartment with while in training prior to shipping out to Thailand. We rejected the first aircraft we were assigned because of an oil leak in the number two engine. That delayed us by another thirty minutes as we checked and preflighted the second aircraft.

The Ho Chi Minh Trail on the eastern border of Laos was only about thirty-five minutes away at our normal cruising speed of two hundred knots. When we arrived, Nimrod 36 was working with a C-130 flare ship. They had located a large convoy of enemy trucks and set fire to five or six of them. However, they were under fire from at least four antiaircraft artillery guns (AAA) that we could spot.

It became our task to suppress the AAA while Nimrod 36 continued to work over the trucks. We spotted a Russian-made ZPU-4, identifiable by its red tracers, two 37 mm guns, and a .50-caliber machine gun, near the trucks. We decided the ZPU-4 was far enough to the west that we could avoid its area of effective fire and still work the trucks. As Nimrod 36 went in for a strafing run, we made a dive-bombing run on the nearest 37mm. We made an approximately forty-degree-angle dive, delivering two rockets fired simultaneously from each wing. It seemed to be a direct hit, but within a few minutes the gun recovered and resumed firing at Nimrod 36. We made another steep dive at the gun, this time delivering a thousand-pound bomb from the bomb bay. As we pulled off target and up from the dive, the tremendous blast of our bomb shook us even from several thousand feet away. No more was heard from that AAA gun.

We went after the second 37 mm next, again firing two rockets from the wing positions. Once more it seemed to be a direct hit, but as before the gun resumed firing within a few minutes. By now we were disgusted with rockets, but confident of the power of the thousand-pound bombs. Consequently we made a steep dive on the second 37 mm and released our second thousand-pound bomb. We felt the familiar jolt of the blast as we pulled off target. No more was heard from the second gun.

The .50-caliber machine gun positioned near the trucks made strafing runs over them especially dangerous. Spotting the white tracers following Nimrod 36 as it made another strafing run on the trucks, we made a low-angle strafing run on the gun using six of our .50-caliber machine guns in the nose. We generally loaded only six of eight guns in the nose to avoid excessive fumes in the cockpit when all eight were fired. We managed to get several good seconds of strafing on target. For several minutes the gun was not heard from, so we began to strafe the trucks along with Nimrod 36. By this time there were several more burning trucks along the road. I am not sure anyone ever got an exact count, but we inflicted severe damage on the enemy truck convoy that night.

Within a few more minutes, however, the .50-caliber was back in action and firing at us. This time we made a very low, shallow strafing run, firing perhaps ten to twelve seconds continually at the gun and pulling up from the target no more than fifty feet from the ground. As we climbed off target I could see the telltale white tracers of a .50-caliber AA gun going up just in front of and behind our right wing. Then there was a shattering clank and thud, and I knew we had been hit. I immediately told McCleskey that the fuel gauge for the right engine indicated we were rapidly losing fuel in the main right tank. The engine began to behave erratically, so we feathered the engine after a few more seconds of distancing ourselves from the gun. We climbed to five thousand feet and headed toward a hill that had been designated a safe place to jettison armament.

Nimrod 36 came up under us to inspect the damage. Besides the now-feathered number two engine, they noted that there was a fire in our wheel well, probably a burning tire, and that there seemed to be fuel leaking onto the fire. We tried one of two fire extinguishers for the area remotely operated from the cockpit, and Nimrod 36 came up under us again to note that it was ineffective. We made a second try with no better results, and that was the last of our fire-extinguishing capability. Our hearts sank a bit at the disappointing news. By this time we were over the uninhabited area, so we dropped our flares, personnel bombs, and remaining rockets. Nimrod 36 came under us again and reported that there was still a fire in the wheel well with leaking fuel still feeding the blaze.

McCleskey, whose previous flying experience was with jet fighter/trainer-type aircraft, had one more trick up his sleeve. I had seen this before in a World War II movie, but I never thought I would have to live through it. He put the aircraft, now flying on only one engine, into a steep dive to try to blow the fire out. I was greatly relieved when we pulled out of the dive at an altimeter reading of 1,200 feet, just 700 feet from the ground. Nimrod 36 came up under us again and reported the discouraging news that the wheel-well fire still raged.

At this point, bailout would seem to be the obvious solution—but since the A-26 had no ejection system, it wasn't that cut-and-dried. There had been numerous fatalities and serious injuries trying to bail out of the A-26, and McCleskey thought it better to attempt a crash landing on the pierced-steel planking runway at NKP. He notified approach control of our condition.

"Control, this is Nimrod 37 declaring an emergency. We're on fire and bringing it in. Have fire and rescue units standing by."

"Roger, 37. Will relay to ensure all available units are on scene. Good luck."

Making a crash landing with one engine, no landing gear, and a fire on the underside of the aircraft near a fuel tank did not seem to be a very good alternative either. Nevertheless, we were within a few minutes of NKP, and we started running the landing checklist. The C-130 flare ship was also following us home and had alerted Air Rescue at Udorn Air Base in Thailand. Two rescue Jolly Green Giant helicopters were on their way. NKP ground crews, fire trucks, and ambulances at NKP were on the taxiway scanning the horizon, waiting for our barely flyable, fiery hulk to come into view.

There was a great deal of adrenaline in my system as I ran the checklist, and I had to try hard to concentrate on my duties and responsibilities. In spite of all we were doing, I was sending up a stream of nonstop prayers. It's amazing how even in the worst of circumstances, one can still find time to call out to God! I had been praying all along, but as we crossed the Mekong River into Thailand, now ten miles from NKP, a favorite Scripture kept running through my mind. "Are not two sparrows sold for a penny? Yet not one them will fall to the ground apart from the will of your Father. And even the very hairs of your head are all numbered. So don't be afraid. You are worth more than many sparrows" (Matthew 10:29-31).

Not one of them will fall—not one of them will fall, I kept reassuring myself. It was then that I felt God's peace quietly descend over my heart.

We started our approach to NKP and, though only seven hundred feet off the ground, Nimrod 36 came under us to make a final inspection. I can still hear their words "Your wheel well is still on fire. My God, your whole wing's on fire. Get out. Get out!"

I quickly blew the canopy so we could bail out. At that moment McCleskey reported difficulty keeping the aircraft stable, making bailout even more difficult.

To bail out of an A-26 after blowing the canopy, you must dive for the wing on your side and pull the cord on your chute when you clear the aircraft's tail. I unfastened my lap and shoulder belts and grabbed hold of my parachute ring. Having always been afraid of not having the presence of mind to find the cord ring on the way down, I had my hand on it and pulled it out several inches as I crouched low and lunged for the right wing. The 130-mph wind stream, however, knocked me back into the cockpit, and I had to untangle myself from the seat harness again.

As the fire increased, the aircraft was becoming more unstable and difficult to handle. At that point I believed I had only the slimmest chance of survival. I made another lunge for the wing, this time with McCleskey giving me a push with his right boot. As I made the second lunge for the wing I prayed the same prayer that Jesus uttered with His last breath: "Father, into your hands I commit my spirit" (Luke 23:46).

A second later I cleared the tail and my chute opened. I looked down and could see the top of a small tree, and then I hit the ground—hard. Disregarding all previous training on getting out of the chute by the quick releases, I unbuckled the chute harness, stepped out of it, and let it blow away. My right foot was hurting, so I remained seated on the ground while I pulled out one of two radios I was carrying and started calling for the rescue helicopters. I thought I was talking to the other A-26, but it turned out to be the C-130 that had followed us.

"This is Nimrod 37 on the ground. Where are the Jolly Greens?" I radioed.

They assured me that two Jolly Greens were already on the way. In fact, they had taken off as soon as the report of our in-flight fire reached them. I felt warmth fill my chest and run down my arms like warm syrup as I thought of their dedication to saving crews in desperate circumstances just like mine.

As I awaited their rescue, praying they would arrive before the enemy, I nervously loaded my revolver. I had never loaded it before for fear of shooting myself in the hip or leg trying to bail out. Although only ten miles from NKP and in Thailand I was in an area that had recently reported as many as two thousand North Vietnamese insurgents, and there had been some casualties in the area. It worried me that I did not hear McCleskey on the radio. I wondered if he had made it and how far away he might be.

Five minutes passed, then ten, and then fifteen. Where were these guys? I was only ten miles away. Another five minutes, another ten. It wouldn't be long now before enemy scouts and search parties would be zeroing in on me. With a damaged foot, I wasn't going to get far trying to evade them.

One of my greatest fears was getting captured—especially by the Pathet Lao. We had learned some terrible things about how they had treated downed navy and air force fliers. If worse came to worse, I decided, I would try to shoot my way out, use my knife, or even throw rocks before I would willingly surrender. I would go down fighting with whatever I had. Then, in the distance, I heard the welcome sound of muffled chopper blades. My eyes lit up as I saw my lifeline—two Jolly Green rescue helicopters approaching from the northwest.

I got on the radio and guided them toward me by giving a gyro GCA (Ground Controlled Approach), telling them to turn left thirty degrees, then corrected back to the right ten degrees, etc. When the first was approaching me I flashed a bright signal light, but the crew did not see it. Fortunately, the pilot of the second chopper spotted me and set down about thirty yards away. Out came a para-rescue medic, Sgt. Duane Hackney. Since I could not walk on my right foot, he helped me into the helicopter. They had nothing for my pain except a couple of complimentary bottles of whiskey, which I quickly downed.

I looked over at Hackney with gratitude. Two weeks before, McCleskey and I had flown combat support for a rescue mission on which one of the pilots from our wing and all of a rescue helicopter crew except Hackney had been killed. This was Hackney's first mission since that night. He later received the Air Force Cross and was to become one of the two highest-decorated air force enlisted men in the Vietnam War.

A short while later we landed at NKP, and I was transferred to a waiting ambulance. To my surprise, McCleskey was already inside. My heart sank as he told me that Nimrod 36 was missing. While surveying our damage and watching us bail out, they were hit by debris from our aircraft as it exploded several seconds after we escaped. My friends Dwight Campbell and Bob Scholl were killed instantly. I hung my head in grief.

Of course, in war there is always a fog over the battlefield and a lot of confusion in spite of the best planning and training. The initial report to the Seventh Air Force in Saigon listed McCleskey and me as killed in action, mixing up the crew members of the two airplanes our squadron lost that night. Later they changed us to missing in action, and finally corrected it to wounded in action, all within a twenty-four-hour period. Fortunately it wasn't until that point that the air force sent out notifications to our families.

My parents lived in the sleepy suburbs of College Park, Georgia. It was a fairly typical middle- to lower-middle class neighborhood. Families knew each other and most of the time got along. There were good schools, low crime, and a peacefully sedate atmosphere. Living near the Atlanta airport, many people like my father worked for the airlines.

The atmosphere in my parents' house altered dramatically that evening when a man in a Western Union uniform climbed their brick porch and rang the doorbell. As they looked at his grave face and outstretched hand, they took the paper from him and quickly tore it open.

Western Union Telegram 24 February 1967

Mr. and Mrs. Leonard L. Scruggs (Report Delivery)
(Western Union Deliver—DO NOT PHONE)
2529 Wood Hill Lane, East Point, GA

I am sending this message to forestall any anxiety that might result from news releases concerning hostilities in Southeast Asia on 22 February 1967. Your son, Captain Leonard M. Scruggs, was injured when his aircraft was hit by hostile fire. He was the navigator of an A-26 aircraft returning to home base when he was forced to eject. He sustained injuries as a result of bailing out. His injuries consist of a fracture of his right forearm. He was treated at the base dispensary and transferred to Clark Air Base, Philippines. I regret the delay in notifying you. The delay was caused by communications difficulties between the overseas area and this headquarters. Hospitalization was required. However, you may rest assured that his life is not endangered. He is in the USAF Hospital, Clark Air Base, Philippines. Mailing address is USAF Hospital, APO San Francisco 96274. I hope you have the pleasure of hearing directly from him in the near future.

Lt. Colonel Joseph C. Luther,
Chief Casualty Division Directorate of
     Personnel Services
Headquarters United States Air Force.

McCleskey had broken both ankles on his parachute landing and was badly scratched up and bloody from scraping along the fuselage as he bailed out. While the telegram described injuries to my forearm, it was the arch of my right foot that was broken with substantial muscle damage. Other than that I escaped with cuts, scratches, and bruises. I believe a part of the debris of the exploding aircraft may have hit me in the right foot. The metal grommet of my boot looked as if it had been hit with a sharp ax. Of course, we were only about seven hundred feet from the ground when we bailed out, so the chutes may not have completely deployed.

25 February 1967

I am in the hospital at Clark. I'll probably have my foot in a cast for eight weeks or so. Hospital life is comparable to prison life. I sure would like to get out of here. There is a slim chance I might get to come home for a little on convalescent leave.

The doctors here have been great, though, along with the chaplains. Right now I am under sedation, so my writing may lack a certain degree of coherence. I'm safe. I hope you don't get any conflicting reports. There was some mix-up. I will tell you all about it when I'm psychologically able. Right now I'm going to get my foot and various scratches, strains, cuts, and bruises well. I'll get the Purple Heart for this, the one medal I didn't want.

In the main hospital room we occupied for the first three days, there were three other casualties besides McCleskey and me: two enlisted marines and one enlisted army specialist. One of the marines had both legs and an arm blown off by a land mine. He talked some in the day and said he was proud to be a marine, but at night he sobbed and cried. Since the tension in the room made it impossible to sleep, I closed my eyes and prayed for him and for his family. I knew this marine was going to have one long hill to climb if he was going to make it when he got home. To this day, I cannot look at a marine and not feel admiration and even a tear for that young man.

12 March 1967

I'm in Ward 16 now. It's an open bay for forty-five people. There is only one shower (one individual stall) for all, so getting cleaned up is difficult. I have a special difficulty taking a shower because I have to keep my cast dry. I have a base pass now, so I can go to the club and things. My physical therapy is going to the pool twice a day. I am not particularly pleased with the progress of my foot. I still can't walk without crutches, or I can painfully hobble around with a cane.

24 April 1967

I had a conversation with Dr. Zeider, an orthopedic surgeon in charge of my care. He said I will very likely have a bad limp for the rest of my life unless the bone density in the arch of my right foot can somehow be restored. He looked rather shocked when I told him, "That's okay. I am just thankful to God to be alive." He gave me two large bottles of Darvon and told me to take four in the morning and try to run a hundred yards, and then to take another four in the evening and try to run again. I have to do that every day. He said I might look like a one-legged spider in the attempt, but I have to do it to regain complete use of my foot. I took his advice and started running. It is painful and awkward, even loaded with Darvon.

Mike

As I spent months in the hospital and recovery reflecting upon all that happened to me, it was impossible for me not to believe that God had some special purpose for my life. I like the way D. A. Carson expressed it when he said, "There are ultimately no loose ends in God's world." Oh, I didn't have all the answers—not by a long shot. But during that difficult time, I began to see more clearly the One who did.

Early May 1967

I'm coming home!!! Thank God, I'm coming home!! Last Saturday night I went to a party at the Officers' Club and unexpectedly, Dr. Zeider was there. He tapped me on the shoulder and said: "Your limp is terrible. I'm sending you back to the States on the next available air-evac." It seems too good to be true. I'll call as soon as I get stateside. I love you.

Mike

RED SKIES OVER THE PACIFIC

Popular Song Titles of World War II

Rosie the Riveter; Remember Pearl Harbor;
Praise the Lord and Pass the Ammunition;
Ac-cent-chu-ate the Positive;
Bell-Bottom Trousers;
A Boy in Khaki, A Girl in Lace;
Milkman, Keep Those Bottles Quiet;
First-class Private Mary Brown;
I'll Walk Alone; Don't Want to Walk
Without You; My Guy's Come Back;
It's Been a Long, Long Time

This Is the Army, Mr. Jones
Irving Berlin, 1942

This is the Army, Mr. Jones,
No private rooms or telephones,
You had your breakfast in bed before,
But you won't have it there any more.

This is the Army, Mr. Green,
We like the barracks nice and clean,
You had a housemaid to clean your floor,
But she won't help you out any more.

Do what the buglers command,
They're in the army and not in a band.

This is the Army, Mr. Brown,
You and your baby went to town.
She had you worried, but this is war,
And she won't worry you any more.

I'll Be Seeing You
Irving Kahal/Sammy Fain, 1944

I'll be seeing you
In all the old familiar places
That this heart of mine embraces
All day through.

In that small café
The park across the way
The children's carousel
The chestnut trees, the wishing well.

I'll be seeing you
In every lovely summer's day
In everything that's light and gay
I'll always think of you that way.

I'll find you in the mornin' sun
And when the night is new
I'll be looking at the moon
But I'll be seeing you.

As Time Goes By (refrain)
Herman Hopfeld, 1931

You must remember this
A kiss is still a kiss, a sigh is just a sigh
The fundamental things apply
As time goes by.

And when two lovers woo
They still say, "I love you."
On that you can rely
No matter what the future brings
As time goes by.

From Guadalcanal to Okinawa

Along with the First Marine Division

★

BOB BOARDMAN

Most of us who enlisted in the Marine Corps in World War II were teenagers. We wanted to be in on the excitement and adventure. The great majority of us had never seen a dead man. Very few of us had attended a funeral. Death was far off, mysterious, vague, and impersonal. Yet here we were rushing off to become intimately involved with the Grim Reaper—to kill or be killed. Boys became men overnight.

But it was more than just excitement and adventure. It was the tales of courage and heroism that really put the bug in me. The First Marine Division had just concluded its participation in the Guadalcanal campaign, the first land offensive against the Japanese in the Pacific. I would join them shortly thereafter, and my life would change forever. But before I can begin to tell you about my experience, and why I joined, you have to know about a man called Mitchell Paige.

Mitchell Paige, Enlisting Magnet

Take all of my factories, all of my business—all but my men—and I'll build again.
Andrew Carnegie

When Platoon Sgt. Mitchell Paige landed on Guadalcanal in 1942, there was no ridge named "Paige's Hill" there. Guadalcanal was a tropical island of swaying coconut palms; coral beaches;

sluggish, fungus-laden streams; and nearly impenetrable, hostile jungles. It was also a place where malaria was as deadly as combat. Only ninety miles long and twenty-six miles wide, this key island in the British Solomon group, seven hundred miles east of New Guinea, was a strategic battleground in the first year of World War II. The airfield on Guadalcanal was essential if America was to further penetrate Japanese-held territory.

On August 7, 1942, the First Marine Division Reinforced (956 officers and 18,146 enlisted) made their historic landing on "the Canal." Together with elements of the Second Marine Division and later reinforced by U.S. Army units, the First endured a four-month slugfest, sometimes in hand-to-hand jungle combat against 40,000 wily, tenacious Japanese soldiers. The victory was costly, with over 1,700 U.S. Marines, navy corpsmen, and soldiers killed. The Japanese were able to eventually evacuate only about 10,000 troops. Over 5,000 American sailors perished in the crucial offshore sea battles.

During the first weeks of battle there, the question from the home front was singular, "Can our marines hold?" It was on Guadalcanal that we first discovered that the Japanese were a formidable foe who would fight to the death. The motto of the Twenty-ninth Japanese Infantry Regiment was "Remember that Death is lighter than a feather, but that Duty is heavier than a mountain."

In spite of this, they underestimated American courage, determination, and ability to fight. In postwar interviews, Japanese officers concluded that "the losses suffered in the Solomons weakened all subsequent Japanese defensive efforts and reduced Japanese naval air strength to a point from which it was never to recover."[1] Captain Ohmae, the Japanese naval planner who helped strategize the Solomons campaign, told U.S. interrogators after the war, "After Guadalcanal I knew we could not win the war. I did not think we would lose, but I knew we could not win."

After the landing on Guadalcanal, the marines unexpectedly and quickly captured the Japanese-built airfield and named it Henderson Field after Maj. Loften R. Henderson, a U.S. Marine

Corps pilot who was killed in the Battle of Midway in June 1942. After that tactical defeat, the Japanese put ferocious effort and manpower into recapturing the airfield and driving U.S. forces from the island. Pivotal to winning back the airfield would be capturing the high ground around the strip, especially one of the key ridges, which had been taken by Mitchell Paige's decimated platoon of marines.

His men were armed with heavy, water-cooled .30-caliber machine guns and other small weapons. Previous casualties and malaria had reduced Mitch's original forty-eight-man platoon to thirty-three. Though they had taken the hill, they were under clear observation by Japanese spotters on Mount Austen. Artillery fire from the mountain had already shattered E Company, which was on the west flank of Mitch's machine gun platoon. Now those artillery guns were going to turn upon his men.

Mitchell Paige noted, "Throughout the daylight hours of October 25, we continued checking and rechecking our rifles, pistols, machine guns, bayonets, knives, and ammunition—and waited with some apprehension for night to fall. We knew that the enemy was aware of our position. All that day, the Imperial Navy sent warships down from Rabaul, New Britain, to shell our positions. Our outfit considered themselves the best machine gunners in the entire corps. We were all in top physical and mental condition, despite a general prevalence of malaria. Long periods of training coupled with the fact that all my guns were equipped with our beloved 'Mahoney System,' as I used to call it, gave us all confidence." (Capt. Mahoney, with Mitch's assistance, had modified the weapons to make them fire more effectively and twice as fast.)

Marine patrols reported that just prior to midnight a large body of enemy troops was beginning to move toward the ridge. These comprised two battalions of the Japanese 124th Infantry Regiment and one battalion of the Fourth Regiment. They were now fulfilling their unit motto about death and duty. Mitch and his small platoon knew that they must hold the ridge at any cost. If the hill were lost, Henderson Field would be lost—and that airfield was the reason they were on the island.

Mitch moved up and down the line encouraging every man. All machine gun and rifle fire was to be held until the enemy could be seen. Mitch said, "At about 0200 hours, in a silence so pervasive that men many yards apart could hear each other breathe, I began to sense movement all along the front. Deep in the jungles below us we could hear the muffled clanking of equipment and, periodically, voices hissing in Japanese. These were undoubtedly squad leaders giving instructions."

The battle erupted simultaneously on both sides. The marines hurled hand grenades toward the jungle edge as the enemy began their charge up the hill. Rifle and machine gun fire crisscrossed in deadly fire. Capt. Louis Ditta's 60 mm mortars exploded into the attacking masses of enemy soldiers no more than thirty yards beyond the marine lines. Some of the enemy gained the top of the ridge and were now in marine positions. It became a series of small life-and-death struggles over the entire ridge top. Bayonets and two-handed samurai swords flashed. The first wave of Japanese attackers failed, but was soon followed by a second assault.

At this point, however, Mitchell Paige's thirty-three-man platoon had a 100 percent casualty rate—every man either killed or wounded. In spite of this, his remaining troops prepared to face the second wave.

Just before dawn, the enemy attacked across the entire hill and was at the point of controlling the ridge. Mitchell was nearly alone now.

"I continued to trigger bursts until the barrel began to steam. In front of me was a large pile of dead bodies. Spent cartridge shells cluttered the area all around my gun. I ran along the ridge from gun to gun trying to keep them firing, but at each emplacement I found only dead bodies. I knew then that I must be alone. As I ran back and forth, I bumped into enemy soldiers who seemed to be dashing aimlessly in the dark. Apparently they weren't aware that they had almost complete possession of the hill."

One enemy soldier, slightly off-balance, thrust his bayonet at Mitch. The point nicked two of his fingers, but Mitch parried the thrust and then killed the soldier with his K-bar knife. In the midst of the raging battle, Mitch Paige acknowledged the providence of the living God in sparing his life time after time. A few minutes after the bayonet attack, Mitch and an enemy soldier raced to an unmanned marine machine gun. Paige got there first, discovered the weapon was unloaded, and frantically tried to load it.

"Suddenly, a very strange feeling came over me. I tried desperately to reach forward and pull back the bolt handle to load the gun, but I felt as though my body was in a vise. Even so, I was completely relaxed and peaceful as though I were sitting in a park. Then all of a sudden I felt a release effect; I fell forward over the gun, loaded it, and swung the weapon around, aiming it at the enemy gunner—aware, as I did, of a strange sensation. At the precise moment that I had been unable to move, the enemy had fired his full thirty-round magazine at me. I felt the heat and thrust of those bullets passing close to my chin and neck. If I had made the natural move forward with my head and arm for the second pull of the bolt handle, those bullets would have ripped through my head. For days I thought about this mystery. That guy had me cold . . . he really had me cold! All I could say was, "Thank you, Lord, You really pulled me out of that one. You put up a shield or something to make that guy miss me."

As dawn broke on October 26, Paige rallied a ragtag band of marines from various platoons for a final assault down the front slope of the hill against the surviving enemy. Cradling a water-cooled but red-hot machine gun in his bare arms, firing from the waist, Mitch and this cadre of men finished the task.

A few weeks later, Maj. Gen. A. A. Vandergrift, commander of the First Marine Division, commended Platoon Sergeant Paige. "Son, that was an important hill that you and your men held. It was the last major Japanese effort to dislodge us and capture the airstrip."

At Mount Martha, in Victoria, Australia, several months after the crucial battle for Guadalcanal, four men were decorated with the congressional Medal of Honor, our nation's highest award. One of them was now 2d Lt. Mitchell Paige, who had received a battlefield commission. His response?

"I don't know what other men say, but I know in my own heart that it's just like being on a ball team. No one man wins these things. Since Guadalcanal, I've said that probably the greatest heroes, the real Medal of Honor winners, were the ones that nobody ever knew about. Yet none of them has ever been recognized. But in my book, they're the heroes. I know what people say when they read 'alone' in my MOH citation. I say, 'No, I had thirty-three men. A piece of my medal belongs to every man in my platoon."

OFF TO BOOT CAMP

You will not see an advertisement that says anything about a college fund. You will not see one that says we will give you a skill. All we say is, do you want to be challenged physically, mentally, and morally? Join the Marine Corps and we'll guarantee you'll be changed, and the change will be forever. That's our commercial.

Gen. Charles Krulak, USMC (Ret.)

The airmail letter from my best buddy was marked "Guadalcanal" and was written on captured Japanese stationery. It was still 1942 and in the early days of World War II. My best friend from high school, Warren Ling, had enlisted in the Marine Corps at age seventeen, just a few months before the attack on Pearl Harbor. Now he was in action on Guadalcanal, the first marine amphibious campaign during World War II, which was reported over the radio and in the newspapers daily.

After hearing combat reports and getting letters from Warren, I went to the Marine Corps office in my hometown of Salem, Oregon, and entered the room where numbers of others waited to enlist. There we met marine recruiter Sergeant Ringland, immaculate in his dress blues, the epitome of a USMC recruiter. We hoped not only for the excitement and adventure of combat, but for the same sharpness of bearing and appearance. The Marines promised to make men out of green, undisciplined youths; we wanted that.

I had wanted to join the marines right after Pearl Harbor and get in on the action, but in those days if you were under eighteen, both parents had to sign release papers. Mom said, "No way," so I waited a year.

Now Sergeant Ringland asked me if I wanted to sign up as a regular or as a reserve. I had no idea what that meant, so he explained. "A regular marine signs on for four years, a reserve for the duration of the war plus six months. Take your choice." His pen was poised, waiting for my answer. As an eighteen-year-old, I had never made a decision like that, affecting my life so far into the future.

"Sergeant Ringland, could I go over in that corner and think about it for a few minutes before I give you my answer?"

In the corner of the marine recruiting office I mulled over these options. Four years sounded like forever to me, so finally I returned to the sergeant and told him that my choice was to become a Reserve. As it turned out, I served in the Marine Corps for four years and two months!

When I turned eighteen and joined the marines, World War II had been underway a year. My dad and I boarded a city bus to go down to the train station, where I would join other recruits on the long journey to Southern California. We sat in awkward silence, each of us lost in a private world of thoughts and concerns about what lay ahead. My mom couldn't bear it emotionally, so she had said her good-byes at the house.

All the way to the train depot, I kept trying to think of what to say to my dad on that final good-bye. I wanted him to know I wasn't afraid to go off to war. Finally, I decided to put on my best tough-guy act. As we shook hands for the last time I said, "Good-bye, Dad! I'll be back!" But I don't think my false bravado fooled him.

Looking back on my life, I see that I appreciated my dad, but we weren't really close. At the train depot we said good-bye, but we didn't hug, just shook hands. I know he loved me and was worried. But like me, he just didn't know what to say.

One of the unique things about serving in the U.S. Marine Corps is that so many marines have nicknames—often ones that fit the individuals to a T. The close quarters of living, training, eating, and fighting a war together brings a keen knowledge of one another. And it all begins at boot camp.

Platoon 1182, number 506095. Like most marines, I will never forget my boot camp platoon and serial number. A few tent rows away, scuttlebutt had it, movie actor Tyrone Power was also a boot. Some of us sneaked over to try to spot him. No luck.

In C Company, First Tank Battalion, First Marine Division, we had our share of characters. When it was learned that the guy with the large handlebar mustache was from Montana, he was immediately dubbed "Sheepherder." Glen Christensen from Minneapolis, at age twenty-seven, was "Old Man," because he was five to ten years older than most of us. A feisty little guy who backed down from no man, friend or foe, he was also called "Banty Rooster." Two men from C Company's maintenance platoon who seemed to do everything together were Brown and Beutow; they became "Bread and Butter." A weightlifter of Polish descent was, of course, "Muscles" or "Ski." Another of my closest buddies, Joe Alvarez, had a proverbial million-dollar smile. He was "Pearls."

It is the human calculus that is so difficult to analyze on the battlefield, and which ultimately makes the final difference between victory and defeat. The United States Marine Corps has produced outstanding leaders for more than two hundred years. Through selection, training, discipline, and the giving of responsibility, the corps has taken America's youth and honed them to the world's finest fighting cadre. Man for man, pound for pound, most marines believe they can match and defeat any foe. In most cases that instilled esprit lasts a lifetime. Wartime accelerates both the need for good leadership and the potential for finding it.

During World War II we came off the farms, out of small towns, from big cities, through a seven-week boot camp, and into training units. Alvarez, Aden, Bahde, Backovich, Barwick, Brenkert, Christensen—we were all privates and were "volunteered" for tanks alphabetically. As lowly privates it was hard to tell by our looks and actions that there was any leadership present. But the months ahead would soon change all of that as we took our place as tank commanders, drivers, and gunners in Company C.

A DOG-TAG CHRISTIAN

Man's extremity is God's opportunity.
John Flavel

A fistfight, a broken window, some stolen shoelaces, and a Gideon-issued New Testament started me on my spiritual odyssey.

It was June 1943. I was part of a replacement contingent of two battalions of marines sent to Australia to join up with the Guadalcanal veterans of the First Marine Division. As a typical young marine, I was searching for adventure and action, not for deep spiritual truths.

Stamped on the metal dog tags around my neck were my name, serial number, blood type, and the letter "P." This meant "Protestant," but was there simply because I wasn't a Catholic. It meant virtually nothing, since I claimed to be an atheist and had absolutely no interest in spiritual matters.

Young men make the best combat troops because they are filled with enthusiasm and a sense of adventure, and don't ask too many deep questions—unless it is just before battle. Although I had occasionally attended church as a youth, I had never read the Bible, and I don't remember anyone ever explaining it to me. But when we boarded the USS Rochambeau in San Diego heading for Australia, the Red Cross workers gave each marine a ditty bag of personal items, including a Gideon's New Testament with Psalms and Proverbs. We tucked these little bags in with our combat gear.

After landing at Melbourne, we took a train a hundred miles northwest to the peaceful inland town of Ballarat, which had a population of about twenty thousand. From the train station we were taken by trucks to Victoria Memorial Park, where my unit—C Company, First Tank Battalion, First Marine Division—was quartered in eight-man tents.

Australia had been in the war since 1939. Most of her able-bodied men were either in North Africa, New Guinea, or POW camps. By the end of World War II over twenty-seven thousand had died in combat. In and around Ballarat we encountered the Home Guard, made up of older men, a few Diggers (the nickname for Aussie soldiers) on leave, and some members of the Royal Australian Air Force.

Although we wouldn't have our first combat experience until December 26, at Cape Gloucester on the east end of the island of New Britain, I was itching for action . . . now! D. I. Bahde from Kearney, Nebraska, a close buddy, and I went out one afternoon for a pub crawl. The more we drank, the bolder we became.

The heel had come off my shoe, so Bahde and I went to a cobbler shop. While the cobbler kindly repaired my shoe—free of charge, because I was a marine—I stole some shoelaces and shoe polish from the front of his shop. As I strode out, we decided to test our skills on some Aussies.

As we passed several Diggers in front of a butcher shop, we imagined that they had made some smart-aleck remarks, and turned to challenge them. At first we stood face-to-face with the Diggers, daring them to repeat their slurs. But I hadn't joined the marines to talk. I wanted action, so I swung at the nearest Aussie. He ducked. I missed him, and my hand went through the plate glass window of the butcher shop.

The glass exploded. It seemed that the sound could be heard all over town, so Bahde and I took off, knowing the police would arrive soon. The first indication of any problem was the feeling of something warm flowing down my hand. Then I saw the gaping wound. I had severed the tendons in my right hand. In one wild swing, my combat on the streets of Ballarat came to a swift end, and I wondered if my Marine Corps experience would also be over.

The bobbies had been alerted. They stopped us and asked for identification. I tried to hide my wounded hand behind my back, but it was no use. The marine military police arrived, and I was taken to Australian Military Hospital #88. The doctors operated immediately, tying the tendons together before they drew up into my arm, which would have left my hand useless. My wrist and arm were immobilized in a plaster cast.

When I awakened from the effects of the ether, I saw wounded and malaria-infected Diggers from the New Guinea battlefield in beds all around me. They merited hospital space and medical attention. And here I was, a nineteen-year-old greenhorn marine who had never been in combat, taking up space because of a disgraceful fight with one of their mates. I was sure these men would ostracize me because of my foolish brawl.

Contrary to my fears, they befriended me! I learned firsthand about the Diggers' famous "mateship." I couldn't use my right hand, so they tied my shoelaces and cut my meat at mealtimes. They accepted me as a "cobber" (a buddy), and their kindness humiliated me all the more.

I was also deeply concerned about whether I would ever be able to use my arm and hand again. It would have been the disgrace of my life if I hadn't been able to rejoin my unit and go into combat with them. I would have lost face and honor, not only before C Company, but also before my family, friends, and the whole nation.

Uncertainty about my future and my strong feeling of shame were two key elements that caused me to begin to seek God. But there was a third factor that added to my guilt. Lying in my hospital bed, I could see my uniform hanging on the wall, the pockets bulging with stolen goods. I was the heel that needed repairing.

During one of Bahde's visits to the hospital, I asked him to bring me the Red Cross New Testament from the barracks. It had always been available to read, but because of the indulgences of the flesh and the spiritual darkness of my mind, I had never opened the book. Daily and unashamedly, I began to read the New Testament. This took courage for a tough, smart-aleck marine!

I don't know what the Diggers around me thought as they saw me reading the Bible. It didn't matter, for this was a life-and-death issue to me. Soon our outfit would leave Australia for real combat in the islands of the South Pacific. Deep in my heart I had a premonition that I would be, and deserved to be, a marine casualty of war. That's when I began to pray.

I knew only two prayers: the Child's Prayer and the Lord's Prayer. I repeated them both many times each day. Jeremiah 29:13 says, "You will seek me and find me when you seek me with all your heart." Fortunately, God looks past the words and looks into the heart for our true motives. He knew I was searching for Him. But I was also beginning to understand that we reap what we sow. Again Jeremiah says, "I the LORD search the heart and examine the mind, to reward a man according to his conduct, according to what his deeds deserve" (Jeremiah 17:10).

I now realized, through my spiritually foggy mind, that what had happened to me on the streets of Ballarat was the climax of a long series of sowing and reaping. R. A. Torrey said, "It is absolutely certain that if a man sins, his own sin will dog him; that it will keep on his track night and day like a bloodhound, and never quit until it catches him and brings him to bay." My sins were dogging me. In utter misery, I knew I needed to get right with God and find peace with Him. I couldn't go ahead in life without somehow, some way dealing with the problem of sin, sowing and reaping.

The day the cast was removed was one of the most dramatic moments of my young life. Gingerly and with great apprehension, I tried to move my thumb. It worked . . . slowly and weakly. For several weeks I went to an Aussie gym to strengthen my thumb and wrist. The feeling and strength slowly crept back, and I was the happiest marine in the First Tank Battalion. It took many weeks, but by the time of my first amphibious combat landing at Cape Gloucester, I was about full strength, although the scar was still very sensitive.

Soon after being released from the hospital, we were sent to Melbourne to await a ship to take us to the South Pacific. In the pages of the Gideon-issued New Testament I discovered that Jesus Christ loved me so much that He had been willing to die for all my sins: the fights, the excessive drinking, using His name in vain, and all the rest. On Goodenough Island near New Guinea, three months from the time I began reading the New Testament,

I accepted Jesus Christ as my Lord and Savior. I discovered the peace of heart that was beyond understanding. That peace and hope would be all I would have to live on in some of the dark days ahead, beginning on the bloody islands of Peleliu and Okinawa.

PREPARING FOR BATTLE

I am only one, but I am one. I can't do everything, but I can do something. And what I can do, I ought to do. And what I ought to do, by the grace of God, I shall do.
Edward Hale

Death and dying are subjects that every man in a combat unit thinks deeply about. Gen. George Patton, U.S. Army, and Marine Gen. Chesty Puller were cousins. Chesty always claimed that Patton should have been a marine! In a speech to his troops before the Normandy invasion, Patton gives clues on the process of conquering the fear of death.

Death must not be feared. Death in time comes to all of us. And every man is scared in his first action. If he says he's not, he's a liar. . . . The real hero is the man who fights even though he's scared. Some get over their fright in a minute under fire. Others take an hour. For some it takes days, but a real man will never let the fear of death overpower his honor, his sense of duty to his country, or his manhood.

Gen. John A. Lejeune, Thirteenth Commandant of the Marine Corps, combat leader, scholar, thinker, educator, and innovator, thought deeply about life and death in battle. Some know him as "the man who charted the course of the corps in the twentieth century." He noted,

In war, if a man is to keep his sanity, he must come to regard death as being just as normal as life and hold himself always in readiness, mentally and spiritually, to answer the call of the Grim Reaper whenever fate decrees that his hour has struck. It is only by means of this state of mind and soul that a man can devote all his thoughts, all his intellect, and all his will to the execution of the task confided to him. Personal fear paralyzes all the faculties, and the attribute of first importance in a commander is freedom from its cold and clammy clutch. There is no substitute for the spiritual in war. Miracles must be wrought if victories are to be won. To work miracles, men's hearts must be alive with self-sacrificing love for each other, for their units, for their division, and for their country. If each man knows that all the officers and men in his division are animated with the same fiery zeal as he himself feels, unquenchable courage and unconquerable determination crush out fear, and death becomes preferable to defeat or dishonor.

For three of their four battles in World War II, the First Marine Division Reinforced was awarded the Presidential Unit Citation. Superb leadership at all levels, unquestioned courage that conquered fear, and commitment to victory over a fanatical enemy were some of the marks of this outstanding cadre of men. I was determined to measure up to this great outfit that had already distinguished itself on Guadalcanal.

As we approached the formidable islands of Peleliu and Okinawa, most of us felt we were likely to have an appointment with death. Only God knew which of our names would be called in the final muster. Each man silently and inwardly prepared himself as well as he could. Some had no premonition; others somehow knew their name would be called.

Each of us made our peace, wrote last letters to loved ones, and reflected upon the mysteries of life. Some read the Bible quietly; others stared in deep thought, while others read the words of Alan Seeger, an American volunteer killed in France in 1916.

I Have a Rendezvous with Death

I have a rendezvous with Death
At some disputed barricade,
When Spring comes back with
    rustling shade
And apple blossoms fill the air—
I have a rendezvous with Death
When Spring brings back blue days
    and fair.

It may be he shall take my hand,
And lead me into his dark land,
And close my eyes and quench my breath–

It may be I shall pass him still.
I have a rendezvous with Death
On some scarred slope of battered hill,
When Spring comes round again this year
And the first meadow flowers appear.

God knows 'twere better to be deep,
Pillowed in silk and scented down,
Where Love throbs out in blissful sleep,
Pulse nigh to pulse, and breath to breath,
Where hushed awakenings are dear . . .
But I've a rendezvous with Death
At midnight in some flaming town,
When Spring trips north again this year;
And I to my pledged word am true,
I shall not fail that rendezvous.
--Alan Seeger

BLOODY NOSE RIDGE
AND PELELIU

No man can answer for his courage who has never been in danger.
Rochefoucauld

On September 15, 1944, the First Marine Division assaulted the coral island of Peleliu in the western Carolines. Nineteen-year-old Pfc. Ivan LeRoy Eims, a marine radioman, manning a .30-caliber machine gun, went ashore with a small group of men before the first wave of soldiers hit the beach.

The only people in front of Eims were the Japanese sitting behind their machine guns and mortars. Watching quietly, they were the silent, hidden enemy. Our amphibious crafts thundered across the coral reef, and the Japanese begin firing and hitting. Stakes in the coral and rising up from the water marked off the exact distance for the Japanese mortar men. Before D day on Peleliu ended, we in the First Marine Divison lost half of our vehicles. In the first eight days of fighting, some units lost 60 percent of their men, wounded and dead.

In a coral cave somewhere on Bloody Nose Ridge, sliding steel doors quietly opened. A Japanese artilleryman had the amphib squarely in his sights. Eims' tank touched the sand and dashed onto the beach, and a Japanese shell ripped through it in a fraction of a second. A direct hit.

Eims yelled, "Let's get out of here!" The crew rapidly evacuated the burning hulk. All around him on the beach, meanwhile, marines were being ripped apart. Eims passed one man whose abdomen had been completely blown apart. Only a thin piece of skin on each of his sides held him together.

Eims raced for cover, now ready to do battle as an infantryman. The sand in front of him went pop, pop, pop as a machine gun sprayed a burst of bullets at him.

"As soon as that strip was laid down, I ran for cover. I didn't get far when I saw what the machine gunner had hit." A marine lay in a pool of blood, riddled from his ankles to his throat by the burst.

Lying there and about to die, the wounded marine grabbed Eims. "Mate, I need help. Do you know how to pray?"

Pray? I don't know how to pray, he thought.

"I didn't know anything about religion. Nothing. But there was another fellow crawling along a little ridge just above us. I reached up and grabbed him, pulled him down, and asked, 'Do you know how to pray?' I had the wrong guy. He cussed me out and kept going, and when I turned back to the wounded man, he died looking me straight in the eyes."

Eims had offered no help. "I didn't know how to help him. That machine gun could have gotten me. A few more feet and I began wondering what happens to a guy when he dies. I wondered where that dead marine went when he died. I didn't know, but I was sure of one thing. If I lived through this, I was going to find out."

But the battle was raging, and he stumbled over another wounded marine. This one had his upper lip shot off. No upper lip, yet he was trying to smoke a cigarette. Eims and a corpsman helped the man toward an approaching jeep. Before they could get near it, the jeep disappeared in an explosion, with the two riders in it.

"There wasn't one large piece of anything left. Just smoke. But some of the shrapnel of that explosion had hit me. There was a hole in my left knee about the size of a lemon. An artery was hanging out like a little finger and pumping blood on the ground in rhythm, like a heartbeat. I shouted, 'I'm hit.'

The corpsman with me was hit too. His left arm was blown off. Staggering over to me, he said in an apologetic tone, 'I'm sorry, but I don't think I'll be able to help you.' Then he keeled over dead."

Eims was finally evacuated to a hospital ship. Of all the horror and bloodshed he saw that day, the one thing that haunted him most was the question of the dying marine, "Do you know how to pray?" He wasn't ready to die, and neither was Eims until he could answer that question.

"Corpsman?" Eims asked the nearby attendant.

"What can I do for you?"

"I think I'd like to read a Bible if you have one available."

Back on Peleliu, Pfc. Claude Franklin made his D day landing. He was a gunner in the 60 mm Mortar Section of I Company, Third Battalion, Fifth Regiment of the First Marine Division. Franklin wrote of his experiences that morning:

I'll never forget the D day landing on Peleliu. As we neared the beachhead, the amphibious tractor that carried my squad got stuck on a huge mass of underwater coral. Shells were bursting everywhere. I saw several other amphibs burning in the water and on the beach. I was scared. We jumped over the side into the surf, hunkered down, and then literally crawled ashore.

Immediately, I heard a command, "Get those mortars set up and firing!" I looked at my mortar tube, and it had sand in it. I reached back to get the cleaning staff off my pack and it wasn't there. The mortar wouldn't fire unless I could get the sand out of the tube. I looked behind me, thinking I might have dropped the staff while crawling up the beach. Almost in panic, I prayed, "Lord, help me find that cleaning staff!" Then I spotted it in the surf! I scrambled back and got it. We hastily swabbed out the tube and moments later had it firing.

Shortly we moved inland amid terrible noise, smoke, and confusion. We realized that we had been separated from the rest of our company. Then we heard a lot of noise and machine gun fire behind us. We spotted two U.S. Sherman tanks and felt somewhat relieved . . . for a few seconds. Then we realized that these tanks were headed right toward us, shooting up everything in front of them with their machine guns and 75 mm cannon. Either we had strayed out into no-man's-land or the tanks had come in behind us instead of on our flank. Someone yelled, "Let's get out of here!" All of the mortar section except Ed Mahoney and me took off running laterally away from the tanks.

Mahoney and I found a partial cover behind a small pile of coral rocks. We were afraid that if we stood up to run, the gunner in the tank would mow us down before he realized we were marines. He was traversing back and forth with machine gun fire and occasional blasts from his cannon. I was terrified, thinking, This is it. I'm going to die. Then a verse I had learned years before flashed through my mind: "Our help is in the name of the LORD, who made heaven and earth" (Psalm 124:8, KJV). So I started praying, "Lord, be with us. Please help us, Lord."

Mahoney and I were flat on our bellies behind the rocks, which were no more than eighteen inches high, when the machine gun started spraying the rocks, sending coral chips and debris all over us. At the same time, a blast from the cannon literally lifted us off the ground. It dazed us for a few seconds. Then Mahoney said, "I'm hit! I'm hit!" He put a hand to his eyes and brought it down covered with blood. Then I remembered the Twenty-third Psalm and started mentally reciting. Yea, though I walk through the valley of the shadow of death, I will fear no evil; for thou art with me.

I suddenly experienced a calmness and confidence that I hadn't had before. I seemed to feel the presence of God. Suddenly the tank veered off at an angle. We crawled around the rocks like squirrels around a tree, to keep from being seen. After the tank passed us, we ran up behind it and knocked on it, and it stopped.

This was my closest brush with death. Mahoney only had a small cut in one eyebrow, probably from a piece of flying rock. I suffered no injuries.

Did the Lord hear my prayer and turn that tank away from us, or did it just happen to veer at that moment? It can't be proven, but I believe our narrow escape was the result of my prayer. And I've been a strong believer in the power of prayer ever since.

Pvt. Charles "Chick" Owen was certain this was the day he would die. It was early morning, D day, September 15, 1944, and Owen had landed in the first wave of marines to come ashore on Peleliu's Orange Beach Three.

He was flat on his stomach in the white sand, pinned down by Japanese gunfire. Ahead of him in the dark jungle and coral ridges were more than ten thousand Japanese trying to kill him. Behind him more marines continued to stream ashore. He couldn't go back and was too scared to move forward. Though all combat marines had been trained over and over to get off an exposed beach, Owen and his buddies were frozen in fear. They felt it would be suicide to move.

Said Owen, "Everyone on that beach was praying, either desperately in their heads or out loud." He saw torn bodies and body parts strewn around him, while bullets were zinging over his head and hitting the sand beside him. He was seeing and hearing the realities of war, not the romantic, exciting picture he had imagined.

Two years earlier, lying about his age, Owen had joined the marines in Georgia . . . at the age of fourteen! Now, at sixteen, he was certain he and his buddies would not survive the first day of battle. Everyone on the beach lay stretched out flat so they wouldn't be a target for the Japanese. Those who did move forward into the jungle crawled as low to the ground as they could. Owen said, "The noise of the incoming fire was such that voice contact was almost impossible; the artillery, antitank, mortar, machine gun, and other small arms fire were dealing out death by the wholesale upon the assaulting marines, particularly those who remained on the beach."

Then Owen saw something he couldn't believe. A man stood up and walked right toward him and his praying buddies. He was a marine major from some other company, armed with a tommy gun and carrying a Japanese shovel slung over his shoulder. This mysterious officer, outwardly fearless, had his major's insignia in plain sight on his collar, rather than hidden on the underside where it would not attract enemy snipers.

As the major came toward the young marines, Owen heard a very loud voice. "I would describe it as a booming voice, one that could be heard over all the accompanying noises of battle, and one I will never forget. It still rings in my ears today: 'Get off this beach or I'll shoot your butt!' "

The major's commanding presence, courage under fire, and bravery were the answer to the young marines' prayers. It was either the Japanese mortars or the wrath of the unknown major. The choice was easy. The men moved inland on the double.

Owen later learned that the next mortar barrage exploded precisely where they had been lying. He says, "If that major hadn't been on that beach, on his own, no one having told him to do it, I would have been dead right there, at age sixteen."

Charles Owen and his outfit moved inland, taking bloody yard after yard from the enemy who had pledged to fight to the death. That same night those persistent Japanese mortar shells, which had been unable to hit Owen on the beach, finally caught up with him. Wounded in the neck, he was evacuated to a hospital ship for a short time, but soon rejoined what remained of his unit and finished the battle of Peleliu.

The commanding general of the First Marine Division had issued a communiqué four days before embarking for Peleliu from Guadalcanal. It stated with great confidence and certainty that Peleliu would be a "short one, a quickie. Rough but fast. We'll be through in three days. It might take only two."

Capt. John Heath, our C Company commander, was directing fire from the back of one of our tanks when a sniper shot him between the eyes. John Heath was one of our finest officers. He had molded C Company into a well-trained, disciplined, tough outfit with high esprit. Most of us simply couldn't believe he was dead. But death comes for everyone at some point. If ever the men of the First Marine Division needed the help and intervention of angels, it was on this terrible island of judgment and multiplying casualties.

The scorching heat was our enemy as well. Peleliu was only seven degrees off the equator. Each day we fought in 110-degree heat. Every marine came ashore with two full canteens of water, but once ashore these were quickly emptied. Water was extremely scarce, especially when the beachhead was so precarious. Some Marines low on water and ammunition resorted to drawing brackish water from the bottom of shell holes with dead, decaying, and bloated bodies only a few feet away.

A two- or three-day struggle? It took over one month to capture this island! Death, the king of terrors, held court on that two-by-six-mile jungle-covered, coral outcropping in the Pacific. He held out his scepter, beckoning forth over ten thousand young Japanese men. No one has ever known the exact count. Death was more selective with the 28,484 men of the First Marine Division Reinforced. Before the invasion, the division had estimated five hundred marine casualties on D day. The first day on that narrow and precariously held beachhead, it cost us over twice that many: 1,148 wounded, 92 killed, and 58 missing in action. In the end 1,252 marines and 404 soldiers from the First Wildcat Division were killed.

Death may have been in charge, but two kinds of angels landed on Peleliu with us as well. The first wore marine uniforms, but were not marines. It may be difficult for a marine to admit, but the first kind of angel were navy personnel.

The U.S. Navy gave the marines their best. Doctors, corpsmen, and chaplains were well-trained angels of mercy. They offered us not only the finest of service physically and spiritually, but they also gave themselves sacrificially. Ask any combat marine how he feels about these "docs," surgeons, chaplains, and navy nurses aboard hospital ships. Many will say without hesitation that we would not be here today if it were not for these rough-clad, tough-talking angels of mercy. There was a poem written then that so completely described them.

Who Taught You, Corpsman?

Who taught you, grimy corpsman?
You who first bound up the nation's
    wounded,
Kneeling on the battlefield,
A specialist in stanching blood
Who knows no bounds to valor.

Who taught you, grimy corpsman,
The Hippocratic lies that the living tell
    the dying?
The gruff thumbs up,
The noncommittal nod.
Do you know you're lying?

Who taught you, grimy corpsman,
To crawl out under deadly fire?
To ease the pain of the last few breaths
With cooling hands
And reassuring smile.

Who taught you, grimy corpsman,
As you fight death in death's own grim
    arena?
I know who taught you, grimy corpsman,
This compassion for the wounded
Must be taught by God.
    —Ken Gruebel

Reprinted by permission of Leatherneck magazine

Tom Lea, a Life magazine war artist, landed on Peleliu fifteen minutes after the first wave on D day, with Headquarters Company, Seventh Marine Regiment. Lea described these navy saviors in action as he came across them in a huge shell hole on the narrow beachhead:

> About thirty paces back of the Japanese trench, a sick bay had been established in a big shell crater made by one of our battleship guns. Lying around it were pieces of shrapnel over a foot long. In the center of the crater at the bottom a doctor was working on the worst of the stretcher cases. Corpsmen, four to a stretcher, came in continually with their bloody loads. The doctor had attached plasma bottles to the top of a broken tree stump and was giving transfusions as fast as he could after rough surgery. Corpsmen plied tourniquets, sulfa, morphine, and handled the walking wounded and lighter cases with first aid. The padre stood by with two canteens and a Bible, helping. He was deeply and visibly moved by the patient suffering and death. He looked very lonely, very close to God, as he bent over the shattered men so far from home. Corpsmen put a poncho, a shirt, a rag, anything handy, over the gray faces of the dead and carried them to a line on the beach, under a tarpaulin, to await the digging of graves.[2]

There was a second kind of angel on Peleliu. In several cases the second type thought it good to team up with the first ones and give a helping, saving hand in the midst of the carnage of battle and death. They also had a penchant for dressing in marine dungarees and helmets.

Joe Marquez from Los Angeles, a tall, athletic basketball MVP-award winner and student body president in high school, had joined the navy in 1943. In San Diego he underwent intense hospital corpsman training. Although he didn't know it at the time, all of his training was for the one unforgettable battle of Peleliu.

Joe was an angel of mercy to marines of the Fifth Marine Regiment. Several owe their lives to him. But in the midst of Peleliu's crisis, Joe encountered the second kind of angel.

I landed on Peleliu on September 15, 1944, with H and S companies. I was assigned to the battalion aid station. My job was to further treat and evacuate the wounded as they came off the lines. My first taste of fear and helplessness came as we were unloading supplies from the Amtrac. The mortar and artillery we were receiving was terrible. Later that day we received another heavy shelling, wounding many and killing some in both companies. One of the marines had an arm and leg blown off, and this affected me deeply because I could not save him. I thought about this marine when I prayed.

Although I felt that I would not be killed, I did have a feeling that I would be wounded. I prayed that I would not be disfigured or suffer the loss of a limb. The longer the campaign lasted the more I thought about the loss of a limb. I told God that if I had to lose a limb to please make it a leg. My father was a paraplegic, and he was able to get around. I felt I could still work as long as I had my arms.

The first night on Peleliu I was unable to sleep, but it didn't matter as I was told to report to duty. The next morning after we took the airfield, I found G Company and stayed with them for three weeks. I enjoyed working with the marines. We seemed to form a bond. My only close call during that period was when we were hit by friendly fire and I received a small laceration on my forehead. After being relieved I returned to H and S companies, where I had some hot chow and two good nights' rest. I was then assigned to Fox Company.

I do not remember any names of the members of the platoon. The lieutenant I remember only as "Meatball." That evening a mortar shell hit us, and we had a couple of wounded, including the other corpsman. The following day we moved up onto Bloody Nose Ridge and hooked up with another platoon. We were still understaffed, but we did have three corpsmen and one lieutenant.

About 4 A.M. on Friday the thirteenth, the Japanese were able to climb the ridge and lob some grenades into our lines. When a grenade exploded I felt my leg rise, and the first thing I thought about was the marine who had lost his arm and leg. I was scared, and I do not know what I would have done if the person next to me had not started yelling that he had been hit. I was able to calm this person, and then I was able to do what I had been trained to do.

I began to crawl around to assess the damage and see who needed to be treated first. One of the corpsmen, Ken, was the most seriously wounded, and I decided to give him a unit of plasma. I could not see his veins in the dark and asked the lieutenant if we could get a flare sent over our area. His reply was, "You're in charge, Doc!" With the light from the flare, I was able to start the plasma. A marine volunteered to watch the plasma so that I could take care of the other wounded.

It was at this time that I heard a voice say, "I'm a corpsman, can I help?" All night long we labored side by side. At daylight some stretcher bearers and a corpsman came on the scene, and the corpsman said, "I hear you need help up here." I told him everyone was taken care of, thanks to the help from the other corpsman. The new man said, "What other corpsman? We are the closest unit to you, and we were just able to get up here." I looked around, but my mysterious helper was no longer there.

To this day I still relive this experience and give thanks to God for seeing me through this terrible campaign. On that fateful night on Peleliu, with so much death, dying, and mutilation all around me, I believe that the corpsman who helped me was a heavenly angel sent by God. I have to believe this until someone proves otherwise—and I don't think anyone will.

Some military strategists decry the value of the Peleliu battle. They say the island could have been bypassed, but hindsight is always twenty-twenty. Who really knows? Fifty years after the battle, some Palauans gave a letter to a returning marine veteran who had been wounded there. The letter was titled "A Rock Tougher Than Bloody Nose Ridge":

Rage, Rage, Rage engulfed the Pacific Islands fifty years ago, and this week commemorated the carnage in Palau as American veterans returned to its battlegrounds. I wonder if we were able to truly honor them for what they did then and what was to follow over the next half-century. Had Palau been bypassed by the American forces, would there be a Palau today; would there be a people called Palauans? Lest we forget, Palau was forcibly taken by Japan eighty years ago this month. Some two years lapsed before the League of Nations mandated the Micronesian Islands to Japan with the proviso of nonmilitarization. America refused membership in that body and refused recognition of the mandate. After the bloody battles of the Palau, the U.S. military initiated a benevolent restoration of the islands followed by an agreement with the United Nations to oversee the development of self-determination for the peoples of Micronesia. In a few days we Palauans will join the world of nations with all of the privileges and the responsibilities that come with our new political status. As the American veterans depart the islands, we Palauans should reflect upon the events of the days commemorating our liberation as well as examine what might have been had these veterans not come in 1944. I say to those veterans of the Battles of Palau, thank you, thank you, thank you; were it not for you, freedom for our people would not have come. God Speed.

Roman Tmetuchl, September 16, 1994

THE BATTLE FOR OKINAWA

Greater love has no one than this, than to lay down one's life for his friends. (John 15:13)

On April 1, 1945, the U.S. Tenth Army, under the command of Lt. Gen. Simon Bolivar Buckner, planned to land three army divisions and two marine divisions abreast on the East China Sea side of Okinawa. My close buddy, D. I. Bahde, and I were in C Company, First Tank Battalion, First Marine Division and were part of the initial assault force of 182,000 men.

We knew the invasion force was huge, but didn't realize that it was 75,000 more men than had landed on Normandy on D day in 1944. To everyone's amazement, the American assault from the sea was virtually unopposed. Total Tenth Army casualties were only 28 dead, 104 wounded, and 27 missing.

But we were facing an enemy, dug into the deepest, strongest piece of rock we would ever face. Lt. Gen. Mitsuru Ushijima, commander of the Thirty-Second Imperial Japanese Army, chose to offer only token resistance on the landing beaches and instead waged a prolonged war of attrition.

Utilizing the natural coral-limestone ridges running east and west across the southern third of the island Ushijima had set a 117,000-man force to digging with pick and shovel. For months before our landing, this workforce (which included conscripted Okinawans) honeycombed the ridges and hills into veritable underground villages with amazing interlocking fields of fire against the enemy. These diggers lived the lives of moles and did not use explosives to enhance their excavations. Their main line of defense was several stories deep with air conditioning, and the entire line stretched six miles across the island. Their underground fortress could hold seventy thousand—the bulk of Ushijima's forces—and was a seemingly impregnable defense.

The general's great hope was that the Imperial Navy, Naval Air, and combined Army Air units would be able to sink the bulk of our navy. This would cut off vital supplies to our ground forces and force our defeat. General Ushijima wanted to make the defense of Okinawa a long, costly, drawn-out affair, in contrast to the invasions of Tarawa, Guam, and the other island battles. Because Japan's overall supplies were short and little was left of their naval forces, he counted on a war of attrition. He hoped that the Kamikaze (Divine Wind) Force would destroy our invasion fleet by suicide attacks, cutting off supplies, thus isolating the invading expeditionary force.

On shore, unaware of this strategy, we watched in awe as our navy pilots and Japanese kamikazes fought in aerial combat, and plane after plane plunged into our vulnerable ships.

The U.S. Navy suffered tremendous casualties. Contrary to all casualty ratios in war, their killed in action (4,907) was higher than the number wounded (4,824) in this battle. Shrapnel from ship and shore antiaircraft batteries fell out of the sky, raining down upon us with deadly effect. The Tenth Army finally found Ushijima and his main forces on the southern third of Okinawa.

Each tank driver was sealed in his compartment—entombed might be a better word. The other four members of each tank crew stood on the back while the tank was driven off the ramp. But the cost was excruciatingly high. From May 11 through May 20, the First Marine Division "would lose 200 Marines for every 100 yards advanced."

One of our other C Company tanks, after crossing the reef barrier off the Hagushi beach, blew off its flotation pontoons in the shallow water. It proceeded to move through the calm surf toward the landing beach, then very suddenly drove into a huge, hidden hole that swallowed it up. Four of the five-man crew escaped from the submerged Sherman; the driver, fighting and clawing against the pressure of the torrent of in-rushing seawater, was unable to extricate himself. The remaining tanks could not get on or through the reef.

Bill Henahan swam to the reef, walked ashore, and talked a bulldozer operator into coming out onto the reef. There, Henahan said, "We unwound the cable from the dozer's winch and hailed a passing LCVP (landing craft, vehicle, personnel), which towed the cable out to our tank. The dozer winched us up onto the reef, and we then drove across the reef to shore. The remaining tanks sailed into the Sixth Marine Division beach area and got to shore safely."

SUGAR LOAF

Offer to God thanksgiving, and pay your vows to the
Most High. Call upon Me in the day of trouble;
I will deliver you, and you shall glorify Me.

(Psalm 50:14,15, NKJV)

During that nearly three-month conflict, the American Tenth Army and the Japanese Thirty-Second Imperial Army fought a no-quarter battle, with Okinawan civilians caught in the middle. The Tenth Army was made up of four U.S. Army divisions and three marine divisions: the First and Second, which had seen previous Pacific battles, and the newly formed Sixth Marine Division, which was made up of a large nucleus of combat veterans from other units. The third regiment of the Sixth Division included numerous veterans from Guadalcanal and Tarawa. The division's ranks were diverse, from high school dropouts to college graduates, from Depression-era dead-end kids to wealthy heirs. Large numbers were still in their teens and few were past their early twenties. A fateful destiny awaited many of these men on an inconspicuous hill not too far away as the Sixth Division moved south. Uncommon courage would become a common virtue.

Patrols of the Sixth Marine Division first came up against a "prominent hill" in front of the main Japanese line of defense. We later named it Sugar Loaf, but the battle for this 165-foot-high, 300-yard-long mound was anything but sweet!

In eight days of intense fighting, Sugar Loaf changed hands more than eleven times. The Japanese knew that if this hill fell, it would be a key to undermining their line of defense and ultimately all of Okinawa. So they desperately reinforced the hill with unit after fanatical unit. The toll on the enemy was great—and ultimately greater than that on the valiant marine infantry and tankers.

Four Marine infantry battalions melted away. Rifle companies all but vanished. With an original complement of 240, they dwindled to between twelve and twenty survivors. Eleven of eighteen company commanders were killed or wounded. Three thousand Marines were killed and seriously wounded. Another 1,289 were lost to sickness and combat exhaustion.

The Sixth Marine Tank Battalion had thirty-three Sherman tanks knocked out in Hell's Half Acre, directly in front of Sugar Loaf. I was in C Company, First Tank Battalion, First Marine Division. We were heavily engaged on the left flank of the beleaguered Sixth, fighting through Wana Draw and Wana Ridge. As is the case in most wars, our unit was deep in our own problems with the same tenacious enemy and had little or no knowledge of the difficulties and sickening losses on our right flank.

Cpl. Jim Day made it up Sugar Loaf on May 14, leading several other marines to a shell crater, where for three days and nights they fought off assaults by the Japanese. Most of his mates were killed or wounded. Day helped four wounded marines one by one to help and safety, but each time returned to clamber up Sugar Loaf. Finally only one wounded Marine remained with him in that precarious position. Wounded by shrapnel and burned by white phosphorus, Day held his ground. When finally relieved after those three harrowing days, the enemy dead around his fighting hole numbered over one hundred. His commanders on Sugar Loaf who would have recommended him for the Medal of Honor were all killed.[3]

Marine infantry and tankers fought together, died together, and helped rescue one another in that inferno. Many helplessly pinned down and wounded "mud marines" were straddled by us in our thirty-three-ton Sherman tanks. We'd open the escape hatch in the bottom and pull the wounded into the hot, cramped, but relatively safe shelter of our tanks. They were then evacuated to our own lines and a battalion aid station.

Platoon Sgt. Ed DeMar, badly wounded and lying helpless on the battlefield, was ministered to under fire by a marine he didn't recognize. Howie Perrault was a tank driver in Able Company. Tankers like Perrault on Sugar Loaf helped save many of G Company's stricken men at the risk of their own lives. A few minutes later, Perrault, now wounded himself, and De Mar lay side by side on the back of another tank. As De Mar turned to thank Perrault, he watched helplessly and in horror as a burst of machine gun fire caught Perrault in the head and killed him.

It took a great deal of intestinal fortitude to be cooped up in a World War II Sherman tank. In essence it was a blind, vulnerable beast for the five-man crew: tank commander (TC), gunner, and loader in the turret, with the driver and assistant driver down in the front part of the armored chassis. The poor ventilation, dust, noise, heat, and stink of diesel fuel inside this steel box were enough to try any man. The TC was forever making use of his periscope, as his vision was extensively blocked.

Sticking one's head out the hatch for a quick look was like playing Russian roulette. It was a full-time job checking for his supporting infantry, identifying the position of his other tanks, and overcoming anxious chatter on air in order to use his radio/intercom. The tank driver was always alert to the intercom guidance of his TC as he peered through the limited vision of a periscope, picking his way along. The danger of minefields, ditches, mechanical failures, thrown track, antitank guns, and fanatical Japanese satchel-carrying suicide troops, were all a constant menace.

It was around 0800 that fateful Father's Day morning of June 17, 1945. The sun already burned hotly in a clear and cloudless sky. Our seven Charlie Company tanks, supporting Lt. Col. Hunter Hurst's Third Battalion, Seventh Marines, were led by 2nd Lt. Jerry "Ack Ack" Atkinson.

Hurst's Battalion attacked south from Kunishi Ridge. Their objective was the left portion of Mezado Ridge some six hundred meters distant. The valley in which the tanks and infantry were to traverse was a fairly open field, filled with clumps of dry sugar cane and ditches—all excellent hiding places for the Japanese infantry and their automatic weapons, mortars, artillery, and observation posts.

We knew from bitter experience that the enemy's top priority was to stop our tanks, no matter what! This valley of death was no different. We soon discovered that the Japanese had our tanks sighted in with their 47 mm and 76 mm antitank guns set up into kill zones, firing in some cases from the flank no more than one hundred meters away. We didn't know it, but we were the proverbial fish in a barrel.

Here's the story, from the perspectives of several of the men who lived it.

LT. JERRY "ACK ACK" ATKINSON
(SECOND PLATOON TANK COMMANDER)

June 17 is my annual memorial day. Why? Because I've been living on borrowed time since that day in 1945.

My platoon was supporting Lt. Col. Hunter H. Hurst's 3/7, pushed south toward Mezado. My buddy Charlie Nelson's Third Platoon was covering our advance from the vicinity of Kunishi on high ground behind us. Sgt. Bob Bennett was my gunner that day. My driver was Cpl. Bob Boardman, a raw-boned Nebraska farm boy, and my loader was Pvt. K. C. Smith.

After receiving the signal from the infantry, my tanks crossed the line of departure south of the town of Kunishi. We led the infantry attack across the cane fields. If I recall correctly, we had four tanks in a line—two of mine and two from C Company. Moving along in third gear, I kept a wary eye on the piles of dried sugar cane and brush in the field. Past experience proved that the Japanese made skillful use of such cover to hide troops, suicide teams, and antitank guns. About halfway across I peered through my vision blocks, checking the infantry's progress; they were supposed to be coming behind me. I couldn't see them, so I stopped our tanks immediately. Bitter experience had taught us that it was fatal to outrun your infantry support.

Another quick look confirmed that many of them were stuck in a ditch about two hundred yards behind—for good reason, too! Heavy enemy artillery, mortar, and flat trajectory fire prevented them from keeping up. Part of this fire was landing on and around our tanks. I was on the left flank with the other tanks running in an irregular line. Sergeant Brenkert's tank was to my right. Suddenly, I heard someone yelling on the platoon SCR 508 talk channel with unintelligible expletives. "They are killing us!"

SGT. BUD BRENKERT

Lieutenant Atkinson's tank was slightly behind and to the left of us. My tank was the first one struck by the antitank (AT) guns.

One shell went through the steel holding piece, which was part of the pontoon apparatus on the front of the tank. The second shell penetrated the left side of the tank under Pop Christensen's seat. The fragments from that shell killed my assistant driver. The third shell struck the side of the tank and traveled through one fuel cell, coming to rest inside the fuel cell on the right side.

The high pressure released when the shell hit the fuel cell caused the vaporized diesel to spew out in large white clouds. I mistakenly thought that my tank was on fire. The Japanese then shifted their fire to Lieutenant Atkinson's tank, setting it on fire. We were unable to move our tank at first because the round that passed under the driver's seat had fouled the gearshift mechanism. Fortunately Pop, my driver, was able to free it up, and we moved our tank alongside Atkinson's, using it as protection from the antitank fire. I told Chris to drop the escape hatch, and we waited for five minutes or so for someone to appear from Atkinson's tank. When no one did, we revved up the engines several times, indicating that we were backing up.

LIEUTENANT ATKINSON

Blam! . . . Blam! . . . Blam! . . . Blam! . . . Blam! Five 76 mm slugs, fired in quick succession, penetrated the armor on the left side of my tank. The first one broke the left track and left front drive sprocket. One round passed behind, barely clipping Bob Boardman's seat. The velocity was such that this 76 mm AT slug continued on, passing through the other side. Another round went through the lower turret into the fighting compartment, just missing our loader, K. C. Smith. Steel splinters splattered about, leaving him with a huge bloody chin gash. The round continued its deadly path, passing under the 75 mm gun mount, almost cutting Sergeant Bennett, my gunner, in two. He was perched against my knees. That same round that killed Bennett struck my left thigh just three inches above the knee, leaving my leg hanging there, held together only with a little bone and sinew. This deadly slug continued through, punching another hole on its way out the other side. Another round went through the turret, tearing up the fuel pressure hoses and spraying the crew with diesel fuel.

The fourth steel AT slug penetrated the engine compartment, opening the fuel cell and wrecking the port side GM diesel engine. White smoke and what I thought smelled like steam filled the fighting compartment. It was time to bail out. I shook Sergeant Bennett. His lacerated lower torso made it obvious he was dead. I pulled myself up through the turret hatch and jumped to the ground . . . mangled left leg and all. The tank was on fire.

Boardman came out through the driver's hatch and K. C. Smith via his loader's hatch. They quickly spotted me lying by the tank. K. C. reached down and put my left arm around his neck. Boardman grabbed my other arm and hand, and they struggled to carry me to safety.

K. C. and Boardman dragged me about fifty to seventy-five feet from our tank, stumbling as they went. A sniper shot Boardman's index finger off. The bullet then traveled through his throat, through the back of my neck, and into K. C.'s face. I felt Boardman drop me, and I fell on my face on the ground as the bullet knocked me out. When I came to, blood covered my face and right cheek. My right arm was useless.

I opened my eyes and saw about six or seven Japanese pushing the sugar cane aside to look at me. I tried desperately to move my right arm to get my .45-caliber pistol, which was in my shoulder holster. I intended to shoot myself to avoid the Japanese cutting me up! Peering through my right eye, I spotted an enemy trench nearby. I wanted to get out into open ground and wait for Charlie Nelson's tanks to rev up their engines and fire their coaxial machine guns over me. The Japanese were looking scared and ducked down in the clumps of sugar cane. I counted to five, then rolled over to the right into the trench . . . lucky for me, no one was there.

This was when I saw Nelson's tanks. I stood up, putting the enemy to my back out of their sight. I waved my left arm and hand to Charlie Nelson's tank. Unfortunately, Nelson's gunner thought I was a Jap and cut down on me with his coaxial .30-caliber machine gun with tracer bullets! One of the rounds went through my left hand. I thought, I haven't got a chance . . . my own men are shooting at me! Desperately I lifted my right leg, the only limb

I had left that wasn't damaged. Luckily, Charlie saw my booted leg with its red ski sock, and two marine infantrymen came running up to me and rolled me onto a poncho. Using it as a stretcher, these brave men picked me up and ran back to Charlie Nelson's tank and placed me on top of the engine compartment. Charlie carried me on the back of his tank to a forward command post.

SERGEANT BRENKERT

It was confusion, disorientation, death, and fire that prevailed out in that field that day. After a while, I took my tank and slowly limped back to the road at the southern base of Kunishi Ridge. As we approached the road, Christensen spotted Bob Boardman in the field. He stopped the tank and helped Boardman climb on. We then proceeded to the top of the ridge where our command post was located.

We took Hoffman out of the tank and discovered that he was dead. Boardman, who was bleeding profusely, was given first aid. We put him on the back of my tank and proceeded down from the ridge and across the no-man's valley to our lines. In the middle of the valley my tank ran out of fuel. We transferred Boardman to an accompanying tank and took him from behind our lines to the Seventh Marines aid station.

CPL. GLENN "OLD MAN" CHRISTENSEN

I recall that morning as if it were yesterday. I was driving Sergeant Brenkert's tank. We were positioned in a ragged line to the right and slightly ahead of our platoon commander, Lieutenant Ack Ack's tank. Our tank was about half way across the cane field when the lieutenant ordered Brenkert to move back because extremely heavy antitank and artillery fire was zeroing in on us. Seconds after hearing this order, our tank was hit.

A 76 mm AT round entered under my seat and hit my assistant driver, Hoffman. He was losing a lot of blood, and I stopped the tank and held his body up. Then, as ordered, I put the tank in reverse and started moving back. The purpose of this maneuver was to take advantage of the protection offered by the embankment at the base of Kunishi Ridge.

Suddenly, Lieutenant Ack Ack called our tank for help. They, too, were being clobbered by a rapid succession of AT rounds coming from our left flank. Evidently the same guns had shifted fire, wreaking havoc on them. Because I was too busy maneuvering our tank, I had one of my crewmen reach down from the turret to keep Hoffman propped up.

Brenkert reported that Lieutenant Ack Ack's vehicle was on fire and told me to pull around and try to pick up the survivors. I worked to shift the tank's transmission, but it was stuck. After several exasperating moments, I pulled out a piece of metal stuck in the linkage and put the tank in first gear. Seconds later, another AT round hit us on the left side, entering the engine compartment and cutting through the fuel cells. I stepped hard on the foot throttle and kept moving. Smoke permeated the tank, blinding and choking us.

Taking a chance, I opened the hatch and steered the tank with my head out. We pulled up alongside Ack Ack's tank and dropped the escape hatch. It was a bad place because we were under heavy fire. The AT slugs sounded like a freight train as they roared past us. I felt something wet and, looking down at my legs, I noticed that diesel fuel from the blown hoses was spewing all over under my feet. It was also dripping out of the open escape hatch onto the ground. I stuck my head down through the hole under our tank looking for Ack Ack's crew. Sadly, no one was waiting to crawl up to safety. Brenkert told us through the intercom that he couldn't see anyone from the turret.

I asked for permission to crawl out and look into Ack Ack's burning tank, but Brenkert replied, "No, absolutely not!" Time was wasting. I closed my driver's hatch. We were blinded again with the smoke and fire. Another call came in asking Brenkert to search for the missing Ack Ack and his crew.

Then another call from Lt. Jerry Jerue, our company CO, came over the air, ordering our tank to return immediately to the base of Kunishi Ridge. Brenkert said that it was up to me to "nurse our tank back." We were spewing diesel fuel, had a simmering engine compartment fire, and were in danger of running out of fuel and being stuck out on the battlefield. I opened up my hatch as it smoked up again. There was no time to lose. With

Brenkert guiding me, I backed up, facing the enemy direction of fire. In this position, once our tormentors were spotted, Brenkert and our gunner could shoot back.

I wasted no time heading to the relative safety of the ridge base. Just about that time Bob Boardman and K. C. Smith, separately hiding from the enemy, came out from behind some bushes and rocks. We picked them up and headed for medical help. Then, as luck would have it, our tank ran out of fuel. Fortunately, another tank pulled up and continued our mission of mercy, getting our comrades to emergency medical attention. At the aid station, the real sad part was struggling to get Hoffman, our dead comrade, out of the assistant driver's hatch, wrapped into a poncho, and laid to rest. That's something I still think about.

POSTSCRIPT: LIEUTENANT ATKINSON

I went through the medical evacuation chain to a rear medical aid station. Eventually, I ended up on an LST (Landing Ship Tank) used as a temporary hospital ship. Oddly enough, the corpsman who took care of me and I were the only people in this area of the ship. Was I so messed up that they figured I was dying? After all, I had seven holes in my body. But this corpsman cleaned me up, wiped the blood from my hair and face. I think he helped me stay alive. I later discovered he lived in Nashville just a few blocks away from my home.

It took me eighteen months to recover physically from my ordeal. Since then, there isn't a day that goes by that I don't thank God for my comrades and my life. I still carry the constant reminder—body scars, a limp, and "what ifs" in my mind. In retrospect, it's clear that halting my platoon in the open field was a mistake. Obviously, we became sitting ducks. The now-famous red ski socks are a story in themselves. They helped save my life. If Charlie Nelson hadn't spotted them as I lay dying in that field fifty-plus years ago, I'd be just another grave marker today.

POSTSCRIPT: SERGEANT BRENKERT

June 17, 1945, was the last time I saw Boardman until he visited me in Michigan two years later. When I shook his hand I noticed part of his right index finger was missing. He told me that when he was wounded, he had tried to show me that finger, as it was killing him with pain, but all I was paying attention to was his throat.

Boardman's postwar life is a story in itself. My six-foot, three-inch comrade speaks with a raspy voice, a reminder of the bullet that cut his vocal cords that fateful day in Okinawa. To show forgiveness, he devoted much of his life as a missionary in Japan. He has also made several missionary trips to Mongolia and previously forbidden areas in eastern Asia. He is a familiar figure at First Marine Division reunions and is also the chaplain of the Marine Corps Tankers Association.

POSTSCRIPT: BOB BOARDMAN

My memories of that hot and bloody day became clouded after a sniper cut down Lieutenant Atkinson, K. C. Smith, and me. Jerry was hit with a clean hole through the back of his neck, and I was shot through the neck—shattering my windpipe—and through my trigger finger. Blood was running down the outside of my dungaree jacket, as well as down the inside of my throat. The agony of trying to breathe made me feel as if I were drowning. I was sure it was my time to die, and this was the bullet with my name on it.

Fortunately, I was ready. My flesh was fearful, but my inner being experienced the peace of God that passes human understanding. I rolled into a shell hole and tried to hurry the process by passing out; then I could go and be with the Lord. But I was unable to lose consciousness. As I lay there I began to realize that I might live, so I decided to try to escape.

Though I had a .45-caliber pistol on my hip, my trigger finger had been shattered. I couldn't draw or use the pistol. I sat helpless, holding my torn neck with my good left hand. I cried out to God for deliverance.

Just then Bud Brenkert's tank came out of the cane field. It was limping along, smoke emitting from the exhaust. I could see that it had been severely hit by AT fire. For this reason, "Old Man" Christensen was driving with his head out of the tank hatch. He spotted me, stopped, and helped me onto the tank.

I was then placed on a stretcher on the back of Brenkert's tank, and we took off looking for help. We weren't out of trouble yet. It was necessary to travel through the sniper-infested no-man's valley to reach the battalion aid station. Sniper and automatic weapons fire kept zipping over the tank. In a selfless act of courage, Bud Brenkert left the relative safety of the tank turret and placed his body across mine, shielding me from the enemy fire. About halfway across no-man's Valley, Brenkert's badly damaged tank finally broke down. We were now exposed and helpless.

Fortunately, another C Company tank, commanded by Sergeant Brantly, pulled up and pulled us out of a tough situation. Brenkert and Christensen carried me in the stretcher over to Brantly's tank. The rest of the crew pulled Hoffman's body out of the assistant driver's seat, placing him next to me on the back of the rescue tank.

Let the world count the crosses. Let them count them over and over. Let us do away with names, with ranks and rates and unit designations, here. Do away with the terms—regulars, reserve, veteran, boot, old-timers, replacement. They are empty, categorizing words, which belong only in the adjutant's dull vocabulary. Here lie only Marines.
Maj. Gen. Graves B. Erskine

I survived three U.S. Marine Corps World War II amphibious landings: Cape Gloucester, Peleliu, and Okinawa. Okinawa, the final battle of World War II, lasted eighty-one days. The cost for the United States was over 12,500 killed and 36,300 wounded. The Japanese suffered over 131,000 military killed.

We didn't know as we fought on June 17 that there would be just four more days before the battle for Okinawa would be over.

Weeks later, I had an unexpected reunion at the San Francisco Receiving Hospital; Lt. Jerry Atkinson was still alive. Each of us had thought that the other had been killed.

Because of the fateful events of that day, I speak in a hoarse voice. When people ask how I contracted my "permanent laryngitis," I always tell them that it was a small price to pay to serve our country alongside these courageous men. We, the living, are grateful to each one who paid the supreme sacrifice. We salute them, and our hearts go out to their loved ones left behind. All who served there were unforgettable men in unforgettable times.

DEATH OF THE GENERALS

Every man must do two things alone; he must do his own believing and his own dying.
Martin Luther

Lt. Gen. Simon Bolivar Buckner, a 1908 West Point graduate, soldiered for thirty-seven years. He commanded the 155,000 ground troops of the American Tenth Army on Okinawa. This included the First and Sixth Marine Divisions with the Second in reserve, plus four U.S. Army divisions.

At fifty-eight, Gen. "Buck" Buckner was a large, physically tough officer and the epitome of an army commander, with his white hair and handsome good looks. He was an excellent student and teacher of battle strategy and tactics and had led the U.S. campaign in the Aleutian Islands in 1943. He was decorated for "exceptionally distinguished and meritorious service" and was basically an infantryman with special skill in tanks.

The general, however, was not without controversy. "He was not known as a man who liked to take risks; his instinct was to grind forward with the relentless use of superior firepower."[4] Several high-ranking navy, marine, and army officers had recommended an amphibious landing to the rear of the fortress-like Shuri Line across Okinawa. This, they hoped, would help alleviate the purely frontal assault. Commandant of the Marine Corps and Medal of Honor recipient A. A. Vandergrif recommended using the Second Marine Division, now waiting in reserve on Saipan.

But General Buckner turned down all recommendations. This puzzled even the Japanese commanders, who noted, "The absence of a landing [by the Americans] puzzled us, particularly after the beginning of May when it became impossible to put up more than a token resistance in the south."[4]

After almost three months of no-quarter fighting, Buckner's Tenth Army had gradually driven Ushijima's exhausted, tattered, but brave remnants of the Thirty-Second Army to the southern end of Okinawa. The Japanese still managed in the final weeks to extract about three thousand American casualties per week. Although the end of the battle for Okinawa was described in an upbeat way back home, the accounts in the press had little basis in reality. To the sweaty U.S. infantrymen, who knew each grueling terrifying day might be their last, each yard of soil cost many of their countrymen's lives.[5]

Buckner, who told the press his troops were in the final stages of "mopping up," elected, against the advice of his staff, to visit a forward area to see for himself. On the afternoon of June 18, accompanied by high-ranking officers, he arrived at a forward observation post of an element of the Eighth Marine Regiment of the Second Marine Division, freshly arrived from Saipan. In a few days the island would be secured and he would report back to the U.S. No doubt he was, as a key general, in line for leadership in the coming invasion of the Japan mainland in the fall.

The marine forward observation post could see the cliffs and beach at the southwestern tip of the seventy-five-mile-long island. The general was positioned between two large boulders about a yard apart and was handed a pair of artillery spotter glasses. All seemed secure and safe.

The Japanese First Heavy Field Artillery Regiment, pride of the Thirty-Second Army, had only one gun left out of twelve. Their spotter, looking through his binoculars, saw what appeared to be a number of high-ranking officers.

After one hour of viewing the battleground, Buckner confidently prepared to depart to visit another unit. At this moment the expert Japanese artillery officer gave word to fire and laid five scarce, precious rounds into this tempting target. One of those five shells hit one of the boulders, showering chips, flying shrapnel, and coral fragments, some of which dug into the general's chest and abdomen. The profuse bleeding could not be stanched, and in ten minutes he was dead. None of the officers accompanying him was scratched. Like so many of his men, the commander had been dealt a dose of combat's vast store of misfortune.[6]

Near the gun that killed General Buckner were the commanders of the Japanese troops, Lieutenant Generals Ushijima and Cho. Their last command cave was only about one mile south of the spot where General Buckner met his fate. The two Japanese generals had gradually withdrawn the Thirty-second Army from much of the almost impregnable Shuri Line during the last days of May in order to make their prolonged but hopeless last stand in southern Okinawa. Their final command cave was a far cry from their former headquarters beneath the rubble of Shuri Castle.

Now their relatively small cave, Hill 89 to the Americans, near the village of Mabuni, was the scene of their final orders and a farewell party for their staff. General Ushijima, in full dress uniform, challenged the survivors present "to fight to the last and die for the eternal cause of loyalty to the Emperor." Cho wore a white suicide ceremonial kimono. With their staff they dined well and toasted one another with Black & White Scotch whisky carefully transported from Shuri. Then they sang "Umi Yukaba," an ancient drinking song that had become like a national anthem to the Japanese.

These were the modern samurai commanders who had attempted to instill into all their defending troops the following resolute battle motto: "One plane for one warship. One boat for one ship. One man for ten of the enemy or one tank."

As dawn approached on June 23, the U.S. Army Seventh Division overran Hill 89. The Japanese generals and remnants of their staff made their way to a narrow ledge outside the cave, overlooking the ocean two hundred feet below. As they stepped outside the cave, Lieutenant General Cho turned to his superior.

"Well, Commanding General Ushijima, as the way may be dark, I, Cho, will lead the way to the outside ledge."

Ushijima replied, "Please do so. I'll take along my fan, since it's getting warm."

James and William Belote recount the last moments of the two generals. Even as the Americans closed in, lobbing grenades toward the movement of the Japanese below on the ledge, "Both knelt on the sheet, facing the ocean since room was lacking on the ledge to perform the ceremony facing north toward the Imperial Palace. Silently each opened his tunic, baring his abdomen. At General Ushijima's side stood his aide, Lieutenant Yoshino, holding two knives with half the blade wrapped in white cloth. The adjutant, Captain Sakaguchi, stood on Ushijima's right, saber drawn. Yoshino handed a blade to Ushijima, who took it with both hands and, with a shout, thrust. Simultaneously, Sakaguchi's saber fell on his neck as prescribed, severing his spinal column. Ushijima's corpse lurched forward onto the sheet. Then General Cho took his turn and the ceremony was repeated."[7]

The Japanese staff officers who witnessed and assisted the generals' final moments all killed themselves with a bullet to the head immediately following the burial of the commanders. A year following Ushijima's death, the Japanese government promoted him posthumously to General of the Army. This seems strange and even bizarre not only to Westerners, but also to certain Japanese, especially when tens of thousands of Okinawan civilians needlessly died in this deadly conflict.

A surviving Japanese soldier of Okinawan birth, Masahide Ota, summed up the two Japanese generals' responsibility best: "The commanders of the Okinawa Defense Forces ended their lives as warriors but could not escape criticism for dragging not only their fine soldiers, but also the unfortunate civilians into the war. It did not matter to others that they had acted "under orders."

I have often wondered if any of those three generals was prepared for his meeting with death. I think missionary Jim Elliot was expressing God's wisdom when he said, "When it comes time to die, make sure all you have to do is die."

Condensed from the book *Unforgettable Men in Unforgettable Times*
Bob Boardman, used with permission

RED SKIES OVER EUROPE

WORLD WAR I

In the first five months of World War I, one out of every ten British soldiers died. By the end of the four years, the Allies suffered eighteen million killed or wounded, the German Axis over eleven million.

My soul is torn asunder, but everything must be put
to fire and blood. The throats of men and women,
children and the aged must be cut and not a tree nor
a house left standing. With such methods of terror . . .
the war will finish before two months. . . .
Wilhelm II, German Kaiser, August 1914

It is a war against all nations. [Now]American ships
have been sunk, American lives taken. . . . There has
been no discrimination. The challenge is to all
mankind. Each nation must decide for itself how it
will meet it. The choice we make for ourselves must
be made with a moderation of counsel and a temper-
ateness of judgment befitting our character and our
motives as a nation. We must put excited feeling
away. Our motive will not be revenge or the victori-
ous assertion of the physical might of the nation, but
only the vindication of right.[8]
Woodrow Wilson to Congress declaring War, April 2, 1917

The lamps are going out all over Europe: we shall
not see them lit again in our lifetime.
Sir Edmond Grey, British Foreign Secretary, August 1914

In Flanders Fields

In Flanders fields the poppies blow
Between the crosses, row on row
That mark our place; and in the sky

The larks, still bravely singing, fly
Scarce heard amid the guns below.

We are the Dead. Short days ago
We lived, felt dawn, saw sunset glow,
Loved and were loved, and now we lie
In Flanders fields.

Take up our quarrel with the foe:
To you from failing hands we throw
The torch; be yours to hold it high.
If ye break faith with us who die
We shall not sleep, though poppies grow
In Flanders fields.[9]

John McCrae, 1915

FROM FARM BOY TO FIGHTER

★

MAJ. DOUGLAS VINCENT MASTRIANO, U.S. ARMY

Have I not commanded you? Be strong and of good courage; do not be afraid, nor be dismayed, for the LORD your God is with you wherever you go.

(Joshua 1:9, NKJV)

On any other day, the beauty of the Argonne Forest would have overcome Alvin York. The fall colors displayed themselves like a kaleidoscope as the first hint of winter stretched across the hills of France. It was early October 1918, and the end of what would be called "The Great War" seemed very far away. The hopes for an early finish following America's entry into the war were not to be realized, and casualties mounted in the millions.

The first hint of daybreak came as crimson streaks across the sky announced the arrival of the sun. But Alvin York wasn't thinking about sunrise. He was wondering why his artillery support hadn't begun. It was supposed to precede their advance against the German army that morning. Even so, the whistle blew at sunrise, and the 328th Infantry Regiment "went over the top." Their mission that morning was to attack the German positions in front of them and seize the Decauville Railroad.

Taking the railroad was vital, as it would sever German support and communications and open the way for a broader Allied attack. The 328th advanced up a funnel-shaped valley that grew increasingly narrow the farther it went. On each side and the far side of the valley were steep ridges occupied by German machine gun emplacements. About halfway into the valley, German machine guns began to pour down gunfire upon them. Soon heavy artillery joined the blistering machine guns, taking a heavy toll on the beleaguered regiment. In the face of such overwhelming resistance, the American attack began to waver and stall.

As York recollected: "The Germans got us, and they got us right smart. They just stopped us dead in our tracks. Their machine guns were up there on the heights overlooking us and well hidden, and we couldn't tell for certain where the terrible heavy fire was coming from. . . . And I'm telling you they were shooting straight. Our boys just went down like the long grass before the mowing machine. Our attack just faded out. . . . And there we were, lying down, about halfway across . . . and those German machine guns and big shells getting us hard."[10]

The survivors sought cover wherever they could find it. Sergeant Bernard Early was ordered to take three squads of men (including York's squad) and work their way behind the German entrenchments to attack the machine guns.

Taking on twenty to thirty machine guns had never been York's idea of what God was planning for his life.

Alvin York was born in the backwoods of Tennessee just two weeks before Christmas in 1887, the third of eleven children born into a poor farming and blacksmith family. While Alvin's parents were both committed Christians, he seemed to moving along a different path.

He won acclaim as a local sharpshooter, and also as a reckless drinker and gambler. "I got in bad company and broke off from my mother's and father's advice. I got to playing up right smart . . . used to stay out late at night, drink a lot of moonshine, and gamble my wages away week after week. I had a powerful lot of fistfights."[11]

As the war was breaking out in Europe in 1915, Alvin attended a revival meeting conducted by the Reverend H. H. Russell. During the sermon, York felt as if lightning hit his soul[12] and was moved to accept Jesus Christ as Lord and Savior. From this point his life was forever changed. He immediately abandoned "smoking, drinking, gambling, cussing, and brawling." He took his commitment seriously, grew in his faith, taught Sunday school, led the choir, and eventually became an elder in his church.[13]

York's old friends tried to persuade him to go drinking, but he continually refused. With the help of the Holy Spirit and a strong personal resolve, he quickly grew in both character and moral courage.

As Alvin grew in his faith, the United States made the decision to enter the war in Europe in 1917. Alvin's world turned upside down that June when he received a draft notice. When he read "Thou shall not kill" in the Bible, he believed a Christian could not kill another human being. Yet he also believed that God ordained governments as instruments to be obeyed.[14] Alvin York summed up this dilemma when he said, "I wanted to follow both the Bible and the government, but I couldn't. I wanted to do what was right. . . . If I went away to war and fought and killed, according to my reading of my Bible, I weren't a good Christian."[15]

With the assistance of his pastor and mother, Alvin York applied for exemption from the draft as a conscientious objector. That request and all three subsequent appeals were denied by the State of Tennessee. This put York into doubt and confusion. He trusted God to get him out of doing something that he perceived was contrary to the Bible. As he said, "I was sorter mussed up inside worser'n ever. I thought that the Word of God would prevail against the laws of men."[16]

So, like thousands of other men his age, York reported for duty. He was sent to the 82nd Infantry Division at Camp Gordon, Georgia. When word of Alvin's objection to fighting spread across his unit, it is fair to say that he was not popular. Providentially, York's company commander, Captain Danforth, and battalion commander, Major Buxton, were both committed Christians. Alvin shared his concerns with them, and both of his commanders respected his beliefs and took the time to fully discuss his concerns.

Together, the three walked through the Bible to debate the issue. The 328th had only a few months to train raw recruits for combat, yet these two leaders sacrificed their time to help York overcome his doubts.[17]

"We talked along these lines for over an hour. We did not get angry or even raise our voice. We jes' examined the old Bible, and whenever I would bring up a passage opposed to war, Major

Buxton would bring up another which sorter favored war. I believe that the Lord was in that room. I seemed to somehow feel His presence there."[18]

For every verse the commanders used to support their position on warfare, York countered. One night Captain Danforth read Ezekiel 33: "But if the watchman sees the sword coming and does not blow the trumpet, and the people are not warned, and the sword comes and takes any person from among them, he is taken away in his iniquity; but his blood I will require at the watchman's hand" (Ezekiel 33:6, NKJV).

With this, Alvin York stood up and said, "All right, I'm satisfied."[19] He resolved to serve his country and his God as a soldier. Armed with this assurance, he sought to excel in all that was entrusted to him. It was this moral foundation of a higher courage that was required that day on the ridge in France above his pinned-down fellow soldiers.

Sgt. Bernard Early and his three squads quickly overran the headquarters of a German machine gun battalion, capturing three officers and fifteen enlisted men.[20] Early's men were contending with the prisoners when machine-gun fire suddenly peppered the area, killing six Americans and wounding three more. The fire came from German machine guns on the ridge. The loss of the nine put Corporal York in charge of the eight remaining soldiers. As his men remained under cover, guarding the nineteen prisoners, York took a deep breath and pushed himself forward alone to take on the German machine guns.

"Those machine guns were spitting fire and cutting down the undergrowth all around me something awful. And the Germans were yelling orders. You never heard such a racket in all of your life. I didn't have time to dodge behind a tree or dive into the brush. . . . As soon as the machine guns opened fire on me, I began to exchange shots with them. There were over thirty of them in continuous action, and all I could do was touch the Germans off just as fast as I could. I was sharp shooting. I don't think I missed a shot. All the time I kept yelling at them to come down. I didn't want to kill any more than I had to. But it was them or me. And I was giving them the best I had."[21]

One of York's prisoners, a German major, emptied his pistol trying to kill York. Failing to injure him, and seeing his mounting battalion losses, he offered to surrender the unit. By the end of that morning, York and his seven men marched 132 German prisoners down to the American lines, to the astonishment of the regiments below.

Several months later York returned to Washington, D.C., to receive the Medal of Honor from the President of the United States. He seemed surprised by all of the fuss made over his actions. For Alvin York, the decision to attack the German machine guns that early morning in France had been settled long before, in the quietness of his heart and the shelter of a tent, with his two commanders and his God.

WORLD WAR II

You ask what is our aim? I can answer in one word: Victory—victory at all costs, victory in spite of all terror, victory however long and hard the road may be; for without victory there is no survival.
Winston Churchill, House of Commons Speech, May 13, 1940[22]

The United States will not be a threat to us for decades–not in 1945 but at the earliest in 1970 or 1980–90.
Adolf Hitler, November 12, 1940; Remark to Russian President and Commissar of Foreign Affairs, Vyacheslav Molotov

Yesterday, December 7, 1941—a date which will live in infamy—the United States of America was suddenly and deliberately attacked by naval and air forces of the Empire of Japan.
Franklin D. Roosevelt
Message to Congress following the attack on Pearl Harbor[23]

*True freedom is to share
All the chains our brothers wear,
And, with heart and hand, to be
Earnest to make others free!*
James Russell Lowell[24]

They endured all and gave all that justice among nations might prevail and that mankind might enjoy freedom and inherit peace.
Anonymous, Normandy Chapel inscription[25]

Posters of World War II

United We Win
Waste Helps the Enemy—Conserve
When You Ride Alone, You Ride with Hitler—
Join a Car Sharing Club Today
Save Freedom of Worship—Buy War Bonds
Loose Lips Sinks Ships
It's a Women's War Too!
Victory Waits on Your Fingers—Keep 'em Flying,
Miss USA
Longing Won't Bring Him Home Sooner—Get a
War Job
We Can Do It!

DAYDREAMS, SHATTERED DREAMS, DREAMS COME TRUE

★

RUTH PRECHT

Jesus said to her, "I am the resurrection and the life. He who believes in me will live, even though he dies." (John 11:25)

They say my Aunt Millie was born with a book in her hands. Although I wasn't there, I'm sure it must be true, for I have rarely known her to be without one. She was always happy to read to her nieces and nephews—and since she was number eleven of twelve children, that meant many eager listeners.

Farm life in the 1920s and '30s didn't provide many books or much time for reading, but somehow Millie always managed to find a book—even if it meant reading the same one over and over again. As for finding the time . . . it was more a question of finding Millie when it was time for work. Her sister Hulda would often complain, "Mom, Millie's reading again, and it's her turn to clean the upstairs!" But Grandma would just say, "Oh, leave her be." She knew that her youngest daughter was born with different dreams in her heart—dreams that might take her far away from the farm life they all knew and loved.

Millie read of knights in shining armor . . . hoping one would someday rescue her from the daily monotony of the farm. She read of princes and princesses and faraway places. But her deepest and most serious dream was that she would one day become a nurse and go to India to serve God among the poor and sick.

Even Millie had to occasionally pick up the broom or drive the tractor to pull the plow—farm chores had to be done rain or shine. But after she ran the plow into the fence one afternoon, her dismayed father found other work for her.

One day her brothers Ray and Ernie watched her daydreaming while driving the tractor and decided to play a trick on her.

They had been loading up the hay onto the wagon, working up a sweat, while she idly drove the tractor around the field. As they neared the house and turned back toward the field again, they unhooked the loader. Millie continued to drive the tractor out into the field without noticing she wasn't pulling anything anymore. It wasn't until she reached the far end of the field and turned around that she realized her brothers were gone. It was an indignant Millie that stormed into the house for dinner that night.

"Just you wait," she told her brothers as they laughed hysterically. "Someday I'll be a missionary in India, and you'll be sorry for the way you treated me!"

After graduating from high school, Millie and her friend Laura returned to their alma mater for a basketball game. The place was packed, so they found seats way up in the crowded bleachers. As they were getting settled, a young man looked up at them with the most beautiful, infectious smile Millie had ever seen. To her surprise, Laura waved and said, "That's my cousin Burdette!" It was the kind of moment that must have inspired Rodgers and Hammerstein to write "Some Enchanted Evening," for Millie was sure she had finally met her Prince Charming.

A few weeks later, Millie's sister-in-law Edna asked her to stay with her for a while. Millie's brother Ruben was in the army, and Edna was left at home with three small children, struggling and lonely. She rejoiced to have another adult to talk to and occasionally send on errands. While Millie was shopping at Gotham's grocery store, the clerk who waited on her was the young man with the infectious smile she had seen at the game.

"Are you by any chance Laura Ott's cousin?" Millie asked him.

"I am," he replied. "And who might you be?" They exchanged a few pleasantries until Burdette had to return to work. From that day on Millie was quick to volunteer to go to the store if Edna needed anything.

One day Laura and Ray, another of Millie's brothers, were going to the county fair. They insisted that Millie come along. Reluctantly she agreed, but not wanting to feel like a third wheel, she soon wandered off on her own. Whom should she run into but the grocery store clerk with the beautiful smile?

Back in those days, most families had only one car. Most young men were not able to know ahead of time when that car would be available for a date. Burdette was no exception. He decided to call on Millie. He didn't want to use the phone, for in those days phones were shared as party lines, and one never knew who might be listening.

So he seized a rare moment when the car was available to drive over to Millie's farm and surprise her. But she was not the only one surprised. One item that Millie had failed to mention during their many conversations was the size of her family, for fear of scaring him off. On this particular day a family gathering was planned to say good-bye to two of Millie's brothers. They were leaving with their units to join the battle in Europe.

Millie's parents quickly involved Burdette in the festivities. The entire family was engrossed in a lively game of Bunco on tables stretched throughout the entire first floor. At the same time, younger children noisily raced among the tables, reprimanded with an occasional "settle down," as the babies alternately cooed and cried for attention. The game ended, and the dining room table filled with food.

As the evening ended, Burdette told Millie, "There are so many of you, and yet you all love each other. Your whole family is so much fun, and your mother is so gracious. I have only one brother, and we can't stand each other. You are blessed to have such a wonderful family."

Yet encroaching on this tranquil scene was a terrible world war that had spread from continent to continent. It was to deeply affect the lives of many, including this happy farm family. A few months after this lighthearted evening, Burdette was drafted. Millie and he kept in touch by letter and, on one of his training furloughs, became engaged. Not wanting to be separated any more than necessary, they were married on his next furlough. It was August 30, 1944.

Weddings then were often very simple—sometimes held in the bride's home with the reception at a large house. Millie's wedding was simple, but definitely not small, with all of her family there. She didn't wear a fancy wedding dress, as there was not time to make one or money to buy one. The reception was held at her family's farm with everyone pitching in to help with the food. The honeymoon was far too short, as Burdette had to get back to the base. Millie saw him once more, and then he was gone—shipped off to France.

Millie happily received her first letter from her new husband and shared at least some parts with the rest of her family. She was thrilled to think of letters arriving from Europe, telling her about far-off places she had never been. It was almost as good as reading her childhood books about knights and princesses in distant kingdoms. But weeks passed without so much as a word from Burdette, and fear became her constant companion, filling her days and haunting her sleepless nights.

"The soldiers can't always post their letters. You'll hear from him soon," she was reminded by her family. Yet, somehow these words from loved ones failed to comfort her fearful heart.

"It makes no sense," she said one day. "In his last letter there were no battles. They were just settling into their tents, having a good time and trying to make the best of things."

Two months passed. Then fear became a reality with the arrival of a telegram from the War Department. At the top of it were the words, "MISSING IN ACTION." Those words, while still frightening, held a frail thread of hope. Millie pursued all the possibilities of what "missing in action" might signify. She contemplated where her beloved Burdette might be at that very moment—in a prison camp, in a hospital, simply unaccounted for, detached from his unit or—no, it simply couldn't be!

Two more months passed. Then another telegram arrived, crushing all of their desperate hopes.

THE SECRETARY OF WAR DESIRES ME TO
EXPRESS HIS DEEP REGRET. YOUR HUSBAND
WAS KILLED IN ACTION IN FRANCE JAN. 1, 1945.

Burdette was twenty-one years old and she, just twenty. They had been married for four months and two days, the day he was killed. And on that day, her dreams were shattered.

Many years later, following the death of my parents, I found a scrapbook belonging to my grandparents—Aunt Millie's parents. Tucked in among the family photos I discovered two letters written by Burdette to my grandparents prior to leaving for France. I was touched that he took the time to write to his new in-laws. The letters felt so precious in my hands, but I knew they belonged to Aunt Millie and not to me. I sent them to her and expressed the fears deep in my heart saying, "I cannot imagine what it was like to be widowed at twenty." Her poignant answer touched me deeply.

Dear Ruth,

I cannot begin to describe what it was like to be a widow at twenty—nor would I want to. Let me just say, after so many months of sympathy and earnest concern from relatives and friends, I just said, "No human, absolutely no one, can console me, so it's just you and me, Lord!" I had inherited Burdette's Starks' Prayer Book, and I prayed it to tatters.

In the fall of that year I entered nurse's training a physical wreck and probably worse mentally. People would say, "You looked like death warmed over and couldn't care less." I shall be eternally grateful to the entire medical profession at Lutheran Hospital, where I received loving understanding and, at the same time, a firm attitude of "life must go on."

I worked my tail off. Polio was rampant, and all the students were afraid of contracting it. So I volunteered for this duty. Why not? I had nothing to live for. In those days we went on duty after only two months of classes and then alternated duty with classes.

During leisure hours fellow students (especially a set of twins, who are still my friends) would often come into my room insisting I eat ice cream they "just couldn't finish," or cookies, or whatever. At the same time they would say with a big grin, "Tell us about your husband. What was he like? How did you meet him? Your first date, what did you do? How did he propose? What was your wedding like?" Nothing was sacred. They wanted to know all, and I bared my soul. We laughed, giggled, and cried. Now that was therapy! You get to the point when you remember only the joy—and the hurt is dispelled. Tears then are more sentiment than grief. Do you think that perhaps I was being graciously bamboozled?

From the older students we learned that the director of nurses was a nice lady—but beware! She was strictly no nonsense—hard as nails—and nobody wanted an invitation to see her in her office. Eight months after I arrived, I got a summons. I wasn't sure whether I should pack my suitcase and head for the bus station or be brave and see her first. I chose the latter. I sat down, and she smiled and said, "I called you here to tell you that I am proud of you. When you walked into my office a year ago to apply for training, you were the worst candidate for nurse's training I had ever seen. I accepted you because I felt you needed us more than we needed you. All the supervisors are saying nice things about your performance—and the improvement in your health is truly amazing." I walked out of that office with a completely changed attitude. There truly is life after death—even here on earth.

Aunt Millie's life did go on. A few years later, while working as a nurse, she met Jack, whom Grandma would later proclaim to be "Burdette back from the dead." She was charmed again by an infectious smiled that filled a loving face. Jack and Millie married shortly thereafter and have been married now for more than fifty years.

Aunt Millie was a dreamer and a doer. She never made it to India, but her younger daughter, Cindy, did. She and her husband established Mission of Joy, which now reaches into the slums of India bringing food to the hungry and healing to the sick. More than a hundred thousand have felt their healing hands during the past decade, and Jack and Millie have helped to raise support for the ministry.

Millie still loves reading. You can still find her in her chair with a book in her hands, glasses far down on her nose, quietly resting and dreaming of far-off places.

WAR AGAINST CHILDREN

If the Germans want to put the yellow Jewish star in Denmark, I and my whole family will wear it as a sign of the highest distinction.

Christian X, King of Denmark during World War II[26]

Nine out of ten Jewish children were murdered, not as a result of some tragic accident or some wild scheme gone wrong, but simply because they were Jewish. Such deliberate and systematic killing of children was unprecedented in human history.

Children of the Holocaust—The Survivors Speak (www.adl.org)

To sum it up, I must say that I regret nothing. . . . I will not humble myself or repent in any way. . . . What was done was not of my own doing. I had the feeling of Pontius Pilate. I felt that it was not with me that the guilt lay.

Adolf Eichmann,
Gestapo chief responsible for implementing Hitler's "Final Solution."
Comments made while awaiting trial in Israel (1960–61) for the murder of six million Jews.[27]

At the concentration camp at Buna, thousands of inmates were assembled to watch the hanging of two men and a boy suspected of blowing up the camp's electric power station. Then the march [past the gallows] began. The two adults were no longer alive. Their tongues hung swollen, blue-tinged. But the third rope was still moving; being so light, the child was still alive.

For more than half an hour he stayed there, struggling between life and death, dying in slow agony under our eyes. And we had to look him full in the face. He was still alive when I passed in front of him. His tongue was still red, his eyes not yet glazed. Behind me, I heard a man asking:

"Where is God now?

And I heard a voice within me answer him:

"Where is He? Here He is—He is hanging here on this gallows."

Elie Wiesel, Auschwitz survivor[28]

THROUGH A CHILD'S EYES

★

DR. ANNA RICH

Anna Rich was a child in the Netherlands in 1940 when the Nazis invaded her country. One-and-a-half million children were murdered by the Nazis during World War II, most of them Jewish. Those that helped these children faced the same fate. Following the war's end, Anna immigrated to the United States and later became an American citizen.

THE BOY UNDER THE BED

Rescue the weak and the needy; deliver them from the hand of the wicked. (Psalm 82:4, NRSV)

"Help me! Help me!" the boy cried as he burst through the front door. His face was pale, his dark locks covered his forehead, his eyes were wide open with fright.

Mama jumped up from the big chair in which she sat, reading me a story. She closed the door behind the boy.

"What's wrong, child?" she asked, putting her hand on his trembling shoulder.

"The soldiers, they are after me. I am Jewish. They already took my family. Please help me!"

Without another thought Mama pulled him into my small bedroom and pushed him under my bed. Then she grabbed the rest of us and ran back into the living room. Only seconds had passed, and we now occupied our original places, just as we were before the boy burst in.

From my first earliest remembrance of my childhood in the Netherlands, Papa would take all of us for a little walk each night. Mama would push the carriage with little Frankie in it, and Papa would hold my hand in his while the two older boys ran on ahead. After we returned home and baths were finished, he would comb the tangles from my hair. I would laugh and giggle and squirm under his firm grip. Then we would gather in the living room around the piano, which was Mama's pride and joy, to sing and laugh and hold hands. Our parents would listen to us say our goodnight prayers, then tuck us into bed. Life seemed so simple, so happy and peaceful.

Mama had rosy cheeks and wore colorful clothes. Her curly hair dangled around her pretty face, and her love for her family shone in her eyes. She stayed at home teaching all of us the important lessons we would need to know in life, while Papa worked very hard as an accountant.

In 1940 war broke out, and Papa was forced to join the army. He was made an officer and had to report for duty. Soon thereafter, the Dutch government demobilized the army—they had decided not to fight the war anymore. Times changed, many men were out of work, and food supplies began to dwindle. Many Jewish families had been captured and transported to the prison camps, as they were called. There was a darkness, a kind of gloominess everywhere.

One day Papa came home with a worried face. He patted us on our heads and said, "Children, I have to speak with Mama. Go into the living room and play quietly. We won't be long." His tone of voice was very serious.

Papa was tall and had curly dark hair. He had a little mustache and his hazel eyes usually had little lights dancing in them. But lately there was a sadness in them instead.

We were as quiet as we could be. Mama and Papa spoke very softly, so softly that we could hear Mama crying softly as Papa tried to comfort her. We looked at each other with frozen faces, faces at least as worried as Papa's had been when he walked through the door. Our parents' behavior mystified us. What could be going on? we wondered.

After a while they came into the living room and sat down with us. "Listen, children, I have to leave for a little while," Papa said quietly.

I began to cry, big tears dripping down my cheeks. "But, Papa, you won't be able to take a walk with me or comb my hair,"

I pleaded with a choked voice.

Mama hung her head down and did not look up as Papa spoke to us. "I have to go far away to find work. I wouldn't leave, but there is no work anywhere around here now. I'm sorry, but if I'm going to take care of you, I have to go."

The drumbeat of war that banged all around us had invaded even our happy home.

As time passed we grew used to Papa's absence, though we cherished each one of the wonderful letters he sent. He never failed to send his love and financial support. Mama would read his letters aloud, and we would talk about how wonderful it would be when we were reunited.

We did not have much, but Mama kept us clean and used our food ration coupons carefully and wisely. She was a woman of great courage and held on firmly to her belief that one day Papa would return. She drew her strength from a deep-seated belief in God.

The year was 1943, and Europe was at war. Jews were being rounded up by German soldiers and taken to concentration camps, where many of them were put to death. More than one hundred thousand were taken from our small country to the death camps . . . and almost thirty thousand of those were children.

The invasion of the Nazis had brought untold grief to everyone living in the Netherlands. Ours was a small, flat country filled with flowers, farms, waterways, and sailboats. Most of all, it was filled with peace-loving and hard-working people. It was forbidden to hide Jews, and anyone caught would suffer the same punishment as the Jews. In spite of this, my mother and many of our neighbors hid them and helped them escape. Such was the case the night the frightened boy ran into our house.

All of us had returned to our places in the living room. We tried to look as casual as possible, but my heart was beating wildly.

"Open this door. Open this door!" a voice demanded as someone banged on our front door.

"Shhh," Mama said to us, putting her finger to her mouth.

She walked slowly and steadily to the door and opened it.

Three soldiers pushed past her into our house.

"Is there a young man in here about this tall?" The soldier held up his hand about as high as Mama's shoulders and looked intently at each of us. "We believe he ran into this house. Search it, men!"

The soldiers began to run from one room to another, rummaging through our things. Their footsteps pounded loudly on the floor above us as they banged open each door.

I knew something terrible was going to happen. I had to do something. I stood up and began to cry very loudly, "You are making me afraid. Go away! Go away!

"Be quiet, you brat!" the officer snapped at me, but I wouldn't stop. The man walked up to Mama, his loud boots stomping on the floor. "Shut her up, or I will!"

Mama walked up to me, wondering what I was doing. I had covered my face with my hands and, peeking through, I could see that the soldiers were about to check the room where the boy was hidden. I began to cry all the louder.

The soldier lost his patience now, walked over, and kicked me viciously. My left knee was gashed, and blood started to run down into my socks.

Mama let go of me now and stood in front of me. She put her finger up to the soldier's face. "You stop this, you coward. Get out of my house!"

I was screaming bloody murder now. The boys were crying too, and Mama was yelling, "Out of here! Out of here!"

The other soldiers stood in the hall, shocked at their leader's behavior. They walked into the room and said anxiously, "Come on. The boy is not here. We checked everything." They tugged on their leader's arm and pulled him toward the door as he continued to yell at Mama to "shut up that brat!"

As the soldiers pulled him through the door, he stumbled over his own two feet and hit his head on the door. He began to spout ugly and vulgar words. Mama just went up to the door and slammed it shut behind them.

I kept screaming for a little while longer, until I was sure those soldiers had gone. Now all eyes turned to me as Mama examined the two large gashes on my knee and the blood that was filling my shoe. I sat down and said to Mama, "Go check on the boy, Mama."

She went into the room and looked under the bed at the frightened boy. "Seems everything is clear now. But lie here a little longer until we can be sure."

She got out our first-aid kit and shook her head. "These need sutures. I will bandage them and take you to the clinic as soon as I can. But first, I need to find out who this boy belongs to."

I nodded and leaned back into the soft chair, closing my eyes.

By now several neighbors had begun to filter into the house. Mama motioned to us not to say a word. It was better not to inform others that the boy was in the house. The neighbors told Mama that the soldiers had taken a whole Jewish family out of one of their cellars where they were hiding. Only one boy had escaped. Mama knew their family and learned where his grandparents were hiding.

She asked the neighbors to leave so that she could get me to the clinic. All of them were very upset about the soldier's actions and comforted me, saying, "We love you, honey. You get well."

Before I left the house, I hobbled into the room to say goodbye to the boy. I knelt down below the bedspread and saw his brown eyes looking out at me. I smiled at him and said, "Stay there a little while longer, and we will find your grandma."

Mama looked at me as I stood up. In her eyes I could see her approval. Though I was only five, at that moment I felt very grown up.

The doctors and nurses at the clinic were very kind and tended to my gash. One gave me an apple and another a piece of candy. The doctor promised me, "You are a very brave girl, and one day you'll grow up to be a beauty." But we told no one about the boy. Mama had taught us we could never be too careful in time of war.

That evening my grandmother came over. She was a small woman and brought clothing with her for the boy. It was old ladies clothing that included a hat with a plume. When he dressed up, we laughed so hard that tears rolled down our cheeks.

Before they left, we prayed that God would safely guide and protect them. We hugged the boy, and Grandmother walked beside him down the sidewalk and back to his remaining family. Later that night we learned all had gone well, but Mama instructed us never to speak of it again—for his safety as well as our own.

We often wondered what happened to the boy under our bed, but in the terror and confusion of those years, we never heard of him again. I think it was enough to know that he had come to our door and God helped us to protect him.

POTATO PEEL SOUP

In this manner, therefore, pray: . . .
Give us this day our daily bread. (Matthew 6:9-11, NKJV)

"Children, Aunt Jannie will take care of you today. Make sure you obey her and don't give her trouble, and I will come home with a filled suitcase!" We looked up at Mama as she donned her rose-colored hat with a quick shove, grabbed the tattered suitcase, and opened the door. She took one last look at her four children, and with a determined look stepped outside as Aunt Jannie closed the door behind her.

Our neighborhood was pretty with cobblestone streets and red brick houses that sported lace curtains and pretty plants behind their shiny windows. They seemed very similar, but their sameness was what made the place where I lived so warm and comfortable—so seemingly safe. I wondered what Mama was up to today.

We had learned that we needed to be a team when Papa was away. We managed to hold onto a little radio that we would secretly listen to, to hear the news of the war. It was on this little radio that I first heard the voice of the President of the United States. I didn't understand his words, but I loved to hear him. He sounded so powerful, so promising and exciting. Mama would translate the words of the President as we waited in breathless anticipation. We prayed the Americans would soon come to help, and Mama always held firm in her faith that they would.

Mama was the only daughter of an English architect and a Dutch seamstress and shop owner. She was raised and educated in an all-girls school in England where they spoke French during all their meals and social activities. She met Papa at church, where they both sang in the choir. Papa had come from a musical family and was studying to become a concert pianist. He soon fell in love with the red-headed, properly educated, socially refined young lady. They were married, and we came along a short while later.

In addition to feeding the five of us, Mama also helped Aunt Jannie and her five children and took care of Grandma, Papa's mother, who had become ill. Food was distributed through a system of food stamps given to every family. It was a kind of rationing, and when the stamps ran out, that was all there was that month. But Mama taught us to be thankful to God even if it wasn't enough. She always said that the Lord worked in strange ways and that He would never leave His children begging for bread.

One of our biggest surprises came the day we received some packages from the Red Cross. I remember the little green tin cans containing chocolate-covered sugar cookies—how wonderful they tasted. There were other agencies that tried to help us as well, but everyone suffered from a want of basic necessities.

But Mama always rose to the circumstances and was very resourceful. When she returned with her suitcase on that particular day, she opened it to reveal a trunkful of potato peelings! That night we celebrated with potato peel soup.

Mama's courage under these circumstances taught us to stand on our own two feet, to do the best we could, and to be thankful in every circumstance. It was something the Lord had taught her, and something she passed on to us. She tried to teach us to see the difficulties as a great adventure that would end up in a surprise conclusion. It helped us to not be so afraid of the war that was raging all around us.

Mama, with all her social graces and proper upbringing, wasn't too proud or too refined to collect potato peelings from alleyways to keep her children alive. She was a woman of great courage and determination. Papa called her "a woman of substance." But to me she was special because she was my mama.

BOMB SHELTERS AND ANGELS

For He shall give His angels charge over you,
to keep you in all your ways. (Psalm 91:11, NKJV)

The war in Europe meant many of our nights were spent in complete darkness. There were times when enemy planes would fly over, and we were told to turn off our lights so that none could shine through the windows. When the sirens would sound, a stabbing pain of fear would rush through my body. We would run for our candle and match, turn off the lights, and close the drapes.

Mama would turn over our sofa and big chair, and we would all crawl underneath. Then she would say "pray" or "sing," and we obeyed. The sounds of planes would get louder and louder, and we would tremble. Our little faces and bodies were so closely huddled together we could hear each other's labored breathing. My two big brothers and I were under the sofa, and Mama and baby Frankie were under the chair, hiding so that the plaster wouldn't fall on us. At least we felt somewhat safer in our little hideaway. It wasn't until the sounds of the bombs and the planes faded away that we could think of coming out. Even then, we could hardly sleep, and fear became our unwelcome but familiar companion.

"Anna, we're out of milk. Go down to the corner and get some and come right back. Here's the money."

My older brothers were in school that morning, and Mama needed milk for little Frankie, who was sick. I was only five, but the store was just a few doors away across the street. I took the coins from Mama's hand and headed out the front door.

"Wait a minute, Anna. Take this silver pitcher and have the man put the milk in it."

"Okay, Mama." I took the pitcher and started to skip away.

"You be careful with that pitcher, now. It's the one my mama gave me."

I liked the way my mama's voice sounded when she talked

about Grandma. Mama said she was a happy woman who would sing and paint pictures and embroider tablecloths.

This was the first time I had been sent on an errand, and I felt very grown up. The merchant was a very nice man. Every time I'd come to his store he'd say, "Come here, darling." Then he'd wink at Mama and let me take a piece of hard candy from a tin box. Today he filled the little milk can and then let me take a piece of lemon candy. "Be careful, don't spill it," he said warmly.

I carefully walked out the door, watching the white milk in the little pitcher slosh from side to side. I walked very slowly, never taking my eyes off the milk. Suddenly a siren startled me as it began to wind up in volume. It sounded so shrill. I had never been outside when the siren went off. I had never been away from my strong Mama when the planes came.

Now I was alone. I couldn't move. I called out, "Mama, Papa, Jesus!" But I was all alone, and my hands were shaking, and the milk began to slosh wildly from side to side. Then the thing I feared most, the thing my Mama told me not to let happen, happened. The little pitcher just couldn't hold the white milk with my hands shaking as they were. But the sirens kept going off, and I was afraid.

People were running from all directions, heading to the bomb shelter. "Hurry, people," a voice boomed. "We only have three minutes till the enemy planes will be here."

I heard many feet running. Then I felt a large warm hand take hold of my little one. I looked up at a strange man, and together we ran down the stairs into the shelter. Even though I'd never seen this man before in the neighborhood, I felt safe with him. As we entered the shelter, I saw many others who were already there.

I began to look around for Mama and couldn't find her. I saw our neighbor, Miss Rosie, holding Frankie.

"Where is my mama?"

"She's looking for you, honey. She'll be here soon."

I began to walk back toward the steps of the bomb shelter. A man stood there talking to a woman at the top of the stairs.

"I'm sorry, lady; we have to close the doors. Your daughter is probably already here."

"I can't come in. My daughter is missing. I have to find her."

When I heard her voice, I screamed, "Mama! Mama! I'm here. I'm here!"

Mama came running down the stairs and grabbed me and began to kiss me over and over.

"Look, Mama. I still have your silver can," I said as I held it up to her, "but the milk . . . I spilled it."

She looked at me, then at the can, and then at me again. She grabbed me tighter and whispered in my ear, "Oh, my baby, my precious one."

I told her about the man I had never seen before, who had taken me to the safety of the shelter. We went from family to family looking for him. He had held onto my hand while I was down there alone. He held it until I had heard my mama's voice and run to her. Where had he gone?

Finally Mama gave up looking for him and asking about him. She looked at me and said, "Honey, it must have been an angel. They're everywhere, and they are sent to protect God's children."

I looked into her strong eyes and never doubted her a bit.

We were in the shelter several days, and I came to like it. They handed out food and fruit and coloring books and crayons. There was a man there who sang and played a harmonica. I followed him around wherever he went.

A nurse came and checked on us, and gave me a smallpox shot. She thought I was looking good, and I remember wondering why she gave me the painful shot if I was looking so good.

In the evenings the radio was turned on, and we heard the voice of the President of the United States. Mama translated for many people in the shelter, and her words gave others hope. Mama said it was good to have hope, because hope keeps you going. She gave out a lot of hope to people in those days.

I worried about my cat, Minnie. I hoped she had found a safe hiding place, away from the planes and the bombs. My brother told me she had nine lives, so if she lost this one, she would have eight more. I hoped he was right.

Several days later, they opened the shelter doors and we returned to our home. I found Minnie—hiding in the storage shed. She seemed to be the same old cat and lay in bed with me, pulling my hair. But she began to hide at night in the kitchen, and we often wondered if she had been as frightened as we were.

I never again saw the man who rescued me that day, though I kept my eye open for him for a long time afterwards. In time I forgot what he looked like, but I never forgot the warmth I felt when he put his hand over mine. I felt safe, and that was something both special and rare during those years of war.

A PAIR OF SHOES

Therefore I say to you, do not worry about your life, what you will eat or what you will drink; nor about your body, what you will put on. . . . For your heavenly Father knows that you need all these things.
(Matthew 6:25, 32, NKJV)

"Oh, God. I know it sounds impossible, but if I could have anything, I'd like my own pair of shoes. Oh, and a puppy too, God? Amen."

"Did you say your prayers, Anna?" Mama asked quietly as I lay down to sleep.

"Yes, Mama."

"Goodnight then, dear," she said as she kissed me.

"Goodnight, Mama."

Things had gotten more difficult for our family than we ever could have imagined. My brother had become sick with dysentery and was put into a children's hospital. My mother had sold everything she had, a little at a time, as she continued to try to feed and clothe us while searching for my papa. It had been more than a year since we had heard from him.

By this time we had lost our home, my cat, and all of the things that had made me feel safe. We lived with my grandma and other relatives for a while, but now we had to return home. Home . . . Home . . . What was that? I looked out the train window, dreaming of our little house that seemed so warm and safe.

My thoughts were interrupted by terrible sounds of bombs and steel colliding as our train was attacked. Many of the cars were derailed, and others turned over. I managed to climb out of a window and began to run. Two soldiers ran after me, pushed me to the ground, and lay on top of me to protect me from the debris flying everywhere. When all had stopped, they lifted me up and took me to a nearby refugee camp.

The soldiers were like knights in shining armor. They handed me two of the largest slices of white bread I had ever seen. They gave me chocolate and gum. The next day the Red Cross managed to locate my mother and reunite us.

We found space on the benches at the train station and began sleeping there. Today, I imagine you'd say we were homeless. I remember crying because I was cold and hungry and had hurt my fingers when they had been crunched in a closing door. The first-aid people were kind to me, and they put a splint on my fingers and gave me a little food. It was winter in Holland, and while our winters weren't severe, they were cold enough to give my brother Aatje frostbite that night.

During the daytime Mama kept us busy teaching us how to read. But I missed my cat and my bed. I became quieter and more tearful, but I still tried to sing and pray each day. I asked God to find my father, to heal my brother, and to give us a home again. I asked Him to bring the soldiers to rescue us. But what I really wanted and needed was my own pair of shoes.

Because of the lack of money and shortage of supplies, my brother and I shared a pair of shoes. Even the pair we shared was on its last legs, consisting of little more than a wooden sole and a leather strap across the toes. So one day I would go to school wearing the shoes, and the next day my brother would attend wearing them. I liked being home with Mama and little Frankie, but I liked being in school during the day much better. So I started to pray fervently for my own pair of shoes. I gave God a lot of reasons why I should have them, starting with how I wanted to be educated like my mama.

My teacher was very kind to my brother and me and would often commend me as a good student. Because Mama had taught me to read when I was four, the teacher allowed me to help her with all sorts of little chores. One day after school she asked me,

"Annie, why have you been missing school so much lately?"

I was too embarrassed to speak and stood in silence. But she was patient and not in a hurry, so she waited. I looked up into her eyes and saw love and concern there, and my heart melted. I looked at my feet and whispered, "Aatje and I must share these shoes."

She didn't say anything for a moment, and I was afraid to look at her face. Then she patted me on the head and said, "I understand, dear. Now don't you worry about a thing."

But as I went home that day my heart was heavy. I felt the weight of the world on my shoulders.

Two days later I was back in school again. It was a wonderful day in which we played a game that I won. Fifty years later, I still remember the joy I felt! As the dismissal bell rang, everyone grabbed their shoes, put them on, and headed out of the door, glad to go home after a long day. I just sat at my desk and watched them go. I looked over at the lone pair of shoes remaining, and they reminded me that my day of excitement was over.

My teacher came from behind her desk and looked at me, a large smile on her face and her hands behind her back.

"Anna, two days ago you told me about your shoes. Well, I was praying that night, and God spoke to me. Do you know what He said?"

I looked at her and shook my head from side to side.

"He told me, 'Anna needs a pair of shoes. Will you buy them for her?' "

Then she took a small cardboard box from behind her and slowly took off the lid. I beheld the shiniest pair of black shoes I had ever seen. She looked at me and then placed the box into my hands.

Tears started running down my face. I threw my arms around her and whispered, "I'm so glad you listened to God."

I walked home that day in a trance, looking at my shiny shoes with every step. When I got to the train station, I ran to Mama, squealing with excitement. I could barely get the story out, and just kept pointing at my feet. "Look at my shoes, Mama. Look at my shoes."

Mama just stood there in shock and joy as she took in the story of the kindness of my schoolteacher.

"God heard my prayers, Mama. He heard my prayers, and look!"

"I know, dear. He knows what we need, and He always provides."

With the faith only a child might have, I added, "And you know what else, Mama? He's going to bring me a puppy!"

"What?!"

A HOME FOR ANNA

He shall cover you with His feathers, and
under His wings you shall take refuge. (Psalm 91:4, NKJV)

Living at the train station was hard, and I kept praying that God would send the soldiers to rescue us. It was 1945, and Mama must have been crazy with worry, because she could find no trace of my papa. She was a strong woman, but these circumstances could break even the strongest. Yet, we held on to our hope and our faith that God would see us through.

Mama felt it would be better for us to live in a children's home for a while until she was able to get our own place back in our hometown. So we went to an orphanage where the boys and girls were separated. It was worse than being cold in the train station. All of us came down with lice, and our hair was cut short. My brother Aatje ran away after only a few days.

At night I would cry and wish I could be back with my mama. We had lived with relatives in Switzerland at one point, and I prayed to go back there too. I missed the people and peace and safety of that country, and dreamed of the fresh air and Swiss landscape. My prayers changed, and I cried out, "Oh, God, why have you sent me here to this place with unhappy children and lice and rats? Have you forgotten me, God?"

I refused to speak Dutch. Most of the time I spoke in the Swiss dialect, so strong was my yearning to leave Holland and be safe again. I heard the headmistress say I was a problem child, and it would be better if my mama would come back and take me away. My brothers tried to comfort me, and Mama visited and told me things would be better soon. I thought of running away, but I didn't want to hurt Mama. Her face was sad, and I knew she missed Papa.

The children at the orphanage were afraid to go to the bathroom at night because of the rats. We could hear the scratchy sounds they made, and it scared us. Yet I didn't want to wet my bed, and I remember asking God to help me.

On night I woke up and had to go to the bathroom very badly. "Oh, God, please help me. I don't want to wet the bed, but I'm afraid to get up. Mama says you give your angels charge over us. Where is my angel?"

All of a sudden I was aware of the presence of a person standing by my bed. I peeked out from under the blanket and saw a very large man carrying a very large ax. I didn't think he was a beautiful angel, and he didn't speak, but I knew he had been sent to protect me.

I got up and went to the bathroom, and he followed me and stood outside the door. When I came back to my bed, he was gone. I told the children and the mistress in the morning about this angel. The mistress looked at me and told me not to lie.

"I believe in God, and I don't lie!" I insisted. Nevertheless, she told Mama to take us out of there as soon as possible. God had not forgotten me!

The Red Cross and housing authorities assigned our family a small apartment on the second floor of a small street in what was termed an "undesirable" neighborhood. Undesirable? They had no idea where we had been. For us, it was a God-sent miracle, and we were overjoyed!

Mama picked us up from the orphanage and took us to the little apartment. We didn't have a stick of furniture, and as we were walking down the street we saw an old chair put out for the trash man.

"Now, that's a mighty fine chair I can clean up nicely," Mama said in a happy tone of voice. All of us worked together to push the chair home and up the stairway. It was very heavy, but together we managed it. We named the chair Ouwe Taaie, which meant "old tough one." At that moment, I decided it would be Papa's chair when he came home.

And that reminded me to pray again. "Please bring my papa home soon, God. My mama needs him, and so do I."

A PUPPY, TOO?

Ask, and it will be given to you; seek, and you will find; knock, and it will be opened to you. (Matthew 7:7, NKJV)

Once we had our own place again, I began to remind the Lord of my desire for a dog. Mama said she had enough trouble feeding us, let alone a dog! But one afternoon I told the butcher that I was praying we might have a dog one day.

"Well, when you get that dog of yours, you come by here and I'll give you a bone each day," he said with a twinkle in his eye. I smiled and ran out, my heart filled with joy. I got home and told Mama that the butcher was going to help feed the dog every day.

She said doubtfully, "It will take a miracle for us to have a dog."

It was at that moment that I knew we were going to get a dog, because God is good at miracles. So I stopped praying for just any dog; I began to pray for a "miracle" dog. And of course, I never forgot to pray for my papa.

One night we had just turned off all the lights and gone to bed when a loud noise outside in the hallway alarmed us. We got up to investigate, and all of us children followed Mama to the door. When she opened the door, there stood a very large dog at the top of the stairs. She quickly closed the door and put her back to it.

"I prayed for food, not a large dog. No way!" she said as she tried to keep us from opening that door.

"Mama, I prayed for a dog, so please let him in!"

She looked at my pleading eyes and my brothers' eyes and only slightly relented.

"Well, for tonight he can stay. But tomorrow, out he goes. Besides, I'm sure he is just lost and belongs to someone."

My brothers were grinning, Frankie was clapping his hands for joy, and Mama was looking worried. I was in love, and promptly named the dog Bobbie. I put my arms around him and kissed him. "Welcome to our family, Bobbie!"

I looked at Mama. "God sent Bobbie to us, Mama." She didn't say a word.

We went back to our beds, and Bobbie followed me. My tiny bedroom was just large enough to hold a child's bed and a small bookcase. We didn't have toys. But now I had a dog!

The next morning my brothers and I took Bobbie for a walk. We passed the butcher, who gave him a bone, just as he promised. Everyone in the neighborhood knew I had been praying for a dog. When they saw me, they laughed at the sight of a tiny girl and a huge dog walking down the street. My brothers and I had sparkles in our eyes and smiles on our faces as we proudly walked with our dog.

Mama told us that night, "I pray for food each day. Why would God send this large animal?" She still had the worried look on her face. I knew she didn't want to go through the alleys looking for food again.

I hugged her and told her, "I prayed for this dog, Mama." She looked down at me and hugged me back.

Then the most amazing thing began to happen. The butcher came to our house the next day. He told Mama that he thought it was wonderful that the little girl had a dog and he would send scraps every day. "I promise," he said happily as he descended the stairs. The next day he did just as he said.

Then the vegetable man showed up at our door. "I'm going to be giving you some extra fruits and vegetables. I promise."

The entire neighborhood knew of Mama's worry about keeping this big, mangy dog, and God put it on their hearts to do what they could to help.

Even the flower man on the corner came outside one day as we passed. He handed Mama some flowers and said, "Come on, Mama. Let the children have this dog, and we will help you."

Funny, isn't it, how God answers our prayers in the most unusual ways? That dog ended up providing food for the entire family, through the kindness of our neighbors and the prayers of a little child.

PAPA

He saved them from the hand of him who hated them,
and redeemed them from the hand of the enemy.
(Psalm 106:10, NKJV)

After many years of terrible war, there finally came to our country a day of freedom, a day of celebration, a day of victory for all of us who had survived. Our family got on a train to go to The Hague, where a very large parade was going to be held to celebrate Victory Day in Europe. I was excited about so many things. The war was over, we were traveling back to visit our relatives in Switzerland, and everyone was together . . . everyone except Papa.

By now, I was a very grown-up five-year-old. But I had butterflies in my stomach. Everyone there was so happy to see us—to see that we had grown and survived the years of terrible war. I was glad to see them, too, yet I had a place inside of me that was sad. I told myself to cheer up, but it wasn't easy.

The war was officially over, and countries were again in control of their farms and land and cities. The Americans and Canadians were planning a parade, and I was excited to see these men who spoke the language of the President. His words had brought us comfort on so many different occasions.

The next day the streets were lined with thousands of people. Troops and tanks began to pass by. We waved and yelled and jumped up and down. These were my heroes.

"Johnny, look at me!" I yelled as I threw them kisses. They smiled back at us and threw kisses back and waved at us. Several soldiers jumped off a tank, and I pushed my way through the crowd to get to the front.

One of them touched my hair. "Look at that curly red hair," he said and stroked my head. "Here, honey, chocolate? Gum?"

I said, "Cigarettes for Papa?"

He smiled and handed me some. "Come to America, will you?" He bent down and kissed me on the cheek. "Good-bye," he said, and I started to cry.

"Good-bye, good boys! Thank you for saving us."

Everyone around us was laughing, but I was very serious, and I cried. Later Mama traded the four cigarettes for a loaf of bread, a tomato, and a banana for the baby.

God works in the most unusual ways, I thought. He gave us food, but first it was cigarettes.

When the parade was almost over, the Salvation Army band came down the street playing their instruments. I ran to them as fast as I could. They were soldiers too, Mama had told me, only they worked for God.

There was a crowd of people around them, and they were playing their wonderful music. One of the dark blue uniformed men started to preach. After that they passed around a plate to collect money. I ran up to the man with the cymbals and asked if I could play them. He said, "Sure, honey," and handed them to me.

I began to play the cymbals. It was hard work, but it was fun. Then when the plate came near me, I grabbed it and yelled, "Repent, everyone, and give your money!"

Everyone gave money, even the passing soldiers. Everyone was laughing; it was such a happy day. That's when I decided, then and there, that I would go to America someday. I would go to the land the President spoke from, and I would preach too. Mama said, "Sure, honey," and patted me on my head.

We left The Hague with a happy feeling about our future, but still I wondered about Papa. I kept reminding God about him. By this time, when I would mention Papa to Mama, she would just shake her head sadly and tell me not to talk about him. But I prayed for him all the time anyway. God will bring him back to me. I was sure.

One evening some months later we were in our apartment. After dinner we had been reading, and Mama made a bowl of pudding. We took Bobbie out for his nightly walk, and then it was time for bed. We prayed, and the boys went off to their room where Mama tucked them in.

I was restless that night, so Mama asked, "Would you like some pudding?" I stared at her, and then out of my mouth came the words, "No, it is Papa's pudding."

We looked at each other in the strangest way. Mama gave me that long, pensive look, as she often did when I would say something "off the wall." She put the pudding back on the windowsill, since we didn't have refrigerators in those days. The cool night air would keep it fresh one more day.

I tossed and turned in Mama's bed that night. I couldn't sleep, so I began to pray. I thanked the Lord for my mama and for my brothers. I prayed for the boy who had hidden under our bed so long ago. I thanked Him for our apartment and for Bobbie and all the people who had helped us: the schoolteacher who gave me shoes, the dog that God sent, and the butcher and vegetable man who kept us fed.

God had provided for us in the most unusual ways. Mama had prayed for food, but first came the big dog, and then came the food. It seemed this was the way God built our faith during those years.

A knock on the door interrupted my prayers. Mama sat up and looked down at me. Her eyes were big and wide open.

"Oh my God!" she said as she jumped up out of bed and ran to the door. I followed her, as did all of the boys. We stood there inside of the door, and Mama called tentatively, "Who is it?"

"It's Papa!" a voice boomed.

Mama yanked the door open, and there he was—tall and skinny with flaming red hair and the most wonderful smile on his face. Mama threw her arms around him and pulled him into the apartment, closing the door behind them. We all hugged and cried and laughed and talked, all at the same time.

I remember him bending over me, touching my hair, and kissing me and holding me tight. "I prayed for you every day, Papa!" was the first thing I could say to him.

He snapped his fingers and said, "That's why that chicken came by the fence every day and laid an egg!

We learned from Papa that he had been taken prisoner by the Germans a short while after he left us to find work. After all those years of torture and near-starvation conditions, he survived to come home to us again.

Papa sat down beneath the windowsill, and Mama gave him the bowl of pudding. He ate it all while we sat and watched him, spellbound by his every movement. Papa was home. Papa was home.

Of course I believed in miracles . . . though all of my dreams were impossible in the eyes of people, God had made every one of them come true.

RED SKIES OVER ASIA
THE VIETNAM WAR

We of the Kennedy and Johnson Administrations who participated in the decision on Vietnam acted according to what we thought to be the principles and traditions of this nation. Yet we were wrong, terribly wrong.
Robert S. McNamara—Secretary of Defense[29]

One of the big lessons of the Vietnam War is, if you are going to be in a war, you better be in it to win and not tie your hands the way we did.
George Schultz, Secretary, Labor and then Treasury under President Nixon[30]

Resulting War Slogans of the Era

War Is Not Healthy for Children and
  Other Living Things
Make Love Not War
Hell No, We Won't Go
Don't Trust Anyone Over Thirty
No Nukes Is Good Nukes
Peace Now!
One Way! ('70s Jesus Movement saying)

A Song of the Times

"Blowin' in the Wind,"
  Bob Dylan, 1963
How many times must a man look up
Before he can see the sky?
Yes, 'n' how many ears must one
  man have
Before he can hear people cry?
Yes, 'n' how many deaths will it take
  till he knows
That too many people have died?
The answer, my friend, is blowin' in
  the wind,
The answer is blowin' in the wind.

SHORT TOUR

★

WILLIAM L. LANDRETH
FIRST LIEUTENANT, U.S. ARMY
OCTOBER 1968–JANUARY 1969

To everything there is a season, a time for every pur-
pose under heaven: a time to be born, and a time to
die; a time to plant, and a time to pluck what is
planted; a time to kill, and a time to heal.

(Ecclesiastes 3:1-3a, NKJV)

I was three weeks in-country, a raw lieutenant fresh from the
States. I was leading an afternoon patrol west of Duc Pho in the
central highlands of Vietnam. While only a short time out, my
radioman informed me, "Eight-one, you got a call from eight-one
papa."

We were redirected to recon the ridgeline where a suspected
Vietcong position was dug in. Our orders were to find it, make
contact with the enemy, and destroy them. It took us most of a
day of backbreaking effort to hump our way up the ridge, chow
down, and set up our night defensive position.

I was eager to earn the respect and confidence of my men—
a formidable task for a green lieutenant. Leading men who
already had more jungle savvy usually generated an undercurrent
of suspicion and mistrust.

The line grunts generally operated with the premise that most
new infantry officers were inept glory-boys, a little reckless, or
both. But I didn't arrive with duty-honor-country in my head. I
didn't care about scoreboards and kill ratios. My primary concern
was not with body counts; what mattered to me was getting each
of my men home in one piece. I was determined to allay their
fears and prove to them that I wasn't going to ask them to do
something I wasn't prepared to do myself.

That afternoon I walked point for the first time, taking the afternoon patrol in a sweep along the west flank of the ridge. The air was hot and heavy, the undergrowth so thick that the trail was wide enough for only one man. Except for the occasional splinter of sunlight penetrating the dense canopy, we were enveloped in a dappled maze of green twilight. As we moved through this shielded green labyrinth, I could smell the scent of wet earth and damp mold, rotting vegetation, and sour sweat.

I threaded my way down the narrow corridor between solid walls of lush plant life, pausing every few paces to listen. Trickles of sweat burned my eyes as I strained to see any trip wires, punji pits, or ambushes up ahead. I was acutely aware of the lethal seriousness of what I was doing. I was filling the vacancy left by the previous platoon leader, who had tripped a booby trap earlier while walking point, sending a jagged shard of shrapnel through his throat.

As I moved nervously down the path, I couldn't shake the uncomfortable feeling that my neck was naked and exposed. At that moment, there were no illusions of Hollywood heroics coursing through my brain—only the rush of adrenaline. With each step, my heart was pounding so hard that I was convinced everyone in the column could hear it. Every new sound or curvature in the trail sent another surge of adrenaline pulsing through my system as I moved stealthily through the steamy, shadowy tangle.

In places there was a double or triple jungle canopy overhead. The trees, foliage, and tangled vines were damp and dripping from the perpetual humidity. Everything seemed to be sweating with nervous anticipation. An oppressive stillness hung in the moist air like an ominous refrain. There were no cries of birds or monkeys. The only life, if you could call it that, were white, inchworm-like ground leeches. They littered the jungle floor in a state of dormancy until the noise of a gentle footfall or the sound of a heartbeat pumping blood through veins awakened them to the approaching meal. Then, like a scene from a bizarre horror movie, thousands of them would raise their heads in unison, homing in on their potential victims, and start inching their way methodically toward us. Our army-issue repellant was the only thing that kept them at bay. It didn't seem to discourage the mosquitoes much, but it was death on those bloodsucking slugs.

The jungle was so impenetrable that we were forced to stick to the trail. If we tried hacking our way through the thick undergrowth, our thrashing would warn Charlie of our approach. It was a perfect setup for a VC ambush, so we snaked along the trail as cautiously as possible. The only comfort was the knowledge that the trail went both ways. Charlie took his chances on it just as we did. Often, our point man and the enemy's point man would surprise each other, empty a magazine, and it would be over in a few seconds—just that fast.

A lot of guys came over thinking that fighting in 'Nam involved slugging it out with the enemy for days on end. That happened only rarely; the jungles of Vietnam didn't accommodate the tactics or rules of conventional warfare. "Firefights" were called such because we expended a lot of firepower in lightning time. Like the speed of a brush fire, the killing flared up, then quickly died down. It happened so fast that some guys didn't have time to react before the shooting stopped. What took time was returning our bodies, now overdosed on adrenaline, back to some sense of normality.

The afternoon patrol included about fourteen men, two squads of six each, the radio operator, and me. We had been out about two hours and hadn't gone very far, as I was moving slowly. I didn't want to make any stupid mistakes. Suddenly I felt a tug on the back of my web gear. The man behind me pulled me back and pointed to our right about thirty feet uphill. There was a crude concrete bunker, covered with jungle growth, with a sinister dark slit staring right at me.

Everything came to a standstill. In that heart-stopping moment, I knew I was dead meat and clearly in the "kill zone." Tense seconds ticked by, but no muzzle flashes were seen or rifle cracks heard. I began to hope there wasn't anyone in the bunker. Maybe it's abandoned, I thought. I couldn't get any lower or move; my legs seemed a little limp. Three or four men checked out the bunker and found it empty.

A few meters down the trail, we spotted a tin-sided one-room building. I motioned the men on line to do a "reconnaissance" by fire. No one fired back. We checked it out and found it empty. A little farther on, we ran into a company-sized complex of about fifteen hooches scattered about fifteen yards apart along the slope of the ridge. Some were barracks, others were aid stations, and one was a regular chow hall. Pigs were running everywhere and squealed in terror as we lobbed in fragmentation grenades to clear the tunnels adjoining the barracks. No VC. By all evidence, they had fled in a hurry when they heard our recon fire a few minutes earlier.

The barracks were dug back about four feet into the damp earth with a huge woven mat, large enough for ten or twelve men to sleep on, suspended lazily eighteen inches above the earthen floor. The hooches had thatched roofs; some were open on one side and others were fully enclosed with just an open door. They all had an attached tunnel that sank into the hillside about six feet deep, made a ninety-degree turn for four feet, and then a final ninety-degree turn with a tunnel exit. These zigzag tunnels served as makeshift bomb shelters.

By the time we had thoroughly cleared the VC encampment, it was nearly dark. I radioed the CO for permission to pull back to our previous night's site—clearly the size of the VC camp suggested that we would be outnumbered if the enemy returned. He denied my request. The CO suspected that we had a good chance of uncovering some weapons or ammo caches in the vicinity and wanted us to hold the position overnight.

I broke the men into three groups of four or five and stationed them in the hooches that seemed the most suitable for a perimeter. Then, under the cover of my poncho liner and with the aid of my flashlight, I plotted our location in the event we had to call for artillery. While calculating the coordinates, it dawned on me that we were on the down-slope of a steep ridge away from our fire support base. At that angle, it would be extremely difficult to accurately adjust artillery fire around our position. With little margin for error, a change in wind velocity or a couple of degree error in the elevation sights of a howitzer, and friendly fire would become deadly.

After the darkness settled in, four of us slipped into one of the bamboo barracks near the trailhead at the edge of the camp. I was tucking the grid map away in my rucksack when one of my men whispered, "Sir, there is someone coming down the trail with a flashlight." We peered through the thatched siding and caught glimpses of a silhouette behind the dancing beam of a flashlight making its way toward us. He stepped over the trip-wire vine I had strung about thirty yards down trail without even noticing the grenade tied to the back of the tree. We were dripping with hot sweat as he headed toward our barracks. He was either going to pass by or turn down the side path leading up to our hooch. He decided to enter our barracks.

I was standing just inside the entrance, concealed in the darkness. The tiny spotlight was pacing across the ground like the probing nose of a bloodhound tracking its prey. I rolled a half-turn out of the doorway with my back on the ground, facing up toward the approaching soldier. In the shaft of light, I could only see his Ho Chi Minh sandals on the dirt trail. A second more, and he would see us. I fired three rounds point-blank into the figure before he crumpled in front of me with his back to my face.

I could see him in the darkness speaking to me with a pleading voice. I didn't understand Vietnamese, but it didn't take an interpreter to tell me he was pleading for his life. He was just lying there in his blood, a young man not so different from me, begging us to have mercy. It scared me and made me sick to my stomach at the same time.

My muzzle flashes and his groaning were giving his friends a good fix on our position. I had little choice. He would die soon anyway. To stop his misery, I fired a final, carefully placed bullet into his spine. Then I grabbed a grenade, pulled the pin, let the spoon fly and tossed it down the trail. I had to discourage any VC who were coming up the path and cover our retreat to another one of the barracks.

When we reached the other hooch, I radioed in to the CO, reported our situation, and requested immediate fire support. Within a few moments a parachute flare popped overhead with its flickering orange ball, followed by four high-explosive rounds with delayed fuses. I had purposely lied about the proximity of my men in order to get the incoming right on top of us. Normally this would be suicide, but I knew that unless we received a direct hit, we would be protected by Charlie's earthen bomb shelters coupled with the pattern of shell bursts that would spread out due to the reverse angle of impact on the hill.

After the initial salvo ripped through the jungle, my radio operator informed me the battery pack on the radio was going dead. Without that lifeline, our chances for surviving the night were slim. The CO told us to conserve energy by "breaking squelch" twice for a fire mission, once to end it. The juice was so low that we couldn't afford to transmit by voice any longer.

Surrounded by a company of VC in the pitch-black jungle, holed up in a dirt cave with only the sound of two static hisses, we were a heartbeat between life and death. I thought of my childhood fears of sleeping in a darkened bedroom, but our predicament gave a new meaning to the word terror. I was gripped by a cold, cramping fear. I was just glad we were huddled in the blackness so my men couldn't see the expression of icy terror on my face.

We waited, listening for movement. After the dust cleared, we could hear a faint rustling in the jungle around us. They were very close—so close we could smell their spicy sweat. The Vietnamese poured a rotten fish sauce called nouc-maum over their food, and once you've caught wind of it, you never forget its distinctive odor. As we sat there drenched in our own sweat, I wondered what we smelled like to them.

After a few moments of waiting for them to filter in from the jungle, I depressed the transmission button twice. Miles away, the gun crews of an artillery battery feverishly loaded huge brass shells into their big guns and rechecked their firing trajectory. With the tug of the lanyards, the Boom! Boom! Boom! Boom! sent their deadly delivery right down Charlie's throat.

Overhead, a lone spotting flare flickered to life, filtering a pale yellow light through the jungle canopy. We braced ourselves and covered our ears as the guttural sound of incoming fire passed in a steep descent overhead. Suddenly bright orange flashes, followed by the deafening Crump! Crump! Crump! Crump!

accented the darkness. The jungle was seized in a violent convulsion of fire and steel. The ground quivered with each impact as everything around us was ripped apart by a hail of flying shrapnel. Pieces as big as my fist tore through the flimsy barracks roof. Slivers of serrated steel scythed their way through broad leaves, branches, and lush vegetation.

Then, that which I feared came upon me. As though someone had ripped open a huge canvas overhead, a torrential downpour came upon us. It was a steady, hard rain, and I could no longer hear or smell Charlie. I was blind and deaf and without a sense of smell. I started to pray—what we referred to as P-&-Ps: prayers and promises. As a boy of ten I had gone forward in a church service and asked Jesus to be my Savior, but the troubled complexities of adolescence and early adulthood had long since erased that former innocence. Now I bartered with God. If He would turn off the rain and just let me live through the night, I would go to a church and support it when I got back home. Almost immediately the downpour stopped, and I could hear Charlie groping around again.

A second time my fingers transmitted the "break squelch–break squelch," and again, gun crews raced to remove spent shell casings and reload their breeches. There were two more fire missions called down on top of us before the sky began to wash with grays. It was 0500. Charlie had given up and slipped back into the jungle.

With the advancing light of dawn, the rest of the company arrived. We blew a hole in the jungle canopy with detonation cord and C-4 (plastic explosive) to provide a landing zone (LZ) for choppers to get in. Some of the rear area brass flew in to survey the tunnel complexes and the rain of destruction we had unleashed on the VC encampment. It was the customary public relations picture-taking for the desk jockey lifers to get feathers in their caps and extol their imaginary contribution to the war effort.

I was left with only the haunting memories of the darkness, the terror, the pleading voice of the wounded soldier, and the snapshots of his wife and kids that I had taken from his body. I tried to console myself with the fact that he would have done the same thing to me if the tables were turned. He had an AK-47, the safety was off, it was loaded with a full magazine, a round was chambered, and the selector switch was on full "rock and roll." But that didn't ease the guilt.

His dying somehow conferred on the VC a humanity that I hadn't acknowledged before. I sensed that I had done something I didn't have the authority to do: I had taken another man's life. Oh, I knew it was either "him or me, kill or be killed," but I didn't feel comfortable playing God. He alone was the Author and Designer of life itself—who was I to take it away?

As I replayed the nightmare in my mind, I also remembered that God had answered my prayers. I didn't know why yet, but I sensed that He had covered me with His hand. Still, the images of the dying soldier sobered me with a profound consciousness of my own mortality and a painful awareness of the value of human life.

Back home life unwinds at a monotonous pace, but in a war zone the mechanics of dying accelerate it. Life can end so abruptly, like that of another North Vietnamese soldier who tried to forage something to eat from one of the throwaway C-rations we had buried at one of our night positions. He fell for the stay-behind ambush set up for VC scavengers. His simple attempt to find food was terminated with a single bullet through his head.

The sight of his wretched remains made me question the sanctity of human life. That body, which once housed the sacred breath of life, seemed so desecrated. It just lay there like a shattered porcelain bowl. The mythical illusions of invincibility so coveted by youth were forever erased from my mind. At that moment I understood that life, even my life, was very temporary. I couldn't help wondering what really happens after the fragile shell we call our body dissolves. Death was so decisive—so final. But what was the ultimate end? War produced a lot of questions for me to consider.

As a reward for our mission's success, our unit was pulled back to the relative safety of a firebase. During Thanksgiving, the army flew in Chinook helicopters loaded with hot turkey dinners in large chow cans. Unfortunately, these cans had previously been used to transport gasoline, and the cooks had not scoured the cans sufficiently before using them as food containers. Within twenty-four hours, the entire base was plagued with a bad case of trots. I'll never forget the sight of two long lines of troopers shifting nervously from one foot to the other behind the sanctuary of the waiting latrines. Every so often, four or five men could no longer maintain control and peeled off for some desperate place to dump. At that moment, we were so vulnerable that a handful of VC could have overrun the entire base.

For the next murky month, we endured the endless misery of rain and drizzle. The relentless drumming pelting poncho liners, sandbags, and tin cans strung along the perimeter wire was like a Vietnamese version of Chinese water torture. We spent most of our time soaked to the skin in flooded foxholes or damp bunkers, or sloshing through dripping jungles, up one unforgiving mountain ridge and down another. It was a sodden month under dirty gray skies, awash in a sea of brownish-red mud, mildew, and monsoon rains.

In January, the rains subsided in welcome respite from the gray monotony. We received word that we would be airlifted the next morning to a village in the rice paddy lands west of Chu Lai. Intelligence (S-2) had information that about ten VC were conscripting forced labor from the local villagers, forcing them to dig cache holes and carry rice.

The job assigned to A Company was to go in and clear out the enemy. One platoon would be set down as a blocking force north of the village while my platoon and another would sweep in from the south, forcing the VC into the ambush. It was the classic hammer and anvil tactic, straight from the pages of a military textbook. It sounded simple in the classroom, but it didn't always come off so flawlessly in the field.

At 0530 hours, we loaded the bulbous green choppers known as "Hueys" in groups of eight amid the usual prayers and nagging question of whether or not it would be a hot LZ. The choppers assembled overhead, then veered off in the direction of the objective, looking like a swarm of dragonflies bobbing up and down in a gentle sea of invisible currents. Against the noise of buffeting winds and the whine of the motors, we were all secretly reassuring ourselves that there would be only ten Vietcong.

Our muscles tensed as we descended over the patchwork of palm groves and emerald rice paddies. All seemed so serene in the early morning stillness. The golden sunrise gilded the surrounding landscape with an almost enchanting beauty, and I could see the saffron-colored roofs of the hooches as we approached the village.

Before we jumped clear, the customary order to "lock and load" was issued. Under the relentless hammering of the chopper blades, none of us could hear the metallic sounds of bolts chambering their rounds. The Hueys set us down in the flooded rice paddies just south of the village just as a copper-colored sun was clearing the eastern horizon.

The Huey I was riding in had accidentally veered off course and dropped us off with the wrong platoon. We jumped out of the hatch into muddy, knee-deep water and headed across the field to link up with the other position. My radio operator, a couple of other men, and I had just reached one of the low dike footpaths bordering the rice paddy when we heard the rattle of rifle fire coming from the village.

The radio crackled to life with word that the point man in the other platoon had been killed. The cluster of men following me were in a crouched position, slogging through the shallow water, when I noticed that the thatched roofs we had observed from the air were camouflaging thick concrete bunkers.

When my fire team reached the second platoon, a number of the men were huddled together crying, overcome with grief at the death of the point man. Some were in a state of semishock, not from traumatic wounds, but from the pain of losing a buddy.

The early morning mist was burning off, bringing the details of the village into clear focus. I could see VC soldiers maneuvering toward a tree line bordering the village. They were jumping like black fleas from bunker to bunker, dodging and running to rifle pits and trenches to take up positions. We'd obviously landed in the midst of a large force of Vietcong and were in imminent danger of being outflanked.

I ordered my men to link up with the other platoon, who were digging in about three hundred yards away on a flat, sandy island ringed by palm trees. It was lying out in the middle of the expanse of rice paddies. We popped a smoke canister to cover our movement while one of the men started firing his 40 mm grenade launcher toward the enemy to keep their heads down. Under the clatter of helmets and web gear, sloshing water, and grunting men, we redeployed. Our dash to the island left us breathless, hearts pounding. I told my radioman to stay behind while I skirted the perimeter to find the other platoon leader. The men were feverishly digging shallow depressions around the sandy island in a circular perimeter.

The occasional snap of rounds, followed by the report of AKs, punctuated the air around us. The sporadic stutter of a machine gun could be heard in the distance. Our situation was rapidly deteriorating. We had to regain the initiative, but our options were limited. I got behind one of the M-60s and started working over the windbreak two hundred yards to our front, where the enemy had taken up positions. I was pumping staggering bursts of six shots a few feet above the rice paddies toward the tree line where Charlie was dug in. The intermittent tracer rounds streaked in quick succession, probing the tree line like a deadly finger.

Somewhere in the distance, a VC mortar crew was releasing an 82 mm round down the mouth of a tube, followed by the hollow cough. About seventy-five yards to our front, a huge geyser of mud, water, and dirt clods erupted, showering the surrounding paddy with a thousand tiny splashes and sending shock waves rippling across the muddy water.

My men were accustomed to fighting in the highlands, trudging up and down jungle ridges. Nobody wanted to hump heavy mortar tubes and base plates, along with a couple rounds per man, up those backbreaking slopes. Because of the density of the jungle canopy, we couldn't fire mortars even if we wanted to. Most of my platoon had never been exposed to the terrifying

KaRUMph! of incoming mortar rounds.

With the first burst, I figured Charlie was firing bracketing rounds to find our range: one long, one short. When they found our distance they would open up for effect. I assumed the first explosion had been the short round, to be followed by another. I thought we had a few precious moments to prepare; I didn't know that the mortar crew had already overstepped us with a spotting round and were now loading their tubes to hit our position.

I moved out to warn my men, who were dug in along the natural berm that ringed the island, to get down. As I passed from position to position, I noticed an old bomb crater gouged into the fringe of the island. I remember having the strongest inclination to dive into the hole, but I ignored the thought and passed by. I was in midstride when an enormous blast of hot air picked me up and slammed me to the ground. There was no sound—just that awful rush of dragon breath. The next instant, I was sitting upright in the dirt with my right leg cocked underneath me and my chin resting on my chest. I remember wondering who had poured hot tomato soup down the front of me.

Then I realized that it wasn't tomato soup, but my own hot blood. I was hemorrhaging from the neck. My throat had been ripped open, jugular vein severed, vocal chords paralyzed, and my right leg lacerated by shrapnel. With each heartbeat, my lifeblood was spurting out of my neck.

I knew I was bleeding to death, yet I had a matter-of-fact indifference to it all. I thought to myself, So this is what it's like to die. It's not so bad after all. Everything was winding down. I couldn't hear anything and was only vaguely conscious of my surroundings in a silent, slow-motion world. The gray-black bursts sounded their final exclamations across the paddies as I faded from this life.

As my life drained out of my wounds, I was overwhelmed by a bright light. It was faint at first, but gradually intensified to such a blinding brilliance that it was like trying to look straight at the sun. The illumination bathed me in a peace that transcended the battlefield. There was no apprehension—just an awesome glory and a deep sense of knowing, as though every question I could ever have asked was already answered.

I felt incredibly light, as though I was suspended in midair. My clinical assumption was that it was due to a rapid loss of blood, but what began to unfold convinced me otherwise. It seemed as if two bands were severed at my shoulders, and I began to rise a few feet above my body. I looked down and saw the top of my head. My navel had ascended to the height of my head. I lowered my chin a little more and could see through my new body. I had a shape and form, but I could see the ground through my chest. It was all so mysterious, yet not menacing. There was no longer any real attachment to my body. The real me was floating upward. It was such an exhilarating and euphoric sensation— as though the sheer rapture of all the joys of humanity were compressed into one intense moment.

Then, a soothing, fatherly voice asked me if there was any reason why I wanted to stay. I remembered that I had been married for only five days before I shipped out for 'Nam. I felt a sense of obligation to my wife not to leave her alone so soon. Suddenly, a commanding voice said, "NO!" and my soul and spirit shot back into my body like a snapped rubber band. The "here and now" quickly colored in around me, and sight and sound returned. The light faded, but that awesome peace remained.

Just then, I heard the voice of a soldier asking, "Anybody hit?" I reached up with my right hand and pinched the surface skin to stop the flow of blood, but it was hard to hold a firm grip with slippery blood all over my neck and trickling between my fingers. I still couldn't speak, so I lifted my left hand over my head and waved for Taylor, my radio operator, to help.

Along with Hernandez, the medic, he started an IV of albumin to help the coagulation of my blood. Taylor then radioed in for a med-evac. However, none wanted to risk landing their dust-offs in a hot LZ and jeopardizing the lives of the wounded they already had on board. Taylor responded, "If you don't come down now, eight-one will die!" I heard the words, but I had such confidence I would live that they didn't even bother me.

The battalion commander was circling overhead and happened to pick up Taylor's transmission. He ordered his personal chopper down to pick me up. Hernandez was also peppered in the back with shrapnel, so they flew both of us to an intermediate aid station to stabilize our condition.

I remember the stone-cold calmness of the door gunner as the chopper tilted its nose forward and climbed across the paddy. I was slumped forward in the bay with my throat laid open when he casually turned, flicked his cigarette, and offered me a smoke. It wasn't just the fact that I didn't smoke that made it seem so strange. Maybe he just did it out of habit—a standard dust-off courtesy, but it felt so melodramatic, like offering a last cigarette to a dying man or supplying a macho prop for a wounded soldier.

When we landed at the aid station, I remember the riveted stares of the onlookers as the medics lifted me off the Huey. I remember the deep concern etched into the haggard lines on the doctor's face. I knew those looks. They were the stare that strains to see the death angel as he completes his gruesome work and the look of morbid curiosity and icy fear that tries to steal a glimpse of the ultimate unknown.

Because of the massive loss of blood, my veins had collapsed. The doctors had difficulty registering another IV needle. But through it all I still maintained a confidence that I was going to pull through. They loaded our stretchers onto another chopper and rushed us to the med-evac hospital at Chu Lai.

When we arrived, the ER was a scene of chaos. Over twenty wounded men were crammed into a room designed to accommodate seven patients. Some were lying on gurneys while others were lying on the floor on stretchers. Doctors were sorting the wounded through triage, with the more critical patients receiving immediate care. I remember a VC in black pajamas lying on a gurney next to me, writhing in agony. I don't think he was high on the priority list.

The doctors were working feverishly on some other grunts while I lay there waiting for my number to come up. Then Hernandez started demanding that someone look at his platoon leader, and within moments a covey of medics were cutting away my fatigues and jungle boots.

That's when the guilt settled over me like a leaden sky. Just a few air miles away my men were in a tug-of-war with death, while I was in the safety of a hospital emergency room. I know it wasn't rational, but I felt I had deserted them in their time of need. It wasn't that I felt so indispensable; it's just that I cared so much for their welfare, much as a protective father feels for his children. That oppressive cloud of guilt stayed with me for the next twelve years.

In a few days I was transported to Cam Ranh Bay, then to Tokyo. Two weeks later, I was flown stateside to Fort Belvoir, Virginia, outside of Washington, D.C. The shrapnel had so damaged my vocal cords that I could barely whisper for a year. In time, the healing process returned my left vocal cord to near normal. I was medically retired from the army in 1972.

I served in 'Nam for only three months, but that short tour was destined to alter the rest of my life. In that space of time, I had acquired an addiction to adrenaline. The intensity of combat keeps your system constantly on the ragged edge. Every sensation is electrified. Your mind functions more smoothly, your thoughts are more lucid, your reflexes more adroit. No artificially induced high can equal it. I found myself taking up skydiving and scuba diving just for the sheer thrill of the rush. I was driven by an insatiable craving to live on the cutting edge. Life didn't seem worth living if you didn't put your life on the line, if you didn't beat the odds.

So I rode the fast lane, slept lightly, and kept a full rucksack by my bed: two hundred rounds of ammo, a high-powered rifle, a .45-caliber pistol, as well as an assortment of knives. I controlled my residual madness better than most, or maybe concealed it better than most, but it was an intimate part of my private life, much like alcohol to the alcoholic.

After five years, my wife could stand no more and ended up divorcing me. I, in turn, was sinking deeper and deeper into a black hole of cynical despondency. I tried EST and transcendental meditation in a last-ditch effort to get my head together, but I was out of control and hopelessly unraveling. I couldn't keep a job for more than two years and was running out of excuses.

I finally reached a point where I longed for an end to my misery. I went to the local vet center in Seattle. They tried their best to help with group therapy and psychotherapy, but all we accomplished was a rehashing of painful memories and a cosmetic catharsis. It was like putting a Band-Aid on a bullet hole. They could diagnose the presence of post-traumatic stress, but they couldn't heal it.

Through it all, I never remembered the prayer and promises I had uttered to God—but He hadn't forgotten me. I had married again, and my beautiful wife, Jan, was a sympathetic sounding board. However, she didn't let me wallow in self-pity; instead, she encouraged me to read the Bible. She stuck with me and loved me even though I dragged her through a nightmarish world of mental and emotional torture. Eventually the paranoia reached a placed where Jan was afraid to go to the bathroom at night for fear I'd shoot her with the .45 I had under my pillow.

It wasn't until I reached rock bottom that I decided to open the pages of the Bible and read. I'd tried everything else the world and psychology had to offer, with dismal results. That Book was the only thing left. Within a few minutes, the awesome power of God's Word brought me to tears. I found myself begging God for forgiveness. He not only forgave me, but did in an instant what the rap groups and therapy never accomplished. I got up from my tear-soaked carpet a healed and restored Christian, transformed and delivered from years of guilt, anger, and fear.

Since that turning point, I've often reflected on the words of a song that Richie Havens sang at Woodstock:

A soldier came down from Dien Ben Phu with tears in his eyes.
He told of many a night when fire was in the sky.
He told of many a morning when the bravest of men would cry,
Knowing that through Satan's earthbound magic,
Many more would have to die.

Those haunting lyrics were written for me. I was the soldier with tears in his eyes, tormented by Satan's earthbound magic.

And I discovered that the battle wasn't isolated to the hellish nightmare of 'Nam. It had followed me back home.

I spent three months fighting green-clad peasants and VC. I came home to fight a twelve-year battle against sin and the enemy of my soul. God preserved me in the first battle and continued to sustain me through all the subsequent ones until He won the victory.

Used with permission.
Condensed from
Vietnam: The Other Side of Glory
Bill Kimball

Postscript
Bill Landreth has now gone home to be with the Lord. The verse He left as testimony is 2 Timothy 4:7, 8 (KJV): "I have fought a good fight, I have finished my course, I have kept the faith: Henceforth there is laid up for me a crown of righteousness, which the Lord, the righteous judge, shall give me at that day: and not to me only, but unto all them also that love his appearing."

POINT MAN

★

SGT. ROGER HELLE, UNITED STATES MARINE CORPS (RET)

*Where can I go from Your Spirit? Or where can I flee
from Your presence? If I ascend into heaven, You are
there; if I make my bed in hell, behold, You are there.
If I take the wings of the morning, and dwell in the
uttermost parts of the sea, even there Your hand shall
lead me, and Your right hand shall hold me.*

(Psalm 139:7-10, NKJV)

Only a split second elapsed between the icy surge of blind terror and the realization of what stood before me. A moment before I had been walking point. Under the scorching glare of the early morning sun, I had paused to wipe the glistening sweat on my face when a hot blast of dragon's breath engulfed me.

I managed to regain my footing, and as I did, I saw a figure standing before me. The Kalishnikov he was holding flashed and jerked upwards as high-velocity rounds slammed into my body, lifting and twisting me backward. I was spinning out of control, and the ground rushed up to meet me. I strained without success to regain my footing. My mind told my body to get up, but it wouldn't cooperate. "Oh, God, he's over me!" The specter of the soldier and the glint of his bayonet on his AK-47 were poised above my chest. And then that long, dark cloud descended.

"Cut the chatter!" the sergeant barked as he pointed the replacements in the direction of a waiting bus with wire mesh covering the windows.

"On behalf of the United States Marine Corps, I want to welcome you to Disneyland east, better known as the 'Nam." We hope that you will enjoy your stay and ride with us again when you return to the land of the big PX." The driver did his best

Hollywood tour guide imitation as we piled into the bus.

"Why the wire over the windows?" the marine behind me called out.

"To keep the friendlies out," the driver said as if we were morons.

"To keep them out?" the same marine continued.

"Yeah," the driver added, "to keep them from throwin' things into the bus."

Another marine joined the conversation. "What do they throw?"

"What . . . do I have to draw you a picture?" the driver asked incredulously. "They throw whatever they get their hands on— grenades, garbage . . . you name it. I was drivin' through the Dogpatch last week, and some kid threw a dead rat at the windshield."

"Too much," the first marine said as he shook his head. "Man, if we gotta keep the friendlies out, what are the bad guys like?"

"Bad," the driver answered quietly. "You guys are in for a real learnin' experience. If Mr. Charles doesn't get ya, the 'Nam will."

I had been in-country less than a week when I learned I was going on my first perimeter patrol. Another new guy, Danny, was sitting next to me smoking his cigarette while I caressed the trigger guard of my M-14.

"Well, I guess this is it," I said.

"Yeah," Danny said absentmindedly.

"Saddle up!" Sgt. Jeremiah Pope snapped as he emerged from the bunker with his radioman. Everyone just called him "Pope." He was only twenty-one but he looked a lot older. Something about the way he carried himself showed that a lifetime separated us. One look in his eyes and you knew that he had the predatory instincts of a killer shark.

"You new guys fall in behind me and Angel." Pope nodded toward Danny and me. "Just keep your eyes open and your mouths closed. All right, check your frags, make sure your tags are taped, and secure any loose gear. I don't want you clowns announcing our arrival to Mr. Charles. Each of you will maintain proper distance with the guy in front of you. I don't want any bunching up. We're going out a couple of klicks (kilometers) and set up an ambush site. Understood?" he asked. No one answered. "Okay. Lock and load!"

The squad headed through the darkness in single file toward a gate in the perimeter wire. "Hold it up!" Pope called in a communications check before stepping off. "Sidewinder One, this is Sidewinder Two, over?"

"Sidewinder Two, we read you clear."

"I'm too short for this crap, Pope," a stocky marine with an M-79 whined as he shuffled past the squad leader.

"Knock it off, Blaine. I'm sick of your bitchin'. In a month you'll be back in the world again. This is just a walk in the woods," Pope reminded him.

"Well, that's just outstanding. I feel better already," Blaine continued. "Maybe you haven't heard, but war can be hazardous to your health!"

"That's old news, Blaine. Your bellyachin' is gettin' old, too."

I felt clumsy and slightly uncoordinated as I struggled to follow the vague outline of the radioman in front of me. It was hard to keep the proper distance in the darkness. I wondered how Danny was doing behind me. I tried to concentrate on each step as we made our way down the sandy trail. The light drizzle subsided, leaving only the muffled sound of men moving through the damp night.

After about an hour of humping, Pope halted the squad and had us set up an ambush site at the intersection of two trails. Word was that the VC were making their nocturnal rounds of the surrounding countryside. They were extorting taxes from the locals and threatening the villagers with reprisals if they helped the "American imperialists."

The night blackness played tricks with my eyes as I scanned the jungle. But I wasn't about to freak out and start shooting at shadows and make a fool of myself. I felt awkward and stupid— like my first day in junior high school. The minutes dragged by in slow motion. After what felt like an hour, I checked the radium dial of my watch to find that just seventeen minutes had passed.

This was the first night of many I would pass waiting for the enemy. It was early 1966, the end of Tet, and the beginning of the Year of the Horse. As time went on I began to gain confidence in my ability, and so did Sergeant Pope. Before long, I was pulling point—on security patrols around the perimeter at first, and then on deeper daytime forays outside the wire. These experiences cultivated my natural instincts as I humped around Phu Bai. I had yet to fire my weapon.

It was 2 A.M. when the sarge rolled through our barracks to kick us out of our racks. "Let's move it. We've got a chopper waiting. Check your weapons and make sure no rounds are chambered. I don't want any of you shooting yourselves before Charlie gets a chance."

I looked at Danny as he was putting his gear together.

"There's something I've got to tell you," he said in a low tone.

"Sure, what is it?"

"I want you to make sure that my brother gets this letter," Danny said as he pulled a folded letter from his shirt pocket.

"But . . ." I started.

"I've got a nagging feeling. Call it a premonition. I don't know what it is, but I'm not going to make it through this one."

"Don't talk like that. It's going to be a piece of cake," I tried to reassure him.

"Just promise me that you'll do it! Okay?" he said forcefully.

"All right, all right." I shoved the letter into my pocket and finished checking my gear.

We sat in silence tightly clutching our weapons as the chopper beat its way through the darkness. Men gritted their teeth or privately prayed as they assumed the various postures of those heading into terrifying uncertainty.

The chopper banked slightly to the left and then began a steep spiral descent. Just above the din of the rotor blades the crew chief shouted, "Get ready!"

"Lock and load! Selectors on semi!" Pope yelled.

My mouth was cardboard dry, my heart pounding like a bass

drum in a rock group. We touched down and Pope yelled, "Let's go! Move it! Go! Go! Go!"

In spite of the potential hazards of an air night assault, everything seemed to go smoothly. We waited near the landing zone, laying in two-man teams until the first hint of light around 5:30. The morning was calm. The sky was clean and blue, and not a cloud was visible. It seemed ironic that such a beautiful morning would greet us while we purposed to hunt down and kill other men.

Wisps of moisture rose from the shoulders of the men in front of me as we emerged through some secondary growth and entered a wide field about a thousand yards across. At the far edge of the field was the jungle. We spread out in a staggered line and swept forward. About a hundred yards into the field another marine came upon sharpened punji stakes, partially concealed in clumps of bushes and low grass. Charlie was close.

"You guys be on your toes," Pope ordered.

As we pressed farther into the field we crawled over numerous small mounds until we realized we had stumbled into a graveyard. A quiet hush fell upon the company as we cautiously moved through the cemetery and closed in on the tree line. Overhead, the steady drone of a Forward Air Controller (FAC) spotter plane could be heard as it passed over the ridge in front of us.

"Viper One, this is Bird Dog, over," the pilot radioed.

"This is Bird Dog, Viper. Read you five-by-five," Captain Jacobs answered.

"I've got some movement along the ridge, Viper One."

"Roger that, Bird Dog. We're in pursuit. Keep in visual contact, over."

"Will do, Viper One. Out."

The company pressed on. Time seemed to slow as the men calculated the distance to the lush curtain of vegetation and coconut palms before them. Dug in before them were not peasant farmers sneaking around the jungle in black pajamas, but a battalion of Vietcong, waiting.

Thoomp! Thoomp! Thoomp! The hollow, metallic cough of mortars drifted from the jungle. I looked over at Danny, whose face was filled with wide-eyed terror.

BOOM! BOOM! BOOM! BOOM! A Chinese .51-caliber machine gun opened up, sweeping the staggered line of grunts. The men flinched in stunned silence for a split second. I turned to Pope just as a .51-caliber round hit him, blowing his helmet into the air and disintegrating the top of his head in a shower of brains and bone. At the same time, a hailstorm of AKs opened up, raking the company with a deadly fusillade of fire.

I looked over at Danny just as he turned to his left. A .51-caliber slammed into his chest, lifting him off the ground and hurling him backward. His M-14 flew out of his hands and tumbled end over end before embedding itself in the sand. I fought to keep my composure.

Karummph! Karummph! Karummph! Deadly gray-black blossoms of .61 mm mortar rounds exploded across the field. I struggled to think, calling upon everything I had been taught as I dived into the sand and started firing on the tree line. This is crazy, I thought as I snapped off the rounds.

Marines were dropping around me as they took hits or scurried for cover. Others were frantically scooping out firing holes in the loose sand with their rifle butts and helmets.

"GUNS UP!" Lt. Leury screamed. "GET THOSE GUNS UP!"

Big Mike was already on the ground with his .60-caliber on bipods, firing measured bursts into the tree line. Tatow—tow-tow-tow. . . TaTow TaTow Tow Tow! He swept the jungle as the weapon spit out a brassy stream of 7.62 casings. The confused sounds of AKs, M-14s, .51s and M-6s reached a deafening pitch as each side tried to gain fire superiority.

I squeezed off rounds as fast as I could pull the trigger, firing blindly at the muzzle flashes that blinked from the foliage. As the last casing spewed out of the ejection port, I grabbed another magazine and inserted it. Ten seconds later it was gone. I yelled in frustration as I crammed another magazine into the rifle and flipped the selector to full automatic. A random burst stitched the soil in front of me, kicking up geysers of sand and dirt.

"Corpsman! Up!" someone screamed, and then another, as men cried out in pain.

Danny, I thought. Pope. I wanted to cry but I couldn't. There was no time. The hate cleared my mind and gave me fresh purpose.

Ssss zzzz whooo. A rocket-propelled grenade (RPG) streaked from the curtain of greens and landed behind Big Mike. KawRUNCH! The grenade exploded in an orange cloud and bowled him over from the concussion.

A second RPG shot from the foliage and exploded thirty feet behind me, causing the ground to heave from the impact.

"Corpsman!" Mike bellowed. A fountain of blood squirted out of his gunner's neck from a severed carotid artery. Charlie Brown was writhing on the ground, grasping his neck as arterial blood pumped from the jagged laceration.

Blaine swore to himself, but rose up and ran toward Mike to help him feed his gun. "Ammo! Ammo!" another gunner called. Blaine scrambled over to Danny's body and grabbed the can of machine gun ammo he had been carrying. He returned to Mike in a zigzag pattern, half stumbling, half running as the crack of AK rounds bullwhipped around him. Mike was behind a cemetery marker, stuttering away on the .60, oblivious to the rounds blowing pockmarks in the plaster headstone. "AMMO UP!" Mike bellowed, then swore as he saw his last belt fed through the .60.

"I'm coming!" Blaine shouted, as he closed the gap. "Aeahh!" he screamed as an AK round hit him below the knee, knocking his leg out from under him and spinning him around as a crimson stream of blood sprayed from his leg. Mike scurried in a low crawl to retrieve the can to feed his gun. Blaine was screaming in pain as he doubled up, squeezing his knee. Mike tried to reassure him as he grabbed the can and scampered back to his gun. He quickly slammed in the fresh belt and started hosing down the tree line.

"Bird Dog! Need marking rounds in tree line, over!" Captain Jacobs yelled.

"Roger, Viper One." The FAC pilot responded coolly as he swooped down low, dipping his nose toward the front edge of the tree line. Whoosh . . . Whoosh! The marking rounds streaked from the rocket tubes. The phosphorous shells landed just inside the tree line, blossoming into graceful umbrellas of molten white streamers.

"Got gunships on line, Viper One. Will stay on station, over!" the FAC pilot radioed.

"Roger that, Bird Dog. May need fast movers. Do you copy, over?" Captain Jacobs opened the terrain map and checked the grid coordinates as he coordinated with the FAC.

"Will do, Viper One."

The sound of gunships making a low pass hammered overhead followed by quick succession of 2.25 rockets streaking from their pods. A string of orange-black explosions ripped through the tree line, splintering trees and bamboo, snapping off palms, and throwing up clouds of dirt and foliage.

The two choppers banked tightly to the right as they pulled up from their first pass, then circled back and came in parallel with the tree line. Their door gunners were chattering away with their swivel-mounted 60s, slashing through the undergrowth with thousands of rounds. Then the Hueys climbed sharply to the left, spilling a glimmering stream of shell casings from the banking gunships in a golden shower, and came in again for one final pass, shredding the vegetation like an enormous blender.

Charlie seemed temporarily stunned by the fury of the gunships.

"Drop your rucks!" The words echoed down the line. "Lay down suppressing fire!" The M-60s opened up again amid the blooping sound of grenades hitting the tree line. "Up and at 'em! Let's rock and roll!" We rose as one and started running toward the enemy, firing fully automatic bursts.

"Unnnh!" A marine next to me grunted as he crumbled in a heap. The dull thud of a high-velocity impact somersaulted another marine from the hit. I ran forward, screaming at the top of my lungs and firing from my hip. Others went down. Men were screaming as the jungle exploded with a wall of return fire. I wasn't thinking now. I was on fully automatic as I rushed the muzzle flashes.

I leaped over a dead marine. KAROOM! I was in midstride when a loud explosion erupted in front of me, blowing me backward in a shower of sand and rocks. I was on the ground spitting out the sand and firing again. I reached for another magazine when I noticed the front of my fatigue shirt was wet with blood. I'm hit! I thought as a wave of panic hit me. I rolled to my back and frantically began to tear at the buttons to check my chest. I didn't feel anything. I ran my hands over my chest and found no bleeding. I rolled to the prone position and realized I was lying on an amputated leg. The blood from it had spattered me when it was blown off in the explosion.

Oh God, I can't stay here, I thought, as I gagged back the hot puke in my throat. Got to get up and move! I got up and started running again.

Squad leaders were yelling "Move! Move! Move!" The men broke into the tree line in hot pursuit of the VC, who were withdrawing through the jungle, dragging their wounded with them.

In a frenzied stampede, marines assaulted the tree line, rushing through broken limbs and tattered foliage that sprang back, snagging weapons and grabbing gear. Rounds slapped through the moist vegetation, ripping through stalks and broad leaves, ferns and trees, clothing and men. The muffled crunch of grenades punctuated the chaos. We were firing wildly now, rushing forward in a panicked rampage. It was five minutes of a sustained heart attack, a fall from a twenty-story building, the wildest roller-coaster ride of our lives—and then it was over.

We were ordered to break off contact. Another company would pursue them with gunship support.

I staggered back through the jungle in a state of dazed exhaustion. Sporadic shots tapered off. Moans filtered through the curtains of green. Marines lay crumpled and sprawled in awkward, dead poses. The acrid smell of burned cordite filtered through the dense air. Shadows lengthened as the sun arched into Laos, leaving the air steamy as it began to cool.

"Water . . . water." The low, plaintive moans of thirsty marines drifted through the air.

I was dazed by the carnage that surrounded me. Danny, I remembered again. Just a piece of cake . . . The words stabbed at my conscience like a hot poker. Our company was a shattered remnant. Forty percent were killed or wounded. Two more would die before they made it to Da Nang. The whole battle lasted less than an hour, but the memories would last forever.

I found Danny sprawled on his back, spread eagle, his arms extended back as if he were reaching for something. His skin was taunt and pasty—the color of pale wax.

"Man, this guy is one messed up muthah!" A marine grinned at me.

"Shut up!" I snapped.

"You know the guy?"

"He was my best friend."

"Oh man, I'm sorry . . . I'm really sorry," he apologized and stumbled away.

I gagged again and swallowed back the urge to vomit as they picked up Danny's body and put it in the rubber bag. They walked to the chopper and heaved the dead weight onto the blood-smeared floor like a sack of potatoes.

Why Danny? I wondered. I had never felt so alone in my life. I listened and watched as the mournful sound of the last chopper receded in the distance with Danny's corpse. The gooks are gonna pay, I vowed to myself. I owe you Danny—and Pope and the rest.

That night in the hooch was the loneliest of my life. My friend was gone. I slumped on my cot and started to unbutton my filthy utility shirt. I touched paper inside my pocket and pulled it out. It was Danny's letter to his brother. I opened it gingerly, read it, and hung my head.

Dear Paul,

By the time you receive this letter, you will know that I am not coming home. It's very hard for me to write this to you or explain what it's like being over here. I don't know if you will understand, but I still feel like I did the right thing. I mean that, Paul, and I want you to know that for sure. Please don't question that or let anyone back home try to tell you different. I know we haven't talked a lot since Mom and Dad died, but for whatever its worth, I know they would have been real proud of how you took care of me and the ranch. You've done real good. Please don't cry for me. Just think to yourself when you see all those stars shining in the heavens at night that your little brother is somewhere up there looking down on you. I want you to know that I will miss you and the ranch and all the good times we shared, even if it was hard at times. I've never told you this, Paul, but I love you. You've been more than a brother to me—you've been my friend.

Your brother,
Danny

I wanted to cry, but the tears wouldn't come. I wanted to sleep, but the memories of the day assaulted me. What if . . . What if I hadn't . . . If only I had . . . Why am I alive? I spent the remainder of the night spinning the questions around in my head without finding their answers until the morning sun crept above the horizon.

Corporal McClure assembled the squad in the morning to discuss the patrol we were going to pull that night.

"Battalion wants us to step up security around Phu Bai. They want us to do a sweep though this pocket of paddy lands. Helle—since you're pulling point, I want you to plot the patrol route, so we can call in reference points in case we need artillery support. Got any suggestions?"

I scanned the map for a moment before responding. "I think we should patrol these small villages," I said as I pointed to his map.

"Okay, map it out."

That afternoon the squad loaded up, called in their comm checks, and headed into the countryside with two additional squads of PFs. (Popular Forces, or Papa Foxtrot forces, were loosely trained Vietnamese national guard forces who fought alongside a number of our marine forces.) It was going to be another searing day in the 'Nam. As the point man, I sifted every shred of stimuli for potential danger as I inched cautiously toward the first village.

I tensed at the sight of a partially concealed man behind the shrubbery of a ten-foot hedge. I motioned Corporal McClure, who was just rounding the intersection, to hold it up. The man was squatting on his haunches in what appeared to be an entrance through the hedge. He was looking down the path in the opposite direction, unaware of my approach. He seemed to be lost in the beauty of the pastel sunset, which had begun to burnish the countryside with golden highlights. I crept closer and then nudged him on the back of his shoulder with the tip of my rifle.

"Choi toi xen can cuoc uca anh (Give me your identification card!)."

The peasant flinched in alarm from the tap of the rifle and sprang to his feet. He was wearing a conical straw hat, old black trousers, and a dull green fatigue shirt.

"Sorry, I do not understand," he replied in Vietnamese, feigning humility.

"Give me your ID card now!" I repeated in Vietnamese. We hadn't patrolled this area of villages recently, so it was customary to check for ID cards that the South Vietnamese government had issued. Without one a person could be hauled in for questioning as a suspected VC. The peasant shook his head as if confused.

Out of the corner of my eye I caught some movement coming from the open area on the other side of the hedge and heard the distinctive singsong chatter of Vietnamese men in the courtyard. I stepped closer to get a clearer look. Two khaki-clad soldiers with web gear were coming out of a hooch set back in the enclosed compound. They were laughing and talking to each other with their AKs slung over their shoulders, unaware of my presence. I turned for just a second, when the first man jumped back and reached into his pants to pull out something.

"Dung lai (don't move)," I hissed between clenched teeth. My chest tightened. A deep breath caught in my throat as I saw the wooden handle of a Chinese grenade halfway out of the man's pocket. He was struggling to get the thing free.

Everything seemed to happen in a splint-second blur. The VC's face was a portrait of wide-eyed terror as he struggled with the grenade. The two soldiers saw movement and were unslinging their assault rifles. I looked down in time to see the man on the ground now, trying to pull the detonator string of the grenade. I shoved my boot on his wrist to keep him from pulling the cord. No time left, I thought as I shoved my M-14 into the chest of the squirming VC. I squeezed off three quick rounds, which imploded in the man's rib cage. Without thinking, I dropped to one knee and aimed through the opening at the two frightened soldiers who were bringing their weapons up to fire.

I flicked the selector to fully automatic and cut loose a fifteen-round burst, which stitched the first soldier in a diagonal line across his stomach and carried over to the other soldier across his upper torso.

Suddenly the village exploded with a flurry of activity as VC sprang to action, spilling out of hooches and scrambling to escape. It was as if someone had kicked over an ants' nest. The popcorn sound of small weapons rattled all around as the force of marines and PFs opened up on the village. Rounds were zipping through the foliage and hooches as the VC raced through the hedges and footpaths to flee.

McClure scurried to where I lay in a prone position firing into the hooch. In a couple of minutes the order was passed down the line to cease fire. A squad of VC tax collectors had melted into the countryside.

Corporal McClure took one look at the VC bodies sprawled in front of me and shook his head, "Helle, you gonna win the war all by yourself? You're some piece of work!" He patted me on the back, and a wave of satisfaction swept over me unlike anything else I'd ever experienced. Suddenly, I was no longer the kid back in Toledo who was always screwing up.

"Whoa! Check this out." Scroggins exclaimed as he admired one of the mint condition AK-47s the uniformed soldiers were carrying.

"It's the first one I've seen any regular VCs issued around Phu Bai," McClure added.

"Hey, if you think that's far out, check out the damage our man Helle has done!" Thumper pointed at the three bodies. "Looks like he single-handedly waxed some of Uncle Ho's finest. Just a little payback, huh, Helle?"

"How did you get the jump on all three, Helle?" Paterson asked in amazement. It wasn't often you saw whom you were shooting at in the blind anonymity of a firefight, let alone got three confirmed kills in a face-to-face shoot-out.

"I just walked up on this one before he knew I was there," I said, casually pointing the barrel of my rifle at the first body.

"That's too much! You just walked up on him, and he didn't even hear you?"

"There it is," I replied matter-of-factly.

"Well, I guess they didn't get the message," Thumper joked.

"What's that?"

"War can be hazardous to your health!"

I basked in the euphoria of my first kill as we walked back to the compound. Minor benchmarks in a person's life back in the sanctuary of America could be fraught with their own unique fears and insecurities—passing your first driver's test, learning to cross the swimming pool on your own, that first solo ride on your bike without training wheels. They were all trivial in comparison to this.

I had looked the monster in the eye and hadn't backed down. In some small way it seemed to validate my manhood. It had also broken the curse I had been carrying: You'll never amount to anything. You're just going to be a bum! Until the corps, it had been a self-fulfilling prophecy. I failed at everything I attempted. But that brief firefight at Son Toi changed all of that. What's more, I thought, plodding across the paddy lands west of Phu Bai, it settled part of the score for Danny.

I continued to pull recon patrols in the mountainous jungles and secluded valleys northwest of the Rockpile, shadowing the enemy and calling in air strikes. For days we slithered through tangled greens, laid buried in rotting humus or hidden in jungle-clogged ravines watching with unseen eyes as thousands of camouflaged North Vietnamese soldiers and porters snaked along trails. I managed to make it back each time, swearing I would never go out on recon again. But after a few days on the Rock, I craved a fresh fix of adrenaline.

When I wasn't pulling recon patrols, I got to know a number of the field officers when they came in for their briefings. One of them was a second lieutenant who was the epitome of a marine. Lieutenant Knox was the kind you would expect to see on a recruitment poster—handsome, sharp, standing ramrod straight in his dress blues and white gloves with his officer's sword smartly drawn at his side. I had seen a lot of young lieutenants come and go during my tour. Most of them were cocky, inflated with their own self-importance, and just a little too gung-ho for their own good. Some of them were more concerned with winning medals than caring for the welfare of their men. Knox was different. He was the kind of officer who didn't have to demand respect—Knox won it easily because he genuinely respected every man in his platoon. He had a quiet strength and an unassuming courage that made him a natural leader.

Knox was tough but never coarse, confident but never arrogant. He was dedicated and fair. I would often find him in the solitude of his bunker quietly reading his Bible or praying. I had seen a lot of guys carrying little Marine Corps New Testaments or wearing crosses and Saint Christopher medals, but these were viewed more as good luck symbols or talismans than anything else. And most of the chaplains who came out to the Rockpile to perform Mass or give short pep talks to the men didn't impress me much with their lofty sermons and tired moralizing. I didn't think I had met anyone who was truly religious.

Lieutenant Knox was different. He was down-to-earth and didn't come across as a kook. He never pushed his religion on anyone, but he affected his men with his resolve and strength of convictions. We gradually became close friends.

"How ya doin', sir? Gunny said you were lookin' for me." I leaned into the lieutenant's doorway, halfway buried in the ground. The bunker smelled of mildew and rot.

Knox was sitting on an empty ammo crate reading a small,

thumb-worn Bible. "Doin' great, Rog. How's life treatin' you?"

"Life sucks, sir, but I'm hangin' in there just the same," I replied. "You sure read that thing a lot. Must be somethin' interesting in it?"

"You oughta try it sometime." He flashed a wide smile. "It won't kill you, ya know." Then he sobered. "You musta have heard the scuttlebutt by now. The battalion is sending a reinforced company on a sweep to flush the enemy out of their hiding places. I'm short a squad leader, and I wanted to know if you'd like to volunteer." He closed his Bible and looked up at me. "I've already cleared it with the captain, and he's got the okay from the colonel. It's up to you."

"Sure, Lieutenant. I've heard that the corps is always lookin' for a few good men." I grinned. I was only too eager to get off the hill.

"That's good. You'll be taking over Third Squad. Sergeant Reid is out with a bad case of malaria. The third herd is a great bunch of guys, and Lewis is the best gunner in the company. "

"Thank you, sir," I replied. I started to leave. "Say, Lieutenant, does that little book really help?

"They don't call it 'the Good Book' for nothin', Corporal."

"I'll keep that in mind, sir. I better shove off. The colonel is probably wondering where I am."

At 20:00 hours, the two platoons assembled. We were pumped up and ready for action. The squad leaders gave the men a final once over, then our two columns moved out. The PF platoon took the northerly route while my marines headed south.

The weather was at the muggy transition time between the end of the dry season and the advent of the rainy. Although the rains had not yet started, the sky was threatening and overcast with dirty gray clouds. The night was hot and sultry, and a smell of impending rain was in the air.

The columns moved with precision and stealth through the darkness, keeping in contact by radio. By 3:30 A.M. we had moved into position. We fanned out just inside the tree line, surrounding an open field about a hundred meters in diameter. There were no sounds coming from the camp, but the pungent smell of wood smoke and fish sauce floated from the clearing, telling us the VC were there.

Sergeant Tre and I had positioned our M-60s and fire teams in an L-shaped ambush with the open end butting up to a steep hill. We were concealed in a double-tier canopy with an open killing field in front of us. The jungle was dripping with moisture that had condensed on the leaves in the early morning air. Crickets, mosquitoes, and flying insects whined and buzzed around us.

The field was covered with shoulder-high stands of elephant grass, stubby trees, and trampled down areas. Camouflaged netting and brush were set up to conceal the base camp from spotter planes. We would strike at first light when we could see what we were shooting at.

Between 4:00 and 4:30 A.M., several VC squads came back from patrols. At one point, the rustling of brush sounded and a squad of eight approached down an animal track. They passed within inches of my men, who were lurking in the foliage, but they were probably too worn out from patrol to notice us. All they wanted was some hot rice and tea.

The camp was a staging area for a platoon of main force Vietcong and a bivouac site for other VC and NVA units passing through the area. The local VC served as escorts to guide other units through the area as they filtered south. That morning there were about sixty VC in the camp. Most were asleep in hammocks strung between spindly trees.

By 4:50 A.M., the clearing began to lighten with the violet half-light of predawn. The camp came to life as a few Vietnamese talked in a low pitch in the still morning air. Word was passed along the line with hand signals to open fire in five minutes. We flipped our selectors to full automatic while the machine gunners chambered rounds and checked their belts. Men glanced at their watches, wiped sweat from their brows, took deep breaths, and tightened their grips on their weapons.

Tatow, tatow, tatatatatat! At 5 A.M., the first M-60 opened up, followed immediately by an eruption of automatic fire that cut across the field at waist level. The startled VC bolted from their sleep and ran in a frantic free-for-all as the machine guns and M-1s mowed them down. The withering fusillade of automatic fire chopped through the shoots of elephant grass like a Weed Eater, neatly trimming the grass in a deadly manicure. Bloop—CRUNCH! Bloop—CRUNCH! Bloop—CRUNCH! The M-79 grenade launchers now began to land in the middle of the frenzied VC.

"FOOORWAAAAARD!" I screamed, and the other squad leaders echoed my command. "Yeaaah!" The marines and PFs rushed through the grass, firing as they went. VC swiveled, pitched, and toppled around them. The onrushing tide of marines stormed across the clearing, overrunning the startled VC in a lightning assault.

"Chieu Hoi! Chieu Hoi!" Frightened VC threw their weapons down and surrendered, begging the marines not to shoot them. The ambush was over in a couple of minutes. The predawn attack had completely taken the enemy by surprise. Our Combined Action Patrol (CAP) unit accounted for twenty-six confirmed VC kills, fifteen wounded, and ten POWs. Only a half dozen VC had escaped. A quick search of the area found two blood trails leading off through the brush.

The attack was a complete success, suffering only three wounded among the marines and one PF seriously wounded. We captured numerous AK-47s, carbines, satchel charges, Chinese grenades, a 12.7 mm machine gun, and several light machine guns. Besides the weapons, we confiscated a ton of rice in burlap bags, medical supplies, maps, important documents, and field radios. We effectively eliminated an entire reinforced platoon and captured so many weapons and stocks of ammo we couldn't carry it all. Some of it we blew up in place, and the rest we concealed until we could return for a more thorough search. We loaded up what we could and started back.

I was basking in the euphoria of my unit's victory and felt that this was my finest moment. I had put it to Charles the way Charles had put it to Danny—point-blank, cold-blooded, and blunt. I felt no remorse, only stone-cold satisfaction. It was payback time, and I had collected.

CAG headquarters was stunned by the overwhelming success of our raid. My unit had done what many larger units didn't accomplish in a year. Rumors quickly trickled down through the grapevine that I was being considered for a battlefield commission. I couldn't have been happier. But I still wanted more.

Three days later, I mustered my men to mount a follow-up attack on the VC base camp to destroy the cache of weapons and ammunition we had left behind. There were a number of tunnels there I wanted to blow to prevent Charlie from using this area again. Around 4 A.M., we assembled in the CAP compound. I ordered each of the men to carry either a block of C-4 or at least two incendiary or white phosphorous grenades. Since I was pulling point on this mission, I felt that I should set the example by carrying the most explosives. My two bags were bulging. I was obsessed with the need to finish the job. The raid had seemed so perfect in its execution and result. This morning's mission would be the final exclamation mark.

The men were smokin' and jokin' and fooling around with each other in the predawn darkness. Their spirits were buoyant with the thrill of victory. They were preening and strutting like prized fighting cocks, ready to get back in the ring. They were bad, and they knew it.

I strapped down the ties on my bags, made some final adjustments, then hefted one on each side, crisscrossed around my neck and shoulders. My bags looked pregnant, but I was dressing lightly. It was early, but the air was already humid.

"You pullin' point with all that stuff?" Monk asked, slurping down the last of some pear juice out of a C-rat can he'd just opened with his P-38 [military issue can opener].

"Is the Pope Catholic?" I responded.

"Whaddaya got in that thing, a tank?" Gopher joked.

"Let's just say there's enough bang in here to finish what we started," I answered.

"Hey, Sarge, just make sure you're far enough away when that thing goes off, so we don't get it too," Spider teased.

"No sweat, Spider. You're so skinny all you have to do is turn sideways and the shrapnel won't have anything to hit! Saddle up!" The men quickly shifted their weight to position their rucks, and then filed off with me at the point. We pushed across familiar terrain, over a green tapestry of rice paddies and untilled fields. By 7:30 we had left the last farmable land and started into the jungle areas where the base camp lay. The morning sun was blistering in its intensity. The sun's heat supercharged the humid air, creating a hot, sticky sauna, which caused men's clothing to cling to their skin like hot flypaper. We were covered with sweat and brine, burning our eyes and blurring our vision.

By eight o'clock I reached the edge of the field about 150 meters across and 50 meters wide. It funneled up to a stand of trees on the far side and was surrounded by a thick wall of tangled brush. We were almost there. All we had to do was cross the field and break through a few yards of tree line, and the clearing was on the other side.

I paused at the edge of the field and carefully scanned the area before resuming point. The fields were covered with knee-high grass, thickets of stubby brush, and small scrub trees. I inched forward a few meters down a trail that cut across the field and then I froze. It was barely noticeable, but three leaves were impaled on a short stick, forming a three-point star at ground level. I knew it was a VC warning that a booby trap was near. I slowly crouched and ran my eyes along the ground, scrutinizing every blade of grass until I saw what I was looking for. A taut nylon fishing line crossed the trail about twelve inches off the ground. I carefully followed the line with my fingertips. I pushed back some blades of grass and found the booby trap in a nearby bush. The line led to an old pineapple grenade, tucked into a bamboo cylinder, tied to a bush. The pin had been pulled. It was waiting for some unsuspecting GI to trip the line and snag it out of the cylinder. Once out, the spoon would fly free and the grenade would go off.

I stood up and motioned to Monk with my hand to watch out for the booby trap. About twenty meters more, I nearly fainted from a sudden jolt of adrenaline. I had just missed stepping on a

Bouncing Betty. My footfall was coming down when I noticed a bent branch just off the trail. The trip wire was concealed in the grass. That was close, I thought. The Bouncing Betty was designed to maim more than kill. Once the detonator was triggered, a small explosive charge popped the mine up to groin level where it exploded, blowing off legs and testicles. I marked the mine with a stick and motioned again to Monk to watch out.

My pace slowed considerably. The morning's euphoria had evaporated as reality settled in. Point was not the place to get cocky, no matter how good you were. Charlie was close.

It was 8:15 A.M. and I was fifty meters from the tree line. I had reached a dry streambed, about two meters across, when I paused to wipe some beads of sweat from my forehead.

Thunk . . . Thud. An object flew out of nowhere and hit me on the thigh. It bounced off of my leg and thudded into the dirt at my feet. I looked down and saw an M-26 fragmentation grenade lying on its side.

It must have fallen off of my flak jacket, I thought. NO! That can't be right. It hit me. . . . It doesn't have a spoon! Ooooh . . .

BLAM! The orange-gray explosion kicked up a cloud of dirt and dead grass, blowing me backward and riddling my body with shrapnel. I felt like I had been hit by a logging truck. I struggled to my feet in a daze.

Forty meters in front of me, an enemy soldier stepped from the tree line with his rifle raised. It was aimed directly at me. I saw the AK-47 blink twice, just a millisecond before the rounds tore into my right elbow and stomach. I toppled backward, landing on my bags.

"OH, GOD!" I cried out in a panicked voice. My entire life flashed before me. I was seized in a swirling whirlpool, sucking me into its vortex. I was blinking from the blood and sun's glare. I couldn't move. The shadow of an enemy soldier towered over me. I couldn't talk. My face was hamburger. My lips were bleeding profusely. I was gulping and spitting blood.

Noooo, I cried out in silence as the soldier drove the bayonet into my stomach. It felt like I had been run through with a red-hot poker.

How much time had passed was unclear. My body was convulsing with waves of pain, and I lay in a fetal position from the intense cramping in my stomach from the AK round lodged in my upper groin. My blood-smeared hand could feel a moist rubbery knot of intestine protruding from the gaping bayonet hole. With all the determination I could muster, I struggled to one knee, then stood, reeling on unsteady legs, like the battered stance of a heavyweight rising from the canvas. It was not an act of bravery, but the sheer adrenaline-induced will to survive.

Blood seeped from the dozens of shrapnel wounds that peppered my body. My right arm dangled at my side, the elbow shattered by the impact of the first round. The remains of my fatigue pants were drenched black from blood. Half coherently, I began the longest trek of my life, holding my intestines in as I half-limped, half-stumbled toward the safety of my own men. I covered maybe ten yards before collapsing.

The initial sound of the grenade's concussion had caused my squad to hit the deck. Only Monk had seen the blast that blew me backward. He watched with relief as I rose to my feet and said to those next to him, "Man, I don't believe this. That is one lucky sucker!" But his relief was short-lived. As soon as I regained my feet, he saw the AK rounds jerk me backward. He swore in frustration, feeling helpless and unable to respond for fear of tripping a full-scale ambush.

He stared in horror at the sight of the NVA officer standing over me—the almost hypnotic scene of the figure raise his bayoneted assault rifle skyward.

"Jesus," he muttered. "He's going to kill him."

The sight of the plunging bayonet was too much for the corporal to stand by and do nothing. Ambush or not, he wasn't going to let that gook get away with it. Monk took aim with his M-16 and squeezed off a burst that tore into the khaki-clad soldier, lifting him off his feet and hurling him backward.

"C'mon, Doc, let's get him." Without questioning, the two marines bolted from their position, under the covering fire of the other men, and darted for me. They were nearly out of breath when they reached my body. Doc held my flak jacket while Monk grabbed my right wrist.

"Careful . . . easy does it !" Doc instructed as they secured my body.

They dragged me back across the field to the safety of our lines. My platoon and the PFs deployed in a tight protective perimeter, concealed by scrub and secondary growth. The enemy chose not to pursue and had melted back into the densely packed jungle on the opposite side of the field.

No sooner had we reached the safety of the platoon than Doc began a heroic attempt to save my life. He tore out his medical kit and extracted a shot of morphine, which he promptly injected into my thigh, then attached the empty Syrette to my fatigues. He tied off the steady stream of arterial bleeding from my right elbow with a green tourniquet. The wound looked like raw hamburger embedded with fragments of splintered bone and exposed tendons. There was no way he could clean the arm properly in the field. All he could do was wrap it with compresses. I was covered with so many wounds it wasn't possible to bandage them all. Everyone was contributing his field dressings to help stop the bleeding.

"Is he gonna make it?" Jenkins questioned.

"Shut up!" Doc snapped, as he tied off another compress.

"He doesn't look good," Jenkins shook his head.

"You heard me," Doc warned.

"Yeah, why don't you quit beatin' your gums, JERKins, and press on this compress!" Carpulucci ordered.

"My name's not Jerkins," Jenkins protested.

"Then stop actin' like one," Monk snorted.

"I'm sorry, Doc. I didn't mean nothin'," Jenkins apologized.

"Gotta get a chopper," I groaned out.

"Keep quiet," Doc ordered.

Wolfman pressed the side band of the handset and spoke. "Gringo One, this is Gringo Two. Gringo One this is Gringo Two. Do you read, over?"

"Roger, Gringo Two. What is your status?"

"We need an immediate dust-off. Do you copy, over?" The radio gave an uncooperative hiss as the incoming voice broke off.

D.J. adjusted the squelch knob as he coaxed the PRC-24. "C'mon, baby, don't quit on me now," he muttered to himself.

"Say again, Gringo Two," the voice came through clear.

"We need a dust-off, Gringo One! Our sergeant is hit bad!" Wolfman shouted into the mike.

"Can't do. All available choppers are committed. Have one outbound in about forty-five minutes, over."

"We need a dust-off now, you mother, or he isn't going to make it! Do you read me?"

An agonizing delay followed before the radioman came back. "Read you five by five, Gringo Two. Gotta hold of a supply chopper en route to Da Nang. He's diverting to your position. About ten klicks out. ETA five minutes. Wants you to mark with yellow smoke."

"Roger that, Gringo One. And thanks, man—I owe ya." The young radioman lowered the hand-mike and sighed a measured air of relief.

"Well, that's a start," Ortez commented.

While the anxious squad waited for the med-evac chopper, Doc took out his bayonet and a pair of tweezers and started scraping away the remaining bits of phosphorous that were still burning in my arm.

"How bad is it, Doc?" I slurred. "Am I gonna make it?" The numbing effect of the morphine had only taken the edge off the pain.

"Lie still and don't talk. You'll be okay," Doc assured me, though his voice was laced with concern.

"I can hear the chopper now!" Ortez shouted. The din of the twin rotors grew louder as the chopper lowered itself into the field. The platoon carried me on a canvas stretcher while Doc held the IV bottles.

I never felt as alone as I lay on the floor of the chopper bay en route to Da Nang's Ninety-fifth evac hospital. Everything was a mishmash of smells, feelings, and sounds: the steady hammering of the chopper blades, the wet clinging sensation of my blood-soaked fatigues, the freezing wind blowing through the open bay, the tight tearing sensation of the tourniquet, the sickening metallic taste of blood, and a dull ache in my gut.

The gurney burst through the double doors of the ER. Though gravely wounded, I was just another casualty among many. The receiving room was filling with casualties from firefights as dust-offs steadily arrived to deposit their human cargoes.

Partly naked marines were sprawled across wooden receiving tables amid an assortment of stainless steel trays, sterile utensils, and rubber tubing, while a collection of plasma bags and saline bottles dangled from overhead hooks. Some were writhing in agony, others were screaming out for more morphine, while others lay quietly dying.

In one isolated corner lay several zippered body bags. They were tagged and waiting for transfer to the morgue unit in Da Nang and eventual transit home. Along one of the walls, a mound of body parts was piled on an abandoned stretcher. Soiled field dressings and discarded bandages littered the blood-smeared floor.

The team of surgeons did all they could to keep me alive, but they had little hope. I was wheeled to an isolated end of the hallway to die in peace, like a broken-down boxcar, shunted off to rust on an abandoned siding. At the foot of my gurney, a black body bag was placed in readiness, neatly draped across my feet.

In spite of the doctor's resignation, something deep inside of me refused to let go. Over the next six days I lingered at the point of death, slipping into and out of an incoherent dreamscape. My mind was a kaleidoscope of bizarre hallucinations, ghostly phantoms, and tortured impressions. At times I was falling backward down a dark shaft. At other times I stood transfixed by the sight of the live grenade lying at my feet. I screamed, but no one could hear, no one could help.

It took five days for word of my condition reach my twin brother, Ron, also a marine in Vietnam. He caught the first available supply chopper to the hospital, where he began a frantic search for his wounded brother. It didn't take long. All of the nurses were more than willing to cooperate with the 6-foot, 4-inch marine, fresh from the bush, standing before them in his salt-encrusted, sun-bleached fatigues. The fierce intensity in his eyes gave sufficient warning he was not to be messed with.

"Can I help you, Sergeant?" the nurse asked.

"Yes, ma'am. I'm here to see my brother, Sergeant Helle."

She looked at him with compassion in her eyes, and with a soft voice replied, "Yes, Sergeant, he's on ward B. If you'll wait just a moment, I'll take you to him."

Before she could rise, Ron strode from the nurses' station. He removed his utility cap as he opened the door and entered the ward. A doctor and nurse were standing at the far end with their backs to him, looking down at a clipboard. Ron had nearly reached them when the doctor turned.

"Can I help you?" he asked in a hushed voice.

"I'm Sergeant Helle's brother. I want to know where he is . . . now!"

At that moment, I was lying a couple of beds down. I had drifted in and out of consciousness for days. My face was badly lacerated and my eyes nearly swollen shut, leaving only small slits to see through. I wanted to say something, but nothing would come out. I couldn't move or talk. I could only listen.

The doctor placed his hand on Ron's shoulder and broke it to him as gently as he could. "Sergeant, I'm afraid your brother isn't going to make it. We've done all that we can."

Ron was stunned as he surveyed me—I looked more like a freshly autopsied cadaver rather than a barely living body. Hot tears flowed down his face. His knees buckled and he fell to the floor, burying his face in the sheets, sobbing, "Oh, God, please, please save my brother."

I could see and hear my brother's cry for heavenly help, but I could do nothing to reassure him. Scalding tears seeped from the slits of my eyelids. Before I blacked out again I prayed a prayer of desperation. "Oh, God, if there is a God . . . please . . . if You'll just let me live, I'll do anything You ask. "

As I lingered between life and death, my parents were notified.

MR. AND MRS HERBEN HELLE, A REPORT
RECEIVED THIS HEADQUARTERS REVEALS

THAT YOUR SON, SGT ROGER LEIGH HELLE
USMC, SUSTAINED INJURIES ON 13 JULY 1970,
IN THE VICINITY OF QUAN NAM PROVINCE,
REPUBLIC OF VIETNAM, FROM HOSTILE FIRE
WHILE ON PATROL. HE SUFFERED MULTIPLE
TRAUMATIC WOUNDS FROM SHRAPNEL AND
BULLETS TO ALL EXTREMITIES. IN THE JUDG-
MENT OF THE ATTENDING PHYSICIAN, HIS
CONDITION IS OF SUCH SEVERITY THAT HIS
PROGNOSIS IS POOR. YOUR GREAT ANXIETY IS
UNDERSTOOD. PLEASE BE ASSURED THAT THE
BEST MEDICAL FACILITIES AND DOCTORS ARE
BEING PROVIDED AND EVERY STEP IS BEING
TAKEN TO AID HIM. YOU ARE ASSURED THAT
HE WILL RECEIVE THE BEST OF CARE.

COMMANDANT OF THE MARINE CORPS

For a week Ron maintained his vigil beside my bed—praying to the only One left who could save his brother's life. For a
week he encouraged me whenever I came to, and when I passed
out, he urged me to hang in there. After two weeks of ICU, the
doctors told Ron that I was going to make it.

My condition stabilized enough for the doctors to risk the
med-evac flight to a better-equipped hospital in Japan. Going to
Tokyo was the beginning of a long and arduous journey home. I
spent a month in Japan, oblivious to the surroundings—lost in a
delirious twilight zone of pain and painkillers. My face felt like it
was constantly on fire. The nurses would fill surgical gloves with
crushed ice and lay them on my face to take down the swelling,
but it still looked like a water balloon ready to explode. Besides
the seventy-two major shrapnel wounds, I was covered with hundreds of small punctures from slivers of shrapnel that had imbed-
ded themselves in my flesh. Until I was able to get a temperature
below 100 degrees, they wouldn't release me to go back home.
There was too much danger of dying en route.

Finally I was loaded onto another C-141 and headed back

home. I don't remember much of that flight except for landing in Anchorage, Alaska. I had only a sheet covering me, since I had so many open wounds, and I thought I was going to freeze to death when they opened the rear ramp. A nurse saw my lips turning blue, pulled off the wet sheet, and got some blankets to cover me. I looked up at her face and managed to say, "Thank you."

After almost twenty-four hours of flying, we landed at Great Lakes Naval Hospital. I was put on a ward where each bed had a small American flag draped at its foot. This was my home for the next six months of reconstructive surgery and physical therapy. It was a physical journey that I had to make, but a spiritual one still awaited me.

In late fall, the paperwork caught up with me, and I was awarded my fifth Vietnamese Cross of Gallantry and a Bronze Star to boot. I was medically retired from the Marine Corps as 100 percent disabled. The hospital issued me a set of crutches, but I wanted to walk out without them. My right arm was still partially paralyzed and I limped, but I was proud to walk out in my uniform.

But the world I left wasn't there anymore.

I took a bus to my parents' old church and hobbled down the sidewalk with my cane, proudly wearing my ribbons. As I approached the steps leading up to the cathedral, two older ladies brushed past me and pulled to an abrupt stop in my path. With a puckered face and absolute disgust one said, "You got what you deserved, you baby killer!" Her voice cracked with contempt.

Her companion spat at my feet and then they strode on. "Actually," the other turned and continued, "they should have killed you!"

I was paralyzed with shock. I felt as though I'd been ambushed all over again.

The church and the people in it obviously weren't interested in me. I had to pour all of my pent-up energy into something. So I applied for a job and was hired as a Pinkerton detective. I liked the hazards of working as a private investigator; it gave me an adrenaline rush similar to what I'd experienced so often in Vietnam.

During this time I met a wonderful woman, Shirley, who filled my heart with love. I married her and thought everything was going to be all right after all. But while the plastic surgeons had done a great job reconstructing my face, no earthly surgeon could remove the scars in my heart. All my working and drinking and love for Shirley couldn't heal my wounded heart, which was hemorrhaging with hate and bitterness and guilt—especially guilt.

I proceeded to turn my wife's life into a perpetual state of misery. I floored my career accelerator and poured myself into that to compensate for the guilt I felt. I was being consumed from the inside with the cancer of bitterness and hate. Shirley begged me to spend more time with her, but I always let her know my job came first. My anger slowly destroyed everything that was good around me. I pursued my work while Shirley's love wilted, shriveled, and died.

Nearly two years passed, and the war in Southeast Asia was still grinding on. I was fighting my own private war, and doing no better than the troops in 'Nam. I was running from my painful memories, but they were gaining on me. I tried to bury them under an avalanche of paperwork and busyness, but the phantoms would always emerge to haunt me.

In desperation, Shirley finally confronted me one morning before I left for work. "Roger, I can't go on like this. We've got to do something. We don't seem to be able to talk. Maybe we could see a marriage counselor or go talk to a pastor together. I'm willing if you are." She was pleading with all her heart.

I could only muster a cold glance and say, "Hey, go ahead, if you need to . . . it's your problem." I closed the door and left for work.

It was Thanksgiving Day. Shirley had hoped against hope for too long. She had nothing left to give. When she found out about an affair I had had while on a business trip, she packed her bags. She turned to me before leaving our small trailer home and said through her tears, "I love you, Roger, but I can't live with you any longer. I'm leaving for good this time."

I stood there in shock as I watched her walk out the door.

As the car drove off, I felt as though I had been run through with the bayonet yet again. The failure I had feared all my life had finally descended upon me like a dark cloud. I had lost my friends in Vietnam, and now I had lost my wife. My remorse was too little, too late.

I wasn't a tough, proud marine anymore. I was a broken man. Night after night I tossed and turned in the cramped loneliness of the empty trailer. I kept myself awake long into the night trying to figure out how to make it up to Shirley. I couldn't eat. I couldn't concentrate. Everything in my life faded from color into a dreary black-and-white.

I finally got up the courage to ask Shirley out to take a walk. It was awkward, and I didn't know what to say.

She broke the ice. "Rog, I've been giving our marriage a lot of thought—"

"Yeah, I know what you mean," I said, cutting her off.

"I'm not finished. I just want you to listen to what I have to say," she said firmly. "Roger, unless we put God first in our lives, we don't have any hope left that our marriage will work." She spoke with a firm conviction that stopped me cold.

"I know, Shirley, but I don't know what to do." I felt like a little kid who had lost his way and didn't know how to get home.

"Roger, I think we should go to church or talk to a pastor."

"I don't know, Shirley. The last time I went to church, two old ladies spat on me and called me a baby killer."

She paused a moment. "Isn't that what they did to Jesus? Spat on Him and rejected Him? I know God cares, Roger. If anyone can understand, I think He can." She looked at me with tears in her eyes. "I know He's the answer. I think He's what has been missing all these years."

As I looked into her eyes, I was transported back to my hospital room in Da Nang. While my brother had knelt beside my bed I had sobbed out the words, "Please, God, if you'll let me live, I'll do anything You ask." It was a promise I had never kept.

That night in the bedroom of Shirley's apartment, we held each other's hands and knelt beside her bed. Broken and spent, I prayed again. "God, I've tried to do it my way. I've really messed things up. I can't do it anymore, Jesus. Please help me and my wife. I love her so much. Please, God, forgive me for the hurt I've caused You. I need Your mercy. I need You, Jesus."

As the warm tears flowed down my face, I felt an enormous weight lifted from my shoulders. That pack I had humped all over Vietnam, the pack that had grown in weight with each new death and each new horror, had fallen to the ground. All of the hate and bitterness and guilt that it held now lay at my feet.

As I held Shirley and she held me, there were no flashes of lightning, claps of thunder, or hosts of angels singing around me. There was just a warmth and contentment I had never known—a deep peace that defied all of my circumstances. And that night, for the first time in almost five years, the nightmares stopped. And I, no longer tortured, began to live.

Condensed from *Point Man*
Bill Kimball and Roger Helle
Used with permission

THE GULF WAR
SANDSTORM FROM THE HAND OF GOD

★

MAJ. DOUGLAS V. MASTRIANO, UNITED STATES ARMY

*Have I not commanded you? Be strong and of good
courage; do not be afraid, nor be dismayed, for the
LORD your God is with you wherever you go.*

(Joshua 1:9, NKJV)

We awoke to yet another dismal and gray day in the southern
Iraqi desert. Since the opening of the ground offensive of Desert
Storm, my regiment had been leading the American main attack
deep into Iraq. Like the cavalry scouts of the old American west,
the Second Armored Calvary led the advance . . . only now with
Abrams tank and Cobra helicopter squadrons. Behind us were a
thousand other American and British tanks—all in search of the
enemy.

We were the eyes and ears of the main body of our army. Our
ultimate goal was to deliver a knock-out blow to Saddam
Hussein's most loyal and motivated Republican Guards. This
would be the day that we faced this formidable adversary.

We began the day's offensive by sending our helicopters six
miles in front of our tanks. As they took up their forward position,
they immediately reported contact with hundreds of Iraqi tanks and
vehicles dug into well-fortified fighting positions. The Iraqis gave
our helicopters a warm reception by firing at them. We returned the
favor by bringing in U.S. Air Force F-16 strikes. Due to their sheer
number, the air strikes did little to deter the combat capability of
these Iraqi soldiers. They had been waiting for over six months for
this day and were ready to give us the fight of our lives.

Our helicopters continued to coordinate with the air force to destroy what they could. Soon it would be our turn to go tank to tank. The dangerous and tricky part of the battle was transitioning the fight from the helicopters to the ground tanks. It was too hazardous to have our helicopters fighting in the same vicinity, so they were ordered out.

As our tanks rolled into position, Saddam's elite troops prepared to unleash their fury. A few meters more and we would be within range of their withering fire. The area was absent any visual cues or landmarks, and the map indicated only that we were near grid line 73 east. So, it probably isn't so strange that the ensuing battle was later referred to as "The Battle of Seventy-third Easting." As our tanks rolled into position, it was hard to believe that the entire regiment was here in this vast expanse of sand.

Just three months earlier, I had wrapped up a three-year tour in Germany. I rejoiced to witness the end of the Cold War and the elimination of the Iron Curtain in Europe. It was a time of promise and expectation. Wide-eyed Eastern Europeans were embraced by West German relatives as they welcomed them to the free world. All over the world, peace was proclaimed, and many American and Soviet military units disbanded. This jubilation was shattered in August 1990 when the Iraqi army invaded and occupied Kuwait. Three months later our regiment was ordered to deploy to Saudi Arabia.

It was an emotionally difficult time for soldiers and families alike. Yet for my family, God seemed to offer a peace in spite of our circumstances. We prayed together before I left; and I was comforted by this Scripture: "Be anxious for nothing, but in everything by prayer and supplication, with thanksgiving, let your requests be made known to God; and the peace of God, which surpasses all understanding, will guard your hearts and minds through Christ Jesus." (Philippians 4:6-7, NKJV)

As we left for the front, my wife, Rebbie, and the wives of other believers in my regiment began to pray for us. They encouraged many others to begin to pray as well. By the time the war began, over twenty churches were specifically praying for the protection and safety of the five hundred men in my cavalry squadron. Their faithful prayers made a difference.

My first direct evidence of God's protection occurred shortly after the war began. One night my driver and I were sleeping in a shallow trench within our perimeter. Since we were at war, and not far from Iraqi positions, our vehicles did not use their headlights. Upon entering the camp perimeter, the procedure was for the passenger to dismount and lead the vehicle through on foot so no one would be accidentally run over. One night, the passenger in a vehicle was too lazy to walk in front and told his driver to drive on anyway. As my driver and I slept, this vehicle headed straight for us.

At that moment, Corporal Trump, one of the few who knew where my driver and I were sleeping, was out on guard duty. He later told me he couldn't escape a nagging voice inside his head to get back inside the perimeter. At first he resisted this urge, since he was on duty and couldn't abandon his post. However, the urgency of this feeling intensified, and he finally gave in.

As Trump neared the spot where my driver and I were sleeping, he saw the vehicle heading straight for us. He shouted down the vehicle and ordered it to a stop—just three feet away from us. The next morning I examined with thankfulness the evidence of the tire tracks that stopped just short of ending our lives. God had kept us safe.

Among these wonderful demonstrations of God's protection, I cherish one the most. The Twelfth Iraqi Armored Division had moved from its position near the Iraq-Kuwait-Saudi border to block the movement of my regiment into Iraq. Part of this Iraqi force clashed with our lightly defended Regimental Support Squadron (RSS).[31] RSS is not equipped for a big fight, since its primary mission is to supply food and fuel. Upon making contact with this Iraqi force, RSS called upon my helicopter squadron for help. We were best suited to counter this threat, since we could respond faster than tanks.

When we received the request for assistance, I was in a

Blackhawk transport helicopter with eight other soldiers. Unfortunately, our one available attack helicopter needed about five minutes to respond. Since we were already airborne, the senior officer in our helicopter decided that we would respond and mark the location of the enemy for our attack helicopters. This was about all we could do, since our Blackhawk was armed only with two M-60 machine guns.

There was not a moment to lose. We arrived at the location, but could find neither Iraqi nor American vehicles in the area. We slowed our speed and increased our altitude to try to locate the RSS unit under fire. However, this maneuver made it easier for the Iraqis to engage us, and within a minute we flew over a group of Iraqi armored vehicles that began a withering fire against us at pointblank range.

Inside the chopper, none of us initially saw the fire and death coming at us in tracers like fingers of death. Then I glanced out of the left door gunner's window, and my eyes were filled with the fire coming at us from below. Everything seemed to move in slow motion as the realization that we were going to die hit me like a hammer in the chest. But the bullets that were coming directly at the cockpit never touched us. God shielded us that day. Meanwhile, the senior officer in the helicopter also saw the enemy fire and immediately alerted the crew to begin evasive maneuvers and get us out of there.

It was clear we had been saved by divine intervention; however, I didn't have time to dwell on this incident of grace. I later attended a service conducted by our regimental chaplain near the ancient Iraqi town of Ur.[32] At the end of the service, the chaplain asked us to stand up and recite the Soldier's Psalm (Psalm 91). As we read verses fourteen and fifteen; the Holy Spirit gripped my heart and brought to mind the incident in the Blackhawk. "Because he has set his love upon Me, therefore I will deliver him. I will set him on high, because he has known My name. He shall call upon Me and I will answer him; I will be with him in trouble; I will deliver him and honor him" (Psalm 91:14-15, NKJV).

The message was clear: the eight other men and I were alive

only because of God's grace and the prayers of His people back home.

As our regiment prepared for the battle at Grid 73, we had to face the unpleasant possibility that the Iraqis would launch chemical weapons at us. In the previous decade Saddam had used them extensively against both the Iranians and his own Kurdish people. Additionally, the prevailing winds blowing from Iraq (northwest) into Saudi Arabia (southeast) seemed to make it an easy decision for a man like Saddam Hussein. If the Iraqis were able to launch their chemical weapons, the wind would carry the toxins deep into the American lines.

It was 1:30 P.M. on February 23, 1991, when my regiment entered Iraq. The ground war had begun. The very instant our tanks entered Iraq, a strange thing occurred. I noticed quite a few little ominous dust devils all around me. But before my very eyes the direction of the prevailing winds began to change; and within minutes the winds had shifted from north to south to 180 degrees in the other direction. With the wind blowing from Saudi Arabia into Iraq, the threat of a chemical attack was greater to Saddam than to our forces. The truly remarkable, miraculous occurence was that the winds stayed this way until 8 A.M. February 28, the very moment the ceasefire went into effect.[33]

The moment the Battle of Seventy-third Easting began, it became patently clear to everyone that the Iraqi tanks were indeed dug in and ready for this key battle. The lead Iraqi unit was only seconds away from firing upon our tanks when a strange occurrence obscured the horizon. A shamal (an extraordinary sand and rainstorm with thunder and lightning) settled upon the battlefield, completely blinding the Iraqi troops.

Despite the miserable weather, the Iraqis remained vigilant to fight, but they couldn't see the American tanks. The storm was on top of both forces, and how we could see and they couldn't wasn't easily explainable. Some think that our technological edge made the difference—our superior infrared capability. However, even with that small difference, the storm was of such a magnitude that we should not have been able to see the Iraqi tanks.

From the distance, through the rain and sand and thunder and lightning, the Iraqi tanks could see only flashes—flashes of death. It was our tanks firing at them. Iraqi tanks burst into flames across the line. Several valiant Iraqi troops returned fire, shooting at the gun flashes that they saw in the distance, but their rounds fell short. As more Iraqi tanks exploded into flames, one after another began to abandon their vehicles. They couldn't fight what they couldn't see. Despite being outnumbered three to one, our regiment broke the back of the lead Republican Guards division.

Had the storm arrived a few minutes sooner, it would have hampered our aviation attacks. A few minutes later would have been too late. The timing was perfect. God's intervention with this mysterious shamal saved numerous American and Iraqi lives and played a decisive role in the defeat and rout of Saddam's best-trained and most-motivated troops. The outcome of this one-sided victory contributed to Saddam's decision to withdraw his two remaining armored Republican Guards divisions.[34]

Thousands of believers continued to pray specifically for my cavalry squadron, and God honored their diligence. Though we had several helicopters go down during the war, not one man among us died. The prayers of God's people are beyond our ability to calculate.

WHAT IS A VETERAN?

Some veterans bear visible signs of their
   service . . . a missing limb, a jagged
   scar, a certain look in the eye.

Others may carry the evidence inside
   them . . . a pin holding a bone together,
   a piece of shrapnel in the leg . . . or
   perhaps another sort of inner steel . . .
   the soul's ally forged in the refinery of
   adversity.

Except in parades, however, the men and
   women who have kept America safe
   wear no badge or emblem.
You can't tell a vet just by looking.

What is a vet?
He is the cop on the beat who spent six
   months in Saudi Arabia sweating two
   gallons a day, making sure the armored
   personnel carriers didn't run out of fuel.

He is the barroom loudmouth, dumber
   than five wooden planks, whose over-
   grown frat-boy behavior is outweighed
   a hundred times in the cosmic scales by
   four hours of exquisite bravery near the
   38th parallel.

She or he is the nurse who fought against
   futility and went to sleep sobbing every
   night for two solid years in Da Nang.

He is the POW who went away one person and came back another—or didn't come back at all.

He is the Quantico drill instructor who has never seen combat but has saved countless lives by turning slouchy, no-account rednecks and gang members into marines and teaching them to watch each other's backs.

He is the parade-riding Legionnaire who pins on his ribbons and medals with a prosthetic hand.

He is the career quartermaster who watches the ribbons and medals pass him by.

He is the three anonymous heroes in The Tomb of the Unknowns whose presence at the Arlington National Cemetery must forever preserve the memory of all the anonymous heroes whose valor dies unrecognized with them on the battlefield or in the ocean's sunless deep.

He is the old guy bagging groceries at the supermarket, palsied now and aggravatingly slow, who helped liberate a Nazi death camp and who wishes all day long that his wife were still alive to hold him when the nightmares come.

He is an ordinary and yet an extraordinary human being—a person who
offered some of his life's most vital
years in the service of his country and
who sacrificed his ambitions so others
would not have to sacrifice theirs.

He is a soldier and a savior and a sword
against the darkness, and he is nothing
more than the finest, greatest testimony
on behalf of the finest, greatest nation
ever known.

So remember, each time you see someone
who has served our country, just lean
over and say thank you. That's all most
people need and in most cases it will
mean more than any medals they could
have been awarded or were awarded.

Remember, Memorial Day and Veterans
Day, and two little words that mean
a lot,
Thank you.
Anonymous

RED SKIES AND FORGIVEN LIVES

*This is certain, that a man that studies
revenge keeps his wounds green which otherwise would heal.*

Francis Bacon

*And whenever you stand praying, forgive,
if you have anything against any one; so
that your Father also who is in heaven may
forgive you your trespasses.*

Mark 11:25, RSV

THE FRUIT OF FORGIVENESS

★

The fruit of forgiveness is evidence of a life given over to God's grace and sovereignty. It is a life that no longer demands rights or retribution, but trusts Him to provide both grace and justice in appropriate amounts for each of His creations. Father Kolbe lived such a life.

Maximilian Kolbe was taken prisoner by the Nazis in May of 1941. He had served as a parish priest in Poland but was soon transferred to Auschwitz and branded as Prisoner 16670. He was assigned to a special work group staffed by priests and supervised by especially vicious and abusive guards. He was put to work carrying building materials to build the crematorium. One guard, referred to as "Bloody Krott," beat him daily for his own pleasure, but Kolbe's eyes always communicated forgiveness.

One prisoner recalled, "Because we were trying to survive at any cost, all the prisoners had wildly roving eyes watching in every direction for trouble or the ready clubs. Kolbe alone had a calm, straightforward look, the look of a thoughtful man. In spite of his physical suffering, he was completely healthy, serene, and extraordinary of character." Another remembered, "Those eyes of his were always strangely penetrating. The SS men couldn't stand his glance and used to yell at him, 'Look at the ground, not at us!'"[35]

His calm dedication to the faith brought him the worst jobs available and more beatings than anyone else. Yet his attitude, words, and bearing showed he bore no ill will to those who committed the worst cruelties and barbaric acts. At one point he was beaten, lashed, and left for dead. The prisoners managed to smuggle him into the camp hospital, where he spent his recovery time hearing confessions.

When he returned to the camp, Kolbe continued to minister to others and even gave away his food rations. When questioned about his actions, he explained, "Every man has his aim in life. Most of you want to return to your wives . . . your families. My part is to give my life for the good of all men."

One man recalled, "He made us see that our souls were not dead."[36]

In July 1941 there was an escape from the camp. Camp protocol, designed to make the prisoners guard each other, required that ten men be slaughtered in retribution for each one who escaped. Francis Gajowniczek, a married man with young children, was one chosen to die. Kolbe volunteered to take his place.

He was put into a starvation bunker where he received no food or drink. On August 14, still alive, Father Kolbe was removed and given an injection of lethal acid. The next day, his body was burned in the crematorium.

ENEMIES NO MORE

★

BOB BOARDMAN

If ever there were two men least likely to become reconciled, they would be Mitsuo Fuchida and Jacob DeShazer. Their countries, Japan and America, were separated by the world's largest ocean. Their backgrounds, languages, customs, traditional religions, thinking patterns, physical makeup, and philosophies of life were as different as those of any two people on earth.

By the end of World War II, nearly sixteen million people on all sides of the conflict had perished. Fuchida and DeShazer were among the combatants determined to inflict the maximum number of casualties upon the other side, even at the cost of their own lives. As implacable enemies, the two men took part in two of the most dramatic events of the Pacific war: Fuchida led the attack on Pearl Harbor, and DeShazer was one of the Doolittle Raiders who launched the first American bombing of Japan. To understand the miraculous nature of their encounter, you must understand the nature of these two men.

Mitsuo Fuchida was born in 1902, the quiet son of a school principal in a small village outside of Osaka. He became a top pilot in the Imperial Japanese Navy. By the attack on Pearl Harbor, he was a veteran of the Sino-Japanese War, having logged three thousand hours of flying time. His diminutive physical makeup belied the tough character of the inner man. Because of his outstanding leadership abilities as well as his flying skills, he was the unanimous choice to be the flight commander of the planes that smashed Pearl Harbor.

Admiral Isoroku Yamamoto, the overall planner and organizer of the attack, handpicked Fuchida to lead the attack from the carrier Striking Force (Kido Butai). The formidable armada, which sailed from Japan's Inland Sea on November 16, 1941, consisted of six aircraft carriers, two fast battleships, two heavy cruisers, one light cruiser, eight destroyers, three oilers, and a supply ship.

At dawn on Sunday, December 7, 1941, 360 planes took off for the surprise attack on America's mightiest naval base. Fuchida arrived over the island of Oahu in his light, high-level command bomber. At exactly 7:49 A.M., he gave the code word Totsugeki (Charge!).

The lead attack planes peeled off to attack. After a few minutes, Fuchida set off a blue flare to signal the other planes that complete surprise had been achieved. Next he radioed Vice Admiral Nagumo: "Tora, Tora, Tora!" (Tiger, Tiger, Tiger!). This was the code for "We have succeeded in surprise attack." Wave after wave of torpedo planes, dive-bombers, high-level bombers, and "zeros"[37] devastated the peaceful Sunday routine of Americans in and around Pearl Harbor.

At Pearl Harbor it was confirmed that eighteen ships had been sunk or badly damaged; 188 planes destroyed and 159 damaged; 2,403 Americans killed. It was a disaster, but it could have been a catastrophe. Luckily, the carriers were at sea, and the enemy neglected to bomb the oil storage tanks at the navy yard and the submarine pens. Moreover, almost all of the sunk or damaged ships would eventually return to battle. The Japanese lost twenty-nine planes and five midget submarines; forty-five airmen and nine submariners died. One, Ensign Sukamaki, was captured when his boat went aground on the other side of Oahu.

As a result of this surprise attack, Fuchida became a national hero. Later, along with Vice Admiral Nagumo, he was ordered back to Tokyo to make a personal report before the Emperor of Japan. Because the Japanese people considered Hirohito divine, a direct descendant of the sun goddess, it was an awesome event for Fuchida to appear before the throne. He was not supposed to speak to the emperor directly, but through an imperial aide. However, Fuchida became so flustered that he replied to the emperor, and later confessed that this experience was worse than the attack on Pearl Harbor!

By the end of the war almost all of Fuchida's flying comrades had been killed in combat. He was at the battle of Midway, a turning point in the war in the Pacific in favor of the Allies. There, Japan lost four aircraft carriers, many planes, and choice pilots. Fuchida was supposed to lead the attack on Midway Island, but he came down with appendicitis and ended up in the sick bay aboard his carrier Akagi, completely frustrated. That sickness no doubt spared his life.

Miraculously, time after time throughout the war, while others were dying around him, Fuchida's life was preserved. God had a special destiny for Mitsuo Fuchida.

Jacob "Jake" DeShazer was born in Salem, Oregon, on November 15, 1912. His father died when he was two years old, and soon afterward his mother remarried. Jake recounts his early life:

"My stepfather had a big wheat ranch. He was a very godly man, and every morning he prayed and read the Bible, tears coming from his eyes as he prayed. But, when I got to be nineteen years old, I rejected the teaching of my parents. I felt at that time that Christianity was like any other religion. I did not know who Jesus was. I tried to get a job, but we were in the Depression, so I ended up in the United States military service as an airplane mechanic. I was in the Army Air Corps, working on the B-25s and taking training to be a bombardier, at the time Pearl Harbor was bombed."[38]

The United States felt an urgent need to strike a retaliatory physical and psychological blow at the Japanese that would let them know what was coming. What better message than to bomb the Japanese homeland? The U.S. Navy devised an ingenious plan for medium-sized American bombers to take off from a navy aircraft carrier, fly five hundred miles to the Japanese mainland, drop their bombs, and then (because of low fuel) crash-land in China.

Lt. Col. James H. Doolittle, aeronautical scientist and skilled pilot, was chosen to lead this daring raid. He had already been commended for many speed records and firsts: He was the first pilot to cross the United States in twelve hours, first to do the almost-impossible outside loop, and first to land an airplane by instruments alone. Since it would be an extremely hazardous mission in which some pilots would surely die, volunteers were called upon to man the sixteen crews. The preparation and training would not only be intense but highly secretive.

When Jake DeShazer first heard of the attack on Pearl Harbor, his reaction was instant: "My heart was filled with hatred and revenge. It seemed like a sneak attack. One month later, I volunteered for the mission with Jimmy Doolittle. . . ."[39]

On April 18, 1942, sixteen overloaded modified B-25s took off from the aircraft carrier Hornet, five hundred miles from the Japanese mainland. Lieutenant Colonel Doolittle's lead plane had only 467 feet of runway on the carrier deck. With throttle wide open, the nose lifted off with just a few yards to spare.

DeShazer was bombardier on the last plane. A seaman on deck lost his footing and was blown into one of the spinning propellers of DeShazer's plane, mangling his left arm. This unnerved the pilot, who pulled a control lever the wrong way. The plane shot off the bow, dipped, and disappeared from sight of the ship. In a few moments the plane regained both control and altitude, skimming across the waves to join the other fifteen planes winging toward Japan.

Each of thirteen planes dropped its cargo of four bombs on Tokyo. The other three planes bombed the major cities of Nagoya, Osaka, and Kobe. The surprise was as complete as the Japanese attack on Pearl Harbor, although the damage was not nearly as extensive. All the pilots of the planes completed their missions and then continued on to either crash-land or bail out in China—except one, who landed safely in eastern Russia.

The other fifteen bombers came down in Japanese-occupied China. Three men were killed in crash landings or bailouts; eight were captured and brought to Tokyo for trial. The rest, including Doolittle, got out alive and headed for safety by various routes to Chiang Kai-shek's lines.[40]

Jake DeShazer was one of the eight captured. All were given death sentences. Three were executed immediately because of the anger of the Japanese over the bombing. The emperor eventually commuted the death sentences of the remaining five, although they were in torturous suspense about their fate for many months. After trials in Tokyo, they were returned to prison in China, where they served nearly forty months.

In their Shanghai prison, the men were kept in overcrowded cells. A small receptacle served for a toilet for fifteen people. For almost twenty months the men were put on a starvation diet. They ate boiled rice soup for breakfast and four ounces of bread each for both lunch and dinner. There were bedbugs, lice, and large rats freely scurrying around their cell. In winter it was bitter cold, and in summer the weather was sweltering. DeShazer recalls:

"In the daytime we had to sit straight up on the floor without any support for our backs. If the guards caught us leaning back on our elbows, they hit us sharply on the head with a bamboo stick. One of the most painful torture methods our captors used was making us kneel for hours on a sharp-edged board. They had formed a triangular board with the razor-sharp edge up. We were forced to kneel on this edge for hours on end. Of course the sharp edge would cut into our knees until we could hardly walk."[41]

In December one of the prisoners, Lieutenant Meder, died from mistreatment. Jake and the other three surviving Americans were allowed to take one last look at his body as it lay in a wooden box just before cremation. On top of the box lay a wreath of flowers and a Bible. Meder's life, and now his death, had a deep impact on his close buddy Jake.

"Lieutenant Meder seemed to understand the Bible well. He had told me that Jesus Christ is the Lord and coming King. That Jesus is God's Son and that God expects the nations and people to recognize Jesus as Lord and Savior. I didn't understand what he meant at the time, but later I remembered his words.

"After Meder's death I began to ponder the cause of such hatred between members of the human race. I wondered what it was that made the Japanese hate the Americans, and what made me hate the Japanese. My thoughts turned toward what I had heard about Christianity changing hatred between human beings into real brotherly love. I was gripped with a strange longing to examine the Christians' Bible to see if I could find the secret. I begged my captors to get a Bible for me. At last, in May 1944, a guard brought me the Book, but told me I could have it for only three weeks."[42]

Eagerly, day and night, Jake read the Bible. His three weeks were nearly up when he came to Romans 10:9. There in his prison cell, he confessed Christ with his mouth and believed in his heart that Jesus is the true Son of God and had been raised from the dead. As Jake pondered the words found in 1 John 1:9, he received assurance of his sins being forgiven:

"How my heart rejoiced in my newness of spiritual life, even though my body was suffering terribly from the physical beatings and lack of food. But suddenly I discovered that God had given me new spiritual eyes, and that when I looked at the Japanese officers and guards who had starved and beaten me and my companions so cruelly, I found my bitter hatred for them changed to loving pity. I read in my Bible that while those who crucified Jesus on the cross had beaten Him and spit upon Him, He tenderly prayed in His moment of excruciating suffering, 'Father, forgive them; for they know not what they do.' From the depths of my heart, I too prayed for God to forgive my torturers. I was determined, by the aid of Christ, to do my best to acquaint the Japanese people with the message of salvation. A year passed by, and while the treatment did not change, I did. I began to love my captors."[43] Jake made a vow to God that, should he survive his prison experience, he would return one day to the land of his former enemy as a missionary.

Lieutenant Meder was like the proverbial grain of wheat falling into the ground and dying (John 12:24). God used his life and death to awaken Jake, but there was another source of power behind the scenes as well. This was a godly mother who had never ceased to pray for her son. She says: "My story is not one of boastful pride, but of witness to the goodness of the God who ever hears and answers the intercessory, pleading prayers of a Christian mother. My son, Jacob DeShazer, is a loving example of what the Lord can do for any mother who really 'gets hold of God' for the solving of every trial and problem in the rearing of sons and daughters."[44]

In 1945, American paratroopers dropped into the prison compound in a dramatic rescue of the emaciated Doolittle survivors. In due time, Jake fully recovered. He attended Bible college in the United States, the first step in fulfilling the vow he had made to God. In college he met Florence, a wonderful young woman, who caught his vision to return to Japan.

In 1948, Jake and Florence arrived in Yokohama feeling apprehensive about how their former enemy would receive them. Because thousands of Japanese had lost loved ones during the war, many of them held a deep-seated enmity toward Americans. But in the immediate postwar years, God mightily used the DeShazers to help reconcile the former enemies to one another and many Japanese people to the Great Reconciler.

One Japanese girl vowed to kill Jake because she had lost her sweetheart in the Doolittle raid. However, during one of Jake's meetings she repented and became a believer. In a meeting in Osaka, four years after Jake's return, two of his former prison guards became believers when they heard his testimony. What drama and emotion there was in that encounter! Could there ever be any more dramatic account of reconciliation?

The answer was to be yes, when we see what happened in the life of Mitsuo Fuchida. Fuchida had come back from the war a miserable, dejected man. Most of his flying companions were dead. Japan had been devastated by the Allied bombings, and his people were defeated and discouraged. Many had lost all their possessions and were close to starvation. Never in Japan's history had foreigners occupied her land. Now all that had changed. What hope was there?

In Fuchida's words: "From Pearl Harbor day, I spent myself as a most patriotic soldier for my mother country. But four years later, Japan had lost the war. I returned to Nara Prefecture disillusioned and took up farming. These were the most miserable days of my life. One day, however, General MacArthur, the supreme commanding officer of the occupied forces, asked me to come to Tokyo to testify at the war trials. I got off my train at the Shibuya railroad station, and there I saw an American handing out leaflets. I took one and read the startling title: I Was a War Prisoner of Japan.

"At that time I was forty-seven years old. I had never heard the name of Jesus. But Jake DeShazer's story inspired me to get a Bible. I read through the pages eagerly, and one day I came to Luke 23:34. Jesus was hanging on the cross, nailed there, yet He prayed, 'Father, forgive them; for they know not what they do.' Right at that moment, Jesus came into my heart. I clearly understood what He had done on the cross. I accepted Him as my personal Savior. Then He transformed me. I was a sinner, but He cleansed me. I dedicated the balance of my life to serving Him."[45]

About this time, Jake DeShazer felt God leading him to begin a fast of forty days. This was no simple thing, as his weight was still low after all he had suffered during the war years. Yet he felt this was the leading of the Lord. Almost immediately upon completing the fast, he met Mitsuo Fuchida. It was a most dramatic moment of complete and emotional reconciliation: one-time enemies now worshiped and served the same God, the Lord Jesus Christ. Only the living God could cause such a transformation in the hearts and lives of two men, once sworn enemies forever— now enemies no more.

From time to time these two men teamed together in meetings throughout Japan, preaching the message of peace, forgiveness, and reconciliation. On May 30, 1976, Mitsuo Fuchida, warrior for Japan turned warrior for God, went into the presence of the Savior he loved and served. Jake attended the funeral of his Japanese brother.

Before he went home to be with the Lord, Fuchida revisited Honolulu, scene of the Pearl Harbor attack, and handed out Bibles to people. He told one American, "I came with bombs once, but now I come with the Bible. Jesus Christ is the reason."[46]

Condensed from the book
Unforgettable Men in Unforgettable Times
Used with permission

A LILY ON THE BATTLEFIELD

★

BOB BOARDMAN

I knew of a daring commander, a favorite of navy and marine enlisted men because of his daring spirit, desire for victory, contempt for the enemy, and vivid language. He was responsible for America's first carrier task force during World War II, which staged the first hit-and-run raids on the islands of Wake, Marcus, and the Marshalls.

While in the First Marine Division during World War II, I steamed into the harbor of Tulagi Island near Guadalcanal, which had been won in a hard-fought battle. The U.S. Armed Forces were using Tulagi as a rest-and-recreation area for the battle-weary men engaged in the South Pacific. As our ship, loaded with marines, moved into the harbor, we saw a large billboard on shore. It said something like this: "Kill Japs, kill Japs, and keep on killing Japs. The only good Jap is a dead Jap. Signed, Admiral ———". When the men on shipboard read it, they cheered.

Though a battle commander must exercise a certain disdain for the enemy, how far should it go? Where is the delicate line between disdain and hatred, between invigorating the morale of the troops and instilling hatred for years and generations to come? The kind of scorn and prejudice that poured forth from that admiral in numerous press conferences and on that Tulagi billboard decades ago still affects certain Americans from that generation.

An American businessman came into my office in the heart of downtown Tokyo some time ago. He was prosperous, well dressed, silver-haired, and in his mid- to late-fifties. I introduced him to three of our Japanese staff. As we briefly conversed while standing in the middle of the office, he asked me, "Do these Japs respond to the message of Christianity?"

I winced and looked to see if any of the Japanese had heard

him. If they had, it did not show on their placid faces as they continued their work. I decided to ignore it, thinking it was just an oversight on my visitor's part, but as we continued talking he repeated the slur. This time I steered him to the door.

Outside, I explained what the word "Jap" stood for and how it brought back harsh memories of the war. He was extremely embarrassed and apologetic and said he had meant no harm by his insensitive remarks. He was, in a very real sense, a brainwashed man of his generation. Our entire national war effort had planted in his mind a subconscious prejudice that endured for several decades.

Another time I was talking to a woman from this same age group at a conference in the United States. When she learned I was living in Japan, she said, "Somehow I just can't enjoy being around . . ."

She couldn't finish her sentence, so I said, "Orientals?"

"Well, yes."

I said to her, "But Jesus was a Middle Easterner."

She was speechless.

Prejudice has a strange inconsistency to it, doesn't it?

Unforgiveness and hatred spread as easily as the worst infectious disease, and no side is immune to its devastating power—I know this personally. But I didn't realize there was such bitterness in my heart until God showed me that He wanted me to go to Japan as His servant. The Lord used the examples of two amazing men to help me give up my resentful spirit. The first man was plenty tough—as tough as any marine. I was in a large meeting in 1951, going through my own struggle, when I heard Louie Zamperini tell his story. Zamperini was a sergeant in the old Army Air Corps. He was a world-class runner, chosen as a member of the All-American college team to participate in the Olympic games in Berlin in 1936. (And while there he shinnied up a fifty-foot flagpole and brought down a swastika as a trophy. Though Hitler nearly had him shot for his antics, he finally allowed him to keep it.)

After the Japanese attacked Pearl Harbor, Zamperini joined

the Air Corps, was shot down in the Pacific, and survived forty-seven days on a life raft. The drifting raft ended up on the Japanese-occupied island of Guam. When his raft approached the shoreline, Zamp and a fellow crew member were too weak to walk; they could only crawl ashore on their hands and knees. They were immediately captured by the Japanese and sent to a prison camp in Japan.

When the prison guards learned that Zamp had been a champion runner, they brutally beat and starved him. For fourteen days in a row, Japanese Sergeant Watanabe, nicknamed "The Bird" by the Allied prisoners, beat Zamp with his heavy web steel belt buckle. Then he made him compete in running events, though he then weighed less than a hundred pounds. If Zamp lost, they beat him; if he won, they beat him harder.

Zamperini had prayed to God for deliverance and mercy on that life raft in the middle of the Pacific Ocean. Now, in prison, he prayed again, but this time with repentance. He told God he would serve Him, if only God would deliver him from the camp.

God kept Zamp alive and delivered him at the end of World War II. When he returned home he became an instant hero—and promptly forgot all of his promises to God. He began to drink heavily, but God wasn't finished with him.

"When I forgot my promises to God in the clamor and excitement and false ambition of postwar living," Zamp says, "I was worse than the prison guards in Japan who had beaten, starved, and tortured me. They denied me the dignity of human treatment, but I denied God in my search for notoriety and material gain."

Zamp finally repented from his willful, materialistic pursuits and returned to Japan to share the Good News of Jesus Christ with the Japanese people. But his supreme test of faith was whether he could visit Sugamo Prison in Naoetsu, come face-to-face with his former guards, and say, "I forgive you, in Christ's name."

During the 1998 Winter Olympics he returned to Japan to carry the Olympic torch through the town of Naoetsu on the way to Nagano, headquarters of the Games. It was here where he was held for most of those thirty months during the war, and his story spread long before he arrived.

The Japanese, and especially the townspeople of Naoetsu, honored and cheered this eighty-one-year-old American—and in a sense apologized to him for the brutality he had suffered at their hands in World War II. His jailor and torturer, "The Bird" Watanabe, still survived. After the war, the Allied War Crimes Tribunal searched for him to put him on trial for atrocities committed against Allied POWs, but he eluded capture.

Louis Zamperini had an appointment to meet his captor face-to-face, but The Bird broke the appointment. The Bird missed his chance to hear the words, "I forgive you."

The second man who taught me forgiveness was a Japanese man born just after World War II ended. His generation had been caught between the traditions of old Japan (some of them good, some bad) and the new, postwar Japan. As a high school student Toru Nagai began to investigate the life, death, and resurrection of Jesus Christ in search of the answers to his many questions. Nagai was hooked, and his mind was transformed. Nagai's belief and mental attitude changed steadily over the course of time.

We met while laboring side by side repainting several churches and landscaping their grounds on the island of Okinawa. There were twelve of us: nine Japanese and three Americans. When we finished we looked forward to some rest and sightseeing. This was the first time our Japanese coworkers had had visited Okinawa, a beautiful coral island seventy-five miles long and fifteen miles wide.

For me, Okinawa was more than just another subtropical island inhabited by a million people. It was the place God spared my life on Father's Day in 1945. Nagai and others on the work camp team requested a personal tour of the battlefield where I had been wounded. The place was a high, steep coral ridge called Kunishi Ridge.

I was somewhat apprehensive about the reactions of my Japanese friends. As I told them the story of my injury, which took place about the time most of them were born, I realized it was their fathers' and uncles' generation against whom I had fought. I told them how our tank, hit by antitank fire, was engulfed in flames and destroyed, how we were pinned down behind enemy lines. I pointed out the caves and ravines where the Japanese soldiers hid and unleashed sniper fire, seriously wounding three of us who had escaped from our tank.

After I had finished the story, and we stood there looking at the battlefield, Toru Nagai quietly slipped away. He returned with a wild lily, complete with bulb. He said to me, "Once our people were enemies with yours. But we want you to know that a change has come in our hearts because of the Prince of Peace. We who are standing here are a new generation. We want to dedicate our lives with you to the cause of sharing Jesus Christ with our people. Please accept this lily as a token of this dedication. Plant it back home in remembrance of this consecration."

I planted the lily bulb in our garden in our home in Tokyo. Each year as it blooms, it reminds me of the reason Jesus is called the Prince of Peace. He brought peace to my heart the same way He did in the life of Toru Nagai.

Condensed from the book
Unforgettable Men in Unforgettable Times
Used with permission

RED SKIES OVER EARLY AMERICA

THE FRENCH AND INDIAN WAR

A Song of the French and Indian War

The Girl I Left Behind Me

The hope of final victory
Within my bosom burning
Is mingling with sweet thoughts
  of thee
And of my fond returning
But should I ne'er return again
Still with thy love I'll bind me
Dishonor's breath shall never stain
The name I leave behind me.
The hours sad I left a maid
A lingering farewell taking
Whose sighs and tears my steps
  delayed

I thought her heart was breaking
In hurried words her name I blest
I breathed the vows that bind me
And to my heart in anguish pressed
The girl I left behind me.

The French and Indians combined to rise up against the American colonists and British army in 1755, beginning with the massacre of eleven missionaries. By 1758, thousands of colonists had been murdered in their homes. When the Susquehanna Delaware joined the Iroquois, they spread death and destruction up and down the frontier in Pennsylvania, New Jersey, and New York. In April 1755, Pennsylvania declared war on the Delaware and offered bounties for scalps and prisoners. New Jersey and other states soon followed suit.

Eight years later, in November 1763, the Delaware and Shawnee signed a peace treaty with the British. Col. Henry Bouquet signed the treaty at Coshocton and the Indians released 206 white prisoners. This story is about two of these captured children and the faith that sustained them.[47]

CAPTURED! BUT NOT FORSAKEN!

★

TRACY LEININGER

But watch out! Be very careful never to forget what you have seen the LORD do for you. Do not let these things escape from your mind as long as you live! And be sure to pass them on to your children and grandchildren. (Deuteronomy 4:9, NLT)

It had been eight years since the Leininger family settled in the American colonies, leaving behind their native Germany. They had endured a long sea voyage and forged their way across uncharted mountain ranges to settle on the very edge of the Pennsylvania frontier. The fall of 1755 brought to the Leiningers not only rich beauty but also a rewarding harvest of corn. On this particular day the whole valley seemed to rejoice in the fullness of the season. The autumn sun settled in the western sky, illuminating the rich tones of the maple trees until they set the valley ablaze with colors of crimson and gold.

The Leiningers couldn't know that across the Atlantic in England and France, papers had been signed that would send the chilling beat of a war drum echoing across the frontier. Two great powers in unyielding opposition; both claiming the territories and the river passage to New Orleans as their own.

A deep, abiding faith was the one heritage the Leiningers strove to instill in their four children. The children knew exactly why their parents had made the arduous journey to this rough new world: "because here we are slave to no man and are free to live as God sees best." As the last glimmer of sun faded from the sky on this autumn day, the Leininger family was united in the comfort of their snug cabin.

Everything was like the day before—everything, that is, except for a dark-tanned figure crouching on the ridge, as silent as one of the oaks that overlooked the creek. From within the shroud of the forest, his dark, penetrating eyes watched the family's every move. His people, the Delaware, along with five other nations, had decided to join the French to drive out the English— and the colonists.

On this night Mr. Leininger read from the family Bible a story about the Israelites and their time of testing in the wilderness. As he closed the Bible his face sobered. "Each of you will have times of testing in your life. But you must always remember—no matter how dense the wilderness or dark the hour, God will never leave you. If your hearts remain true to Him, God promises you this blessing."

Though Regina didn't fully understand the meaning of his words, she heard the sense of urgency in his voice. Her mother began softly singing an old German hymn, and the whole family joined in.

> Alone, yet not all alone am I
> Though in this solitude so drear
> I feel my Savior always nigh;
> He comes the weary hours to
>   cheer
> I am with Him and He with me
> I therefore cannot lonely be.

When the girls had snuggled deep beneath their warm quilts, Mrs. Leininger pulled back the curtain and sat on the edge of their straw-ticked mattress.

"Please, Mama," whispered Regina, "will you sing my song once more? I always have good dreams after you sing."

Her mother laughed and placed another kiss on Regina's forehead. Then her melodious voice filled the cabin with its soothing tones. "Alone, yet not all alone am I. . . ."

As the morning sun quietly lifted over the green hills, Mrs. Leininger and her son John left for their daylong journey to the mill. They would not return until the next day, leaving Barbara and Regina to mind the house chores.

Christian spent the morning working in the cornfield with his father. As the sun stood high against the blue sky they knew it was time to join the girls for lunch. As they sat down to pray and enjoy their midday meal, the cabin door swung open. Two strong Indian braves strode briskly into the dark cabin. They were mostly bald, except for a few eagle feathers attached to a tuft of hair in the center of their heads. Their faces were painted with stripes, hardening their sharp features and accentuating their sullen eyes. They wore various leather straps across their strong painted chests, and from the straps dangled all sorts of weapon implements.

Mr. Leininger motioned for them to take a seat, but the warriors stood silently surveying the room. After what felt like hours, the older brave pointed at Barbara and said, "Squaw, give whiskey!"

Mr. Leininger quickly informed them, "We have no whiskey. Surely our Indian brother would like to smoke some tobacco instead." The warriors seemed satisfied with the tobacco and sat by the hearth quietly smoking a full pipe of tobacco. The Leininger men returned to the table and continued to eat their lunch, pretending not to be bothered by the odd actions of their guests.

Regina and Barbara retreated to the far end of the cabin and sat on the edge of their bed, finding comfort in distancing themselves from the painted warriors. Suddenly a shot rang out, and Regina saw her father falling to the floor. He clutched at his chest, crimson surging from beneath his hand. Almost at the same moment the other brave leaped like a panther toward Christian, knocking him from his seat and pinning him to the floor. The struggle lasted but a brief moment—Regina saw the brave reach for his tomahawk with one hand and secure his grip on her brother's scalp with the other. Shrieking, Regina buried her face in Barbara's lap and wrapped her arms around her sister in terror.

For a moment all was silent. Then the Indians started plundering the cabin, ripping the bedding and setting the wooden frames of the cabin on fire. The braves opened the wooden chest that held their family's treasured possessions. They were so focused on the shining contents— the gold-leafed Bible, father's brass pocket watch, grandmother's broach that came all the way from Germany—that for a moment the braves seemed to forget the girls huddled in the corner.

"Regina," Barbara whispered, "We have to run."

Taking Barbara's hand, Regina attempted to sneak through the smoke and debris. But it was no use. The braves' keen eyes caught their slightest movement.

A few quick strides and the strong warriors stood towering above the trembling girls. Yanking them by the arm, they dragged the girls from the smoke-filled cabin and darted for the shelter of the nearby forest. The sight of her older sister was the only source of comfort Regina received as she was carried farther and farther from home.

At last they emerged into a clearing at the top of the ridge, where they joined a group of other Indians who were talking excitedly among themselves.

Barbara wrapped her arms around her sister and gently smoothed her tangled hair. "Everything will be all right," she whispered. "Mama and John will be home from the mill soon, and they won't let them keep us forever."

For a moment Regina's heart calmed, but uncertainty still gripped her. There were too many warriors for John and her mother to overcome by themselves. Far below she could see their valley stretching to the horizon. She could hardly believe how far the Indians had already taken them. In the distance black, charred structures dotted the valley. From each of them streaks of smoke funneled up into the sky. Her heart sank. Had the Indians burned their neighbors' houses too?

There was a rustling at the edge of the clearing. Two more braves along with several new captives emerged. Regina recognized Marie, their nearest neighbor.

"Marie!" she called without thinking.

One of the braves walked toward her. "No speak in white tongue." The Indian glared down at Regina. "White father and brother dead—you Indian maiden—now speak Iroquoian, tongue of Allegheny and Delaware masters." The brave looked around at the other white captives that huddled in little groups about the camp to make sure they all understood the meaning of his words.

Before long the braves gathered all of the captives together in a long line. Using coarse rawhide, they bound them by their wrists. All the next day and the day after that, they sat bound hand and foot, watching helplessly as more grief-stricken women and children were added to their group. Each evening the braves gave the captives small portions of coarsely dried meat and wild black-berries.

All Regina could do was pray and wait to be rescued. By now John and her mother would surely have returned from the mill and begun searching for them. They would not rest until she and Barbara were safely home.

But no one came. Three days later the Indians awakened the party before dawn and forced them to begin a merciless march through the tangled underbrush of the forest. They walked at a brisk pace from dawn until dusk, pushing deeper and deeper into the heart of the Blue Mountains.

After five days of penetrating what seemed to be the very depths of the vast forest, the Indians finally stopped to rest. That evening the braves gave the captives their meager allotment of dried meat and allowed them to bed down early for the night. As the moon rose high in the night, and the Indians talked in louder and more excited tones, Regina dared to speak for the first time since the day they were captured.

"Do you—do you think that we will ever see Mama again?"

Barbara gently ran her fingers across her sister's anxious brow. "Yes, dear, we will see her again. Until then, we must be brave and remember what she and Papa taught us. God will always be with us—even in our darkest hour."

They were silent for a moment.

"The Indians may have taken us away from home, but they can never take away our faith in Jesus Christ—no matter what happens. Even if something were to happen to me, never forget that God is with you." She looked at her sister in the moonlight.

"Regina, do you remember how Mama calls you her little song-bird? Promise me you'll never lose the song in your heart, no matter what happens."

Barbara's words stirred Regina's heart. For the first time since they were captured, she smiled. Regina began to whisper the words to her favorite song, "Alone, yet not all alone am I. . . ." For the first time in her nine-year-old life, Regina understood the deeper meaning of the song. Within the words she found strength and comfort. These Indians could take away everything and everyone they knew, but they could not take away her Savior.

Regina wrapped her arms around her sister's neck. "I promise I will never forget—I will never lose the song in my heart."

With the rising of the sun Regina's life changed forever: her sister was torn from her and dragged down a nearby path heading due west. Both girls watched helplessly as they were forced to leave each other. How long would this separation last? Would they ever see each other again? As Barbara disappeared from her sight, Regina felt a strange mixture of incomprehensible loss and unexplainable peace. In spite of everything, she knew she would never be alone.

The Indians, however, allowed no time for sentiment or reflection. A warrior thrust a small child, no more than two years old, into her arms. "This your baby now!" he informed her.

Regina looked at the little girl. At first she was afraid of the responsibility. She was only nine years old! But as the days passed, she was thankful to have little Susanna to look after. It helped take her mind off her own plight.

Regina's captors were Delaware, and their party headed northwest to the forks of Beaver River, a cold and rigorous journey. Regina thought she would never survive. By the time the warriors finally reached their destination, both her shoes and her clothing had been ripped from her body by the dense underbrush and jagged mountainous terrain. The fall winds blew away any warmth that remained in the air, and winter settled in on the little village.

Life there was grim. The white captives were gaunt and weak from their labors, and almost all the Indians suffered from the harsh effects of a poor autumn harvest. Regina and Susanna were given to an old Indian woman who had lost her family to either a battle or epidemic. At first, Regina was grateful to be given shelter and clothing, but soon the harsh reality sunk in. She was now a slave to a poor, bitter woman who had neither husband nor children to provide for her needs.

Many nights Regina went without food, and she wondered if her weak, shivering frame would live to see spring. Her mistress scolded her harshly and at times even beat her, but Regina did her best to bear it with courage. She remembered how Papa taught her that Jesus was also beaten. She knew she could not give up. If she did, what would happen to Susanna?

As the months passed she understood more Iroquoian, the language of the Delaware. She heard much talk of the war with the English colonials and hoped that someday soon the army would come over the Allegheny Mountains and rescue her.

Finally winter melted into spring planting, followed by numerous summer activities. Then there was the busy fall harvest and the cold winter days spent skinning and tanning hides and scouring the woods for roots or anything edible. It was during their jaunts in the woods that Regina felt closest to her Savior. Often she would quote Scripture and sing her favorite hymn.

The Indians did not allow the captives to speak their own language, forcing them instead to accept the Indian language and religious beliefs. They even dyed her skin with walnut juice. But Regina knew she could not turn her back on the God of her fathers, no matter how much her captors tried to make her forget her past. As soon as Susanna was old enough, Regina brought her into the woods and taught her Scriptures and sang her favorite songs. Many times as she sang, her thoughts drifted back to her mother on the last night they were together. At first Regina remembered her mother's kind face and blue eyes, but as the years passed her memories dimmed.

After nine and a half long years, the British army and American militia defeated the French and Indians, and the peace treaty mandated the return of all white captives. The news quickly traveled east, breathing renewed hope into Mrs. Leininger's heart. Barbara had escaped three years after the fateful Penn's Creek Massacre and was reunited with her mother and brother John. They had moved farther east and settled closer to Philadelphia.

Deep within her heart Regina's mother believed her daughter was still alive, and not a day went by that she did not hope and pray for Regina's return. But would she be among the 206 captives that were handed over to the militia under Colonel Bouquet? And if she were among the freed captives waiting at Fort Carlisle, would Regina remember her family—her own mother? Mrs. Leininger had heard stories of captives returned to their families only to find that they remembered nothing of their childhood and longed to return to the Indians who raised them. These were the hopes and fears she wrestled with as she traveled back across the western frontier to Fort Carlisle. She was thankful to have Barbara and John there for support.

They anxiously searched each face as they walked in front of the long rows of captives. Many turned their heads in fear or looked at the ground in confusion. Some had walnut-stained skin, others looked so pale that they blended with the snow. Some were thin and sickly from the long journey.

Barbara remembered how anxious and fearful she was returning to the English at Fort Pitt. When she and the four other captives escaped, they crossed more than two hundred miles through the wilderness. They arrived half-starved, cold, and fatigued.

"You must remember, Mama," Barbara said reassuringly, "some of them have not seen white people in over nine years." But as she looked at the disheveled group, she wondered if they would be able to recognize Regina. After all, she would now be eighteen—a young Indian woman. That is, if she had even survived.

Mother approached someone who seemed to be about Regina's age. Speaking softly, she reached for the girl's arm. "Do not fear. I will not harm you."

The girl shrank away.

"Do you know your name, child?" Mother spoke in German, but it was no use. It was evident that the girl did not understand English or German.

They spoke to several other captives, but their hopes were repeatedly dashed. Finally Mother turned away with tears in her eyes. "I am afraid we will have to tell Colonel Bouquet that Regina is not here."

Barbara's heart grew sick at the thought of being so close only to return, knowing they could have passed her by. "Dear Lord," she prayed silently, "after all these years of hoping and praying, please—oh please, lead us to her."

A man's deep voice interrupted her prayer, and suddenly they were looking up into the face of Colonel Bouquet.

"Have you found your daughter?" The colonel's face was kind and expressed his deep concern. "Did she have any birthmarks, or perhaps a scar? Or is there a family heirloom she might recognize, like a locket or a trinket of some sort?"

"No, no. None at all. The Indians took most of our valuables during the massacre. What they did not take was lost when they burned our cabin to the ground." Mrs. Leininger closed her eyes as if to shut out the memory and quickly brushed away her tears.

The colonel thought for a moment. "Perhaps you can think of a childhood memory she might have held onto all these years—a term of endearment, a song?"

"Mama! Do you remember how Regina loved to sing, and you used to call her your little songbird?"

Her mother nodded, and renewed hope shone in her eyes. "Yes—yes, you're right!" she said. "I used to sing 'Alone, Yet Not All Alone' to Regina every night before bed. It was her favorite song."

"That's perfect! Why not walk back through the rows of captives and sing it?" Colonel Bouquet urged. "You never know what might trigger her memory."

Mrs. Leininger walked back through the rows of helpless captives, softly singing the hymn. "I am with Him and He with me, Even here alone I cannot be."

Barbara watched the faces of the captives as they passed, and though many seemed comforted by her mother's calming tones, none was especially moved. Then suddenly she heard a loud cry, and a tall, slender girl rushed into her mother's arms.

As the tall girl joined her mother in the song, Barbara knew—it was Regina!

Tears of joy filled Barbara's eyes as she stumbled blindly toward her mother and sister. Together they finished the last verse of Regina's song.

With a voice full of emotion, Regina whispered in Barbara's ear: "The Lord was with me. I remembered our promise. I remembered our song!"

Epilogue

Susanna's parents were victims of the massacre at the beginning of the French and Indian War. No surviving relatives were found, and the Leiningers raised her as their own. At the Fort Carlisle reunion, Susanna was about the same age and size that Regina had been when she was captured.

The first repatriation of captives in 1761 involved six hundred women and children. About half refused to be repatriated and stayed with the Shawnee, Delaware, and Iroquois. Time, loss of all loved ones, loss of language, fear of not being accepted again, and the youth of the children taken into captivity all played a part in this tragic result. Regina's and Barbara's stories of repatriation were exceptional. In 1763, very few of the 206 were reunited with their families.

Regina helped her mother raise her adopted sister, Susanna, and for the rest of her life served the people in her town. She was known throughout her community as a woman of great kindness, whose willingness to help those in need was unmatched.

She was buried beside her mother. On her tombstone in Berks County, Pennsylvania, are these words:

Regina Leininger
As a small child held Indian captive
1755-1763
Identified by her mother's singing the hymn
"Alone, Yet Not Alone Am I"

Condensed from the book by Tracy Leininger,
Alone Yet Not Alone
Published by His Seasons. Used with permission.
www.hisseasons.com

THE REVOLUTIONARY WAR

Revolutionary War Songs

Yankee Doodle
(Written by an Englishman in
    ridicule, but adopted and sung
    with pride by the Colonists)
Yankee doodle, keep it up,
Yankee doodle dandy.
Mind the music and the step,
And with the girls be handy.

The Cruel War
I made my decision,
I will join up too,
Oh Johnny, dear Johnny,
I'll soon be with you.

We women are fighters,
We can help you win,
Oh Johnny, I'm hoping,
That they'll take me in.
The cruel war is raging
Johnny has to fight
I want to be with him
From morning till night

I'm counting the minutes
The hours and the days,
Oh Lord, stop the cruel war,
For this, my heart prays.

On June 1, 1774, Wednesday, the same day the British blockade of the Boston Harbor was to begin, the colonies called for a day of fasting and prayer "to seek divine direction and aid."[48] Washington's diary entry that day was: Went to church and fasted all day.[49]

On July 4, 1775, in his general orders as commander in chief of the Continental army, Gen. George Washington gave the order from his headquarters at Cambridge:

> It is required and expected that exact discipline be observed, and due Subordination prevail thro' the whole Army, as a Failure in these most essential points must necessarily produce Hazard, Disorder and Confusion; and end in shameful disappointment and disgrace.

> The General most earnestly requires, and expects due observance of those articles of war, established by the Government of the army, which forbid profane cursing, swearing and drunkenness;

> And in like manner requires and expects, of all Officers, and Soldiers, not engaged on actual duty, a punctual attendance of Divine Services, to implore the blessings of Heaven upon the means used for our safety and defense.[50]

THE CRUCIBLE OF VALLEY FORGE

★

PETER MARSHALL[51]

Everyone therefore who acknowledges me before others, I also will acknowledge before my Father in heaven. (Matthew 10:32, NRSV)

Suffering. Pain. Hunger. Nakedness. The First Continental Army faced the worst want of circumstances in the winter of 1776 just outside an obscure town in Pennsylvania called Valley Forge. For the first time, Americans as a whole were confronted with the hard facts of their circumstances. Locked in a desperate struggle for survival, they were slowly being backed toward the precipice of surrender by a more powerful adversary. Though they were contesting every inch of ground, there was now some question as to how long America's will to endure would hold firm.

A month earlier, the Continental army had been badly mauled at Brandywine as they tried in vain to stop the British march toward Philadelphia. More than twice as many fresh enemy troops as had been captured had arrived in the Colonies, and America's chief city had now become an armed British camp. Liberty and independence, once seemingly within grasp, were becoming a forgotten dream.

Such were the thoughts that may have weighed on Washington's mind as he sat on his big gray horse and watched his men file silently past on that cold and dismal December 19. They were on their way into Valley Forge, the site he had chosen for their winter encampment. He had decided that Trenton was too dangerous, and Wilmington, Lancaster, or Reading would have afforded the British access to too much territory. Valley Forge was barely fifteen miles from Philadelphia, yet because it lay in the fork where Valley Creek ran into the Schuylkill River, it was easily defensible. With open fields nearby for drilling and ample wood for fuel and shelter, strategically Washington could not have chosen a better location.

Few of the men who shuffled past him through the snow had ever heard of Valley Forge—a name that would be chiseled in the cornerstone of this nation's history. Nor did they care; they were exhausted, hungry, freezing—and had long since given up hope of meat for supper, a warm bed, or a dry pair of stockings. Many did not have a pair of stockings left. Their footgear consisted of strips of blanket wound around their feet. All too quickly the blanket would wear through, and they would be walking through the snow barefoot. In the entire dwindling army of eleven thousand men, there may have been fewer than a dozen properly equipped for the terrible winter that lay ahead.

As they passed by, their heads down in protection against the icy wind, no drumbeat marked the cadence of their steps. There was only the rattle of leafless branches overhead. There were no complaints, no greets, nor did their general attempt to encourage them with hearty words. They knew he was there, and that was enough.

Though he did not speak, the tall figure on the still horse, whose own shoulders were hunched against the cold, was grieving for his men. As the pale afternoon light faded and gave way to a moonless starless night, perhaps he sensed that they were marching into the dark night of the young nation's soul. For now came the time of testing, the time that sooner or later seemed to come to every covenanted body of Christians on this continent. The first Pilgrim and Puritans had faced their starving times; their grandsons had suffered through the horror of a massed Indian uprising. And now it was Valley Forge—the ordeal which, in later centuries, would become known as our "crucible of freedom."

Snow fell early that winter—and stayed. Extreme low temperatures saw the Schuylkill freeze over, and preserved every inch of snow that lay on the ground till the roads were clogged with drifts several feet deep. Shelter now became a matter of desperate urgency.

Washington himself had designed the huts they would sleep

in—log cabins of the simplest construction. Sixteen feet long, fourteen feet wide, and six feet high, these cabins would be easy to heat and could shelter a dozen men on four triple-decker bunks. With shake shingles, no windows, no flooring, and holes under the eaves for ventilation, they were so simple that they could be put up quickly by men not possessing woodsmen's skills.

Practically every able-bodied man at Valley Forge was put to work on them, and upward of seven hundred cabins were erected in less than a month. Not until the last man was thus quartered did Washington quit his own leaky tent for the relative comfort of Isaac Potts' house, which was to serve as his headquarters. Doctor Thatcher and the general's staff must have been immensely relieved at this move, having dreaded to think what would become of the army—and the nation—were their leader to be felled by influenza. And disease was taking a fearful toll of their numbers; they would lose one in four that winter to flu, smallpox, typhus, and exposure.

But Washington did not spare himself. Early in the morning he would begin making the rounds of the camp, and would spend most of the day riding from one regiment to the next, talking with the men. As Dr. Thatcher commented: "The army . . . was not without consolation, for his Excellency the commander-in-chief . . . manifested a fatherly concern and fellow-feeling for their sufferings and made every exertion in his power to remedy the evil and to administer the much-desired relief."

Yet there was precious little that even the General of the Army could do. Congress, comfortably ensconced some ninety miles to the west in York, no longer benefited from the leadership of the best men in America. Men like Adams, Franklin, Jay, Hancock, and Livingston were all vitally employed elsewhere, and their places had been filled by lesser men who were consumed with petty bickering and united in their jealousy of Washington. They convinced each other that his needs were exaggerated. Instead of sending the wagons of victuals and winter clothing for which he pleaded, they would merely print more paper money. With this he was supposed to pay his troops and purchase what he needed. They chose to remain oblivious to the reality of the situation, which was that after several months of both armies feeding off the land, the countryside was exhausted. What scant provender did remain was finding its way into Philadelphia, where the British paid in gold.

From the beginning, life in Valley Forge was grim. The huts were smoky and dark, and the newest men in each hut were given the bottom bunks closest to the door—the ones that got cold first when the night fire burned low. In the morning, the men took turns taking the bucket and padding down to the frozen creek to fetch cooking water. Meal after meal, their food consisted of "fire-cake"—wheat or cornmeal poured into a kettle of water, mixed, and ladled out on a big stone in the middle of an open fire, where it baked. Sometimes there was a bit of salt pork, too, or some dried fish, when the wagons got through. As for winter clothing, it was in such scarce supply that Washington had to issue a general order threatening punishment to anyone cutting up a tent to make a coat out of it, for they had to save every tent they could for next summer.

As the winter wore on and the list of sick and dead mounted, life in Valley Forge became an unbearable nightmare. Now there were men who were literally naked, because they did not have even rags to wrap around themselves. A committee from Congress (they finally sent one in the middle of February) was shocked to find how many "feet and legs froze till they became black, and it was often necessary to amputate them." Exposure to the elements combined with the starvation diet to ensure optimum conditions for the diseases that now ravaged the camp.

Washington himself, throughout his life given to understatement, wrote: "No history now extant can furnish an instance of an army's suffering such uncommon hardships as ours has done and bearing them with the same patience and fortitude. To see men without clothes to cover their nakedness, without blankets to lie on, without shoes (for the want of which their marches might be traced by the blood from their feet) . . . and submitting without a murmur, is a proof of patience and obedience which in my opinion can scarce be paralleled."

Yet the nightmare grew worse. When, in mid-February, the entire camp was down to their last twenty-five barrels of flour, Washington wrote: "I am now convinced beyond a doubt that unless some great and capital change suddenly takes place . . . this army must inevitably be reduced to one or other of these three things: Starve, dissolve, or disperse, in order to obtain subsistence."

And on February 16, a civilian named John Joseph Stoudt would write in his diary: "For some days there has been little less than a famine in the camp. . . . Naked and staving as they are, we cannot enough admire the incomparable patience and fidelity of the soldiery, that they have not been excited by their suffering to a general mutiny and dispersion. Indeed, the distress of this army for want of provisions is perhaps beyond anything you can conceive."

This, then, was the miracle of Valley Forge. That the men endured was indeed amazing to all who knew of their circumstances. But the reason they endured—the reason they believed in God's deliverance—was simple: they could believe, because their general did believe.

Washington made no secret of his Christian faith. In his general order calling for divine services every Sunday, he said, "To the distinguished character of a Patriot, it should be our highest glory to add the more distinguished character of a Christian." And others, such as the pastor of a nearby Lutheran church, Henry Muhlenberg, would note his faith with approval: "I heard a fine example today, namely, that His Excellency General Washington rode around among his army yesterday and admonished each and every one to fear God, to put away the wickedness that has set in and become so general, and to practice the Christian virtues. For all appearances, this gentleman does not belong to the so-called world of society, for he respects God's Word, believes in the atonement through Christ, and bears himself in humility and gentleness. Therefore, the Lord God has also singularly, yea, marvelously, preserved him from harm in the midst of countless perils, ambuscades, fatigues, etc., and has hitherto graciously held him in His hand as a chosen vessel."

When it came to prayer, however, Washington preferred to pray in private, and it is doubtful that he ever prayed more fervently than he did that winter. One of the numbers of accounts of people accidentally discovering him in prayer involved the general's temporary landlord, Isaac Potts.

Potts was a Quaker and a pacifist. One day he noticed Washington's horse tethered by a secluded grove of trees, not far from his headquarters. Hearing a voice, he approached quietly and saw the general on his knees at prayer. Not wanting to be discovered, he stood motionless until Washington had finished and returned to his headquarters.

Potts then hurried to return to the house himself to tell his wife, Sarah, "If George Washington be not a man of God, I am greatly deceived—and still more shall I be deceived, if God do not, through him, work out a great salvation for America."

Something else happened that winter that says much about the quality of Washington's faith. A turncoat collaborator named Michael Wittman was captured, and at his trial, it was proven that he had given the British invaluable assistance on numerous occasions. He was found guilty of spying and sentenced to death by hanging. On the evening before the execution, an old man with white hair asked to see Washington, giving his name as Peter Miller. He was ushered in without delay, for Miller had done a great many favors for the army. Now he had a favor to ask of Washington, who nodded agreeably.

"I've come to ask you to pardon Michael Wittman."

Washington was taken aback. "Impossible! Wittman has done all in his power to betray us, even offering to join the British and help destroy us." He shook his head. "In these times we cannot be lenient with traitors; and for that reason I cannot pardon your friend."

"Friend! He's no friend of mine. He is my bitterest enemy. He has persecuted me for years. He has even beaten me and spit in my face, knowing full well that I would not strike back. Michael Wittman is no friend of mine!"

Washington was puzzled. "And you still wish me to pardon him?"

"I do. I ask it of you as a great personal favor."

"Why?"

"I ask it because Jesus did as much for me."

Washington turned away and walked into the next room. Soon he returned with a paper on which was written the pardon of Michael Wittman. "My dear friend," he said, placing the paper in the old man's hand, "I thank you for this."

Such charity did not weaken him in the army's eyes; the men loved him for it; as did his officers. No one who had served with him could understand why there were generals and congressmen who wanted to see him replaced. But then, the latter did not know how it was at Valley Forge. "The greatest difficulty," said the young Marquis de Lafayette "was that, in order to conceal misfortunes from the enemy, it was necessary to conceal them from the nation also."

Despite the necessity for secrecy, across the nation pastors were beginning to catch the spirit of the tremendous spiritual struggle that was being waged at Valley Forge. More and more sermons were likening Washington to Moses. There were the obvious parallels, of course, but there was also the similarity in his choosing to partake of the same hardships as his men.

"By faith Moses, when he was come to years, refused to be called the son of Pharaoh's daughter; choosing rather to suffer affliction with the people of God, than to enjoy the pleasures of sin for a season; esteeming the reproach of Christ greater riches than the treasures in Egypt" (Hebrews 11:24-26, KJV). Thus did Washington covenant himself with his men in the suffering of Valley Forge, while a day's ride away, the British sat warm and full-bellied, enjoying after-dinner brandy by the fireside.

In the crucible of freedom, God was forging the iron of the Continental army into steel. And now there was a new strength and determination in the camp, as revealed in this piece by an anonymous Valley Forge soldier, which appeared in the Pennsylvania Packet: "Our attention is now drawn to one point: the enemy grows weaker every day, and we are growing stronger. Our work is almost done, and with the blessing of heaven, and the valor of our worthy General, we shall soon drive these plunderers out of our country!"

The soldiers who came through Valley Forge were tempered into the carbon-steel core around which an army could be built. In the tempering process, God sent almost as unlikely an agent as Squanto had been to the Pilgrims—a ruddy-cheeked, bemedaled German with a passion for drill and a twinkle in his eye. This was Friedrich Wilhelm Augustus Baron von Steuben, a former captain in the Prussian army and staff officer of Frederick the Great. Well recommended by Ben Franklin in Paris, von Steuben volunteered his services to the American cause. Washington quickly recognized his expertise and assigned him the task of making a professional army out of the Continentals.

Von Steuben proceeded with typical Prussian thoroughness. There was no drill manual, so he set about to write one. Then one company of men was trained until they responded almost instinctively to the various commands. With these men, he demonstrated to the rest of the companies how to drill.

In musketry, this by-rote precision was especially important. "Prime firing pans . . . charge muskets . . . remove ramrods. . . ." There were many steps to firing a musket, and if, in the heat of battle, one step were overlooked, there would be a gap in the volley. (There were, for example, instances of soldiers forgetting to remove their ramrods from their barrels and actually firing them at the enemy. A flying ramrod had been known to kill a man, but the soldier's musket was useless thereafter.) By the time spring came, von Steuben had drilled the men to the point where they could produce a crisp volley every fifteen seconds.

Arising at 3 A.M. and on the parade ground by sunrise, the Prussian was a demanding drillmaster. He had a saving sense of humor, however, and his oaths were frequently punctuated by laughter. When driven to distraction by the repeated fouling up of one company or another, he would swear at them in German till he was out of breath, then call on his interpreter to carry on in English. His perseverance bore fruit; as March turned into April, the Continental army began to march as one. And their newly acquired precision was more than a little responsible for their steadily improving morale.

From this time forth, Washington never needed to worry about another year-end enlistment lag; men were now signing up for three-year tours. But regardless of the contracted length of their tour, the veterans of Valley Forge were in for the duration and would not think of leaving until the job was done. And when the hardest assignments came—the frontal attacks, the bayonet charges, the flanker details—the Valley Forge men were the ones invariably chosen.

On the first of May, intelligence reached the American camp that France, having become convinced that the Colonial army could stand up to the full might of the British military establishment, was at last coming into the war on the side of America. The dark night was over; the French were allies! With that news, volunteers and supplies began pouring in from all over the country. And now, thanks to Valley Forge, there was an army—a real army—ready to receive them.

But Washington took no credit upon himself for the saving of the army and their new French allies. Instead he gave glory to God and said to his joyous troops: "It having pleased the Almighty Ruler of the universe to defend the cause of the United American States, and finally to raise up a powerful friend among the princes of the earth, to establish our liberty and independence upon a lasting foundation, it becomes us to set apart a day for gratefully acknowledging the divine goodness, and celebrating the important event, which we owe to His divine interposition."

Abridged from *The Light and the Glory*
by Peter Marshall and David Manuel[51]

THE CIVIL WAR

Songs of the Civil War

When Johnny Comes Marching Home
When Johnny comes marching home again,
Hurrah! Hurrah!
We'll give him a hearty welcome then
Hurrah! Hurrah!
The men will cheer and the boys will shout
The ladies they will all turn out
And we'll all feel gay,
When Johnny comes marching home.

Tenting Tonight
Many are the hearts that are weary tonight
Wishing for the war to cease,
Many are the hearts looking for the right
To see the dawn of peace.
Tenting tonight, tenting tonight
Tenting on the old camp-ground.

We've been tenting tonight on the
   old camp-ground,
Thinking of days gone by
Of the loved ones at home that gave us the hand,
And the tear that said, "Good-bye!"

After taking command of the Confederate army in June 1862, Gen. Robert E. Lee engineered an unbroken string of victories against the Union army. After three years of war in the south, Lee moved north into Pennsylvania to feed and clothe his troops while weakening Lincoln's political support for continuing the war. Learning of the proximity of the Union army, Lee concentrated his scattered forces at Gettysburg.

The Union army, under Gen. George Meade, retreated after an opening skirmish but paused on the heights of Cemetery Ridge. At the southern end of the ridge was a small hill called Little Round Top. It was here that General Lee attacked in order to outflank the Union army and dislodge them from the heights. The three days of battle at Gettysburg resulted in severe casualties, with more than 44,000 killed or wounded. Lee's failure to take Little Round Top resulted in his decision to make a frontal assault on Cemetery Ridge with 15,000 men under General Longstreet. In the space of twenty minutes, the Confederate army sustained more than 7,500 casualties and Lee, for the first time, was forced to retire from the field of battle in defeat.

Abraham Lincoln, just sixty days prior to this monumental battle, called the nation to a national day of prayer and fasting with these words: "We have become too self-sufficient to feel the necessity of redeeming and preserving grace, too proud to pray to the God that made us. . . . It behooves us then, to humble ourselves before the Offended Power, to confess our national sins, and to pray for clemency and forgiveness. . . . I request all the people to abstain on that day from their ordinary secular pursuits, and to unite at their several places of worship and their respective homes in keeping the day holy to the Lord."[52]

HILL OF COURAGE

★

MAJ. DOUGLAS VINCENT MASTRIANO, U. S. ARMY

Be strong and courageous; do not be afraid nor dis-
mayed . . . before all the multitude that is with him;
for there are more with us than with him.
(2 Chronicles 32:7, NKJV)

The dog days of summer had descended upon Col. Joshua L. Chamberlain, who found himself a long way from his home in Maine. As the commander of the Twentieth Maine Infantry Regiment in the Union's army, he led his men toward a small town in Pennsylvania where they would join other Union forces facing Robert E. Lee's Confederate army of Northern Virginia. Little did Chamberlain know how greatly his role on the hills outside the small town of Gettysburg would influence the outcome of the larger Civil War.

It was only the year before, in 1862, that Chamberlain volunteered to serve in the Union army. He had been content with his life as a professor of rhetoric and modern language at Bowdoin College. But as the war slipped from one year to two, he became increasingly restless about his own role in this terrible conflict. He had always supported the cause of freeing the slaves and restoring the Union. When the end of the war seemed in doubt and the outcome vaguely clouded, he felt compelled to join the army and "do his part."

Upon entering, Chamberlain was offered command of the Twentieth Maine. However, lacking any military experience, he declined this prestigious appointment and instead agreed to serve as the deputy commander. This was uncharacteristic; most appointed commanders at the time lacked military experience and perfected their skills on the battlefield, often at the cost of their men. Chamberlain learned to serve rather than be served and used this time to study the art of war. One of the tactics he perfected during this period would be instrumental on the day he was vastly outnumbered on the hills of Gettysburg.

Chamberlain's brigade commander, Col. Strong Vincent, guided the Twentieth Maine to their place in the Federal line on the low slope of a hill called Little Round Top. As the regiment occupied its position, Colonel Vincent told Chamberlain the importance of the location. He said, "I place you here! This is the left of the Union line. You understand. You are to hold this ground at all costs!"[53]

The Twentieth Maine was the end of the Federal line; there were no Union troops to their left. If he failed, the Union army would be defeated. An ominous feeling engulfed Chamberlain as he felt the weight of this knowledge on his shoulders. In spite of this, he reflected upon an ancient encouragement and promise from the Bible: "Be careful for nothing; but in every thing by prayer and supplication with thanksgiving let your requests be made known unto God. And the peace of God, which passeth all understanding, shall keep your hearts and minds through Christ Jesus" (Philippians 4:6-7, KJV). He wrote of the calm that brought to him: "My mind and heart are at peace; Jesus Christ is my all sufficient savior."[54]

After taking their positions, Chamberlain had only a few minutes to organize his men. He could hear the fierce fighting just up from Little Round Top, where Confederate regiments from Alabama and Texas endeavored to break the Union line. Like a torrent, the Confederate attack rolled down the hill, hitting the other regiments in Chamberlain's unit first; starting with the Sixteenth Michigan, the Forty-fourth New York, the Eighty-third Pennsylvania, and finally, his Twentieth Maine. Despite the valiant Confederate attack, the Union line held.

Chamberlain knew this was only the beginning of the battle. As he expected, with each Confederate attack his line became weaker. Each onslaught rolled upon his embattled regiment like a wave crashing onto the shoreline, leaving behind increasing numbers of dead and wounded. Yet amid the din and smoke of battle, Chamberlain stood like a rock and led his unit with a clear mind.

He felt that "most likely I shall be hit somehow at sometime, but all 'my times are in His hand,' and I cannot die without His appointing. I try to keep ever in view all the possibilities that surround me and to be ready for all that I am called to.[55] I am in the right place, and no harm can come to me unless it is wisely and kindly ordered so. I try to be equal to my duty and ready for anything that may come."[56]

This confidence in God's divine protection enabled him to inspire his men as he stood bravely exposed to each onslaught. Three times, history records, a providential hand protected him in this battle. The first happened early in the fight when a shell fragment struck his right instep. After this, a Confederate minié ball struck his left side squarely on the scabbard of his sword, merely bending it against his leg. The final instance occurred when a member of the Fifteenth Alabama had Chamberlain in the sight of his rifle. Years later the man wrote Chamberlain of that day and moment.

> I want to tell you of a little passage in the battle of Round Top, Gettysburg, concerning you and me, which I am now glad of. Twice in that fight, I had your life in my hands. I got a safe place between two rocks and drew bead fair and square on you. You were standing in the open behind the center of your line, fully exposed. I knew your rank by your uniform and your actions, and I thought it a mighty good thing to put you out of the way. I rested my gun on the rock and took steady aim. I started to pull the trigger, but some queer notion stopped me. Then I got ashamed of my weakness and went through the same motions again. I had you, perfectly certain. But that same queer something sat right down on me. I couldn't pull the trigger and gave it up, that is, your life. I am glad of it now, and hope you are.

> A member of the Fifteenth Alabama.[57]

Despite his brush with death and the tide of battle turning in favor of the Confederacy, Chamberlain was unmoved. He continued to motivate his men by walking up and down the line, encouraging them to fight on. Who could have guessed that this humble Maine professor would be made of such mettle?

The courage displayed that day was but a manifestation of a deeper personal moral courage and character. As a Christian, Chamberlain lived his life with purpose and self-discipline. He strove to uphold the ideals that set Christians apart. Daily choosing to do what was morally right throughout his life, Chamberlain became a man of courage long before the battle at Gettysburg. As he said: "War is for the participants a test of character; it makes bad men worse and good men better."[58] It wasn't difficult for him to perform noble things on the battlefield when he had developed the habit of nobility in his personal life.

> The lesson impressed on me as I stand here . . . is that in a great, momentous struggle . . . it is character that tells. I do not mean simply nor chiefly bravery. Many a man has that . . . what I mean by character is a firm and seasoned substance of soul. . . . We know not of the future, and cannot plan for it much. But we can hold our spirits and our bodies so pure and high, we may cherish such thoughts and such ideals, and dream such dreams of lofty purpose, that we can determine and know what manner of men we will be whenever and wherever the hour strikes, that calls to noble action. This predestination God has given into our charge. No man becomes suddenly different from his habit and cherished thought. We carry our accustomed manners with us.[59]

In addition to the Twentieth Maine's mounting casualties, Chamberlain soon faced another serious concern. As he peered through the smoke, he saw more Confederate units arriving and beginning to move against the undefended area on Chamberlain's left. From all evidence, it appeared the Confederates were about to attack Chamberlain simultaneously from the front, side, and rear. If this happened the Twentieth Maine would be defeated.

To contend with this threat, Chamberlain ordered his regiment to assume an L-shaped formation. With this formation, he was able to meet the first three successive Confederate attacks against his front and flank. However, like an incoming tide, the Confederates gained ground with each attack. By the fourth attack, it was clear that the Twentieth Maine could not endure. With 136 of his 386 men down and the remainder nearly out of ammunition,[60] the end was now almost a foregone conclusion. Chamberlain had fought valiantly and with skill. But no army could fight without ammunition . . . or could they?

Realizing the severity of the situation, Chamberlain looked at his remaining men and later recorded that moment:

> Not a moment was about to be lost! Five minutes more of such a defensive and the last roll call would sound for us! Desperate as the chances were, there was nothing for it but to take the offensive. I stepped to the colors. The men turned toward me. One word was enough, "Bayonets!" It caught like fire and swept along the ranks. The men took it up with a shout, one could not say, whether from the pit, or the song of the morning star! It was vain to order "Forward." No mortal could have heard it in the mighty hosanna that was singing the sky. Nor would he wait to hear. There are things still as of the first creation, "whose seed is in itself." The grating clash of steel in fixing bayonets told its own story; the color rose in front; the whole line quivered for the start; the edge of the left-wing rippled, swung, tossed among the rocks, straightened, changed curve from scimitar to sickle-shape; and the bristling archers swooped down upon the serried host—down into the face of a thousand! Two hundred men![61]

The Confederates were stunned by this mass of men charging at them from the hills above, all the while shouting, throwing rocks, and pointing their empty guns and steely bayonets. The numerically superior Confederate forces facing Chamberlain first broke, then ran. The Union's left flank was now secure, and the tide of battle, deadlocked until now, turned in favor the North.

With resolute faith, Chamberlain stood firm upon the solid foundation of Jesus Christ as the fierce battle raged around him.[62]

Outnumbered, outflanked, and out of ammunition, Chamberlain refused to yield. He had committed himself to God's trustworthy hands and so could muster such inspirational courage. The bayonet charge into a numerically superior foe went against all conventional wisdom, yet the audacity so surprised the advancing Alabama regiments that it caused them to flee. With two hundred men and their bayonets, against a thousand loaded rifles, Chamberlain engraved his faith and deeds for the generations.

RED SKIES TODAY

*The price of freedom has always been
paid for by the few to benefit the many—
from Calvary to Checkpoint Charlie—
from the Revolutionary War to the present
war. The cost has always been too high.
The currency, always blood.*

*Now we are engaged in a great struggle
for no less than our continued survival as
the clouds of war gather. Many are
watching to see whether we will rise up
and defend the blessings of freedom for
ourselves and a generation yet unborn.
Courage is the call in this hour, and
freedom will be its fruit for those with
brave hearts under today's red skies.*

ONE CORRIDOR AWAY

★

COL. PENNY BAILEY, U.S. AIR FORCE

*Because he has set his love upon Me, therefore I will
deliver him; I will set him on high, because he has
known My name.* (Psalm 91:14, NKJV)

As a young girl raised in the South, I was taught all the proper manners and etiquette of a lady. So when I announced to my family that I felt led to serve God and country by joining the air force, it came as quite a shock. Needless to say, the military was a big change from what I was accustomed to, and I had a lot of adjustments to make. Through a lot of prayer and guidance, God has blessed me tremendously while I serve Him and my country.

My military supervisors immediately recognized my training in etiquette and put me to work in protocol for various senior military leaders. In protocol, we are responsible for planning, coordinating, and implementing plans for distinguished visitors to this country and for executing various ceremonies and special events.

During the past several years I've served as the deputy director of protocol for the chairman and vice chairman of the Joint Chiefs of Staff—the highest ranking general officers in the United States Armed Services. I was excited and greatly honored by the selection; however, I was very nervous about working in the Pentagon and living in Washington, D.C. I had never been to a city that large, nor had I worked so closely with political leaders. The first week on duty set the stage for the level of dignitaries I would meet throughout my assignment: I planned visits for actress Connie Stephens, Senator John Glenn, and astronaut Buzz Aldren. The office I worked in was directly across the hall from the vice chairman's office, which put me in daily contact with him and his staff.

My husband is a military physician also assigned to the Pentagon. On September 11, 2001, he and I drove into work about 6:30. At about seven o'clock, our youngest daughter called me at work and told me she was too sick to go to school. This is a girl who loves school, so I knew she must be feeling pretty bad—so my plan was to finish up early and get home to her.

I had one appointment that day, to show an air force major general where he could hold a conference in the Pentagon. When the general arrived, I escorted him to the opposite side of the building and showed him the army's conference rooms. We walked farther down a hall. The general turned to go even farther into the army corridor, when I suddenly heard myself saying, "Sir, I need to get back to my office."

I was so surprised at what I had said that I began mentally searching for what had prompted me. I concluded that it must be because I needed to check on my daughter. There was a great urgency inside me as we quickly walked back together. As we entered the door of my office, there was a loud noise and commotion outside. I went out to see what was going on and found people running down the hall. I grabbed someone to ask what was going on, and learned that there had been an explosion in the building. Since we were all aware of the attacks at the World Trade Center, I immediately told my supervisor, and we cleared out of our office.

I stayed in the building for some time helping out as I was able. The first thing I noticed in our area of the building was that all the phone lines were ringing. So when there was time, I answered phone calls and called family members of the staff to let them know that their loved ones were all right. As arrangements were made to deploy key staff personnel, the Chairman and the Secretary of Defense to a restricted site, I continued to assist until all the staff personnel were on the helicopters. Then I left the area and began to look for my husband, Jim.

It was amazing to see that in spite of the chaos, confusion, and fear that terrible morning, there were selfless acts of courage and kindness. One senior officer related,

A man at the top of a narrow stairwell noticed a woman waiting in a wheelchair. He picked her up and called out to those behind him, "Someone bring her chair."

A voice from the top of stairs called out, "I've got it." At the bottom of the stairs the woman was placed back in her chair—that had been carried down by an army general.

Everywhere you looked, people were pitching in and doing whatever was required. I headed out to the front lawn of the Pentagon where I was told the medical personnel had set up. Not finding Jim there, I asked if there were another medical unit setup and was told to try the center courtyard. So I headed back into the building, which was now filled with smoke, and made my way to the courtyard.

I walked all around five acres and found no trace of Jim or anyone else from his clinic. Again, I inquired if there was any other location where medical personnel were located and discovered that a few were at the crash site. Determined, I focused on the black smoke billowing into the air. I had to work my way through police, firemen, Pentagon personnel, and media, but two hours later I found him. He was at the crash site, working away on wounded and injured there.

We stayed with the medical group until 8 P.M. However, other than a couple of people my husband took care of immediately after the attack, there were no other patients. The explosions were too significant, the smoke too toxic, and the fire too hot for many survivors. We finally headed home to our three children, who were anxiously waiting for us.

In the shock and disbelief of it all, I didn't think about the preceding minutes before the crash until a week later. Then, as I began to replay what I had been doing at the time of the attack, I realized that the air force general and I had been on the side of the Pentagon where the airplane hit—just one corridor away.

I wondered about my surviving that day when so many others perished. It seemed I had been divinely blessed, and yet I felt uncomfortable about it. A friend who has lived through several combat near-misses wrote to me about how he deals with it.

Each of us who survives such things must at some point ask the question, "Why and for what purpose? Why me and not those others who were equally deserving of life? How can I live with 'living' without feeling such incredible guilt?"

I ask because I must continue to ask, because I have survived—not well, not completely, yet here I am. Having
looked into the silent mask of a child's face in the aftermath
of a café bomb, I wondered, Wasn't there more she could
have offered in life than in death—at least more than me?
Yet there I was, standing as a silent sentinel as they
wrapped her in cloth and carried her away.

In the end, all of my questions remain, and none is
answered. I have chosen to safely deposit them into His
hands for safekeeping until I can ask Him one day in person. Until then, I have to live with surviving.

I didn't need to call my daughter that day; I needed to get out
of the area. That strong urge for me to get back to my office was
God protecting me and the general who was with me. I believe
He had my daughter stay home from school so I would feel a
need to check on her. I had no idea at the time there was any danger. But God knew—and even when I didn't even know I needed
Him, He was there.

I think He was also there that day for those who didn't survive—for those who were delivered into His presence. Like my
friend, I have begun to learn to live with surviving, and make
each of my God-given days count—every single one of them.

AFTER THE TERROR— HOW SHALL WE LIVE?

★

COLONEL JEFFREY O'LEARY, U.S. AIR FORCE (RET)

Be strong and of good courage; do not be afraid, nor be dismayed, for the LORD your God is with you wherever you go. (Joshua 1:9b, NKJV)

I watched in silent horror as the black plumes ascended into the face of the blazing mid-day sun. The smoke twisted and curled, making black wreaths out of the ashes of the innocent, ascending by the thousands into the face of God. I wondered how much hate it took before one could so callously summon the voracious appetite of death. And then I remembered. I had been here before. Not standing outside the Pentagon as it burned or watching with eyes glued to the horror in Manhattan, but on the streets of Jerusalem, where I first faced this shadowy specter as a peacekeeper in the summer of 1990.

The air was cool as a light breeze ruffled the leaves on the trees that hovered above me. I opened the morning edition of the Jerusalem Post as I sat outside a café in Ben Yehuda shopping mall near the Old City. The air held a tinge of fragrance from the small pots of flowers that had been carefully placed around the stone walkways. Even at this early hour, the outdoor shopping mall was filled with tourists looking for souvenirs. I was in no such rush for bargains or trinkets to show I had been to Jerusalem. I was not a visitor but a peacekeeper stationed in Israel, one of about a thousand peacekeepers assigned to Israel, Egypt, Syria, and Lebanon in the early 1990s.

I smelled the fresh bread being prepared for Shabbat at a bakery across the street. I made it a habit each Friday to walk down to the local merchant and purchase hot bread as it was pulled from the ancient ovens. I pulled a piece from a loaf and read the recounting of yesterday's news in Israel and America. I cautiously picked up my glass of Turkish coffee with my thumb and forefinger. The coffee, served in small clear glasses, was so hot one could barely sip it. It was potent enough to awaken the weariest traveler who had stayed up too late the night before sampling the pleasures of the city.

I looked across the mall at the tourists seated there and chuckled as they burned their mouths and hands trying to manage the sizzling drink. Israeli soldiers patrolled the shopping mall in groups of two, semi-automatic weapons slung over their shoulders. They were casually observant as they watched for signs of unusual activity or trouble. It was a strange sight for someone from America—military troops in the streets—but it didn't faze the Israelis or the Palestinians. It was just another day in Jerusalem.

Across from me and down three doorways was another café packed with weary tourists who had dropped their packages and sat down to rest and refresh themselves. I watched them relaxing and enjoying themselves under the trees that sheltered their tables, talking excitedly in various languages about their morning's purchases and the sights they had experienced.

In a loud voice a man at a table suddenly called out to another who was running from the café. Then someone else called out, and I looked up to see a lot of people trying to leave that café. I got up from where I was seated to see what the commotion was. Others started to run, but it was too late. The morning peace exploded in a cataclysm of violence. For some, everything changed forever that day when the blue skies turned red and the marketplace was covered with debris and blood. Children, like fallen sparrows, lay still, and smoke from the burning café ascended slowly into the heavens.

It seemed to me to be a strange war—a war without clarity, without ranks, uniforms, or leaders. This war was made in shadows and darkness, where murder without remorse stalked a people unaware. This wasn't a war of the present but a war of the past, where ancient animosities were dug up like corpses and held up so all could rage against the injustice. Consuming the daily bread of hatred, these people poisoned their future and the hope of their children. And when this hatred had filled that land, it looked to the West with the same voracious hunger and fell from the sky on an early September morning eleven years later. And the black smoke ascended from the funeral pyres of our children. And for the first time in many years, we as a nation began to pray.

I stumbled away from both scenes, numbed by the horror and visage of death. And still hatred and homicide are not satisfied as this savage war rages. I've watched as the number of human bombs increased while the ages of the bombers decreased. Now children have been infected with death's wish for their own demise. I wondered how they could understand the destruction they were calling down upon themselves and their fellow human beings. To walk in the marketplace after the bombing, amid the crying and screaming of those not yet dead, would give even those with the most callous conscience pause for reflection. I read as a physicist tried to explain what occurs when one of these bombs detonates.

An average bomb—the kind strapped around a . . . terrorist's waist, covered by a shirt—would likely detonate at a rate of about 28,000 feet per second—or about 22 times faster than a 9 mm bullet leaving the muzzle of a handgun. That means the surrounding air pressure—normally 15 pounds per square inch—would spike to 2,200 pounds per square inch. Such heat and pressure will melt iron. A person sitting near-by would feel, momentarily, a shock wave slamming into his or her body with an "overpressure" of 300,000 pounds. Such a blast would crush the chest, rupture liver, spleen, heart and lungs, melt eyes, pull organs away from surround-ing tissues, separate hands from arms and feet from legs. Bodies would fly through the air or be impaled on the jagged edges of crumpled metal and broken glass.

The wounded from such an event are horrifically injured by thousands of small pieces of nails and screws. In the news, only the bomber and the dead are ever mentioned. But what of those who survive—the walking wounded? What about the parents and relatives who lose their children, in

Jerusalem or in Washington or New York City? There are precious few words that can adequately describe what it is like to survive the aftereffects of such an event.

FIRST COMES SHOCK

Isn't that how things happen in our lives? We are in the moment, in the experience of the pleasures of God's creation, and something intrudes with terrible consequences. We didn't ask for it, we may not have even contributed to it, and yet our lives are changed—permanently, sometimes irreparably.

You're sitting in your office, perhaps an office like mine at the Pentagon or fifty stories up in the city of New York. Without warning, an airplane flying three hundred miles per hour slices into the building like a hot knife into soft butter, and the safety of the world you once knew disintegrates like breadcrumbs. Perhaps it's a ringing phone that brings the devastating news that a parent, spouse, sibling, or child has been killed in such an attack.

You didn't ask for these things. In fact, had you known they were about to occur, you would have prayed and pleaded with God for His mercy. You stumble through the next day and the day after that. A car backfires and you jump. The news on the television set blares about a similar event, and you start to shake and your heart beats as though you just ran a hundred-yard dash.

You move through the day as though walking through a thick marsh; each moment and each movement seem almost surreal. Time passes, and you can't remember how much you've used and how much you have left. A friend says hello to you three times before you realize someone is talking to you. You live in a new world called shock and confusion and move more slowly than everyone around you.

Your world has changed, and you can't find the words to describe it. And more than anything, you feel completely alienated from all those things you once knew and held dear. Even those closest to you seem far away, as though an invisible shield has come between you and them. You mind seems to be stuck, like a broken gear or a frozen computer, and you can't figure out how to get it going again.

THEN COMES ANGER

You want to strike back. You ask a thousand questions. Who could have done this? I wonder who could have the heart to willingly murder children and people who have no relation, other than by birth, to someone's ancient grudge. When a young girl of seventeen smiles and pulls a detonator cord from her waist, how can you find words to explain it? How can you turn away from hatred if she has killed someone you love? Those who survive combat or random acts of terror, live on with broken bodies as well as broken hearts.

In my year serving in Israel and Egypt, I saw the aftereffects of two car bombs and survived thirty-nine missiles that Iraq fired at Israel during the Gulf War. My friends call me "lucky," but sometimes I feel great guilt. Why did I survive when so many others, equally deserving of life, die? You wonder if it is okay to feel happy, knowing that friends or loved ones perished. And when the anger subsides, you begin to search for meaning—for some semblance or logic or rationality among all the madness.

THEN, PERHAPS, COMES UNDERSTANDING

I spent six months in the Sinai in a jeep patrolling vast quantities of sand on the eastern side of the Suez Canal. Part of our aim was to spread good will wherever possible. In this region, it was the custom of the desert to offer tea to those passing by. So it was with this mindset that I stopped at a Bedouin camp I passed on a late summer afternoon.

I was greeted warmly and escorted into a large tent where I was served a glass of hot tea by one of the men. I carefully held the hot glass between my thumb and first finger to keep it from burning my hand. My calluses weren't as thick as my hosts, and the heat on my fingers kept my attention. My host surprised me by speaking fairly comprehensible English, which I appreciated since my Arabic was quite limited.

As we neared the end of our tea, our conversation took an interesting turn. My host pointed at another Bedouin across the camp and said, "Do you see that man over there tending the camels?"

I looked and said, "Yes."

"He's a camel thief," he said with disgust in his voice.

I was surprised. "Why do you have a camel thief tending your camels?"

He ignored my question and said, "He comes from a long line of camel thieves. His father was a camel thief, his grandfather— they're all camel thieves. In fact, he's stolen my family's camels."

I thought about this for a while, confused. "Well, if he stole your camels, why don't you just go get them back?"

He replied with less volume, "Well, it happened long ago."

I drank the rest of my tea and pondered his statement. Now I was really confused. Another question, though, and I'd be on dangerous ground. My mind danced between practicing diplomacy and satisfying my curiosity. Curiosity won out.

"How long ago did this happen?" I asked carefully.

My host spit out, "Eight hundred years, but he's still a camel thief, and so is his entire family!"

And with that, he got up and stormed across the camp. I watched him trail away in the dust and looked at the other men sitting in the circle. They avoided my eyes and stared at their feet. I took this to mean our conversation and teatime had ended.

I mounted my jeep and was struck by the realization that peace would be a long time coming to the Middle East. If such hatred was harbored within the same Bedouin tribe, how much more was nourished between Arab and Jew?

There is enough anger and memory in much of the world to fuel war for a thousand years. The Chinese have a saying, "Before setting out on revenge, first dig two graves." I don't think that proverb captures the true destructiveness of hatred. From my experience, I would say, "Hatred turns on all who welcome it; in time it will murder you as well as those you love."

There is an enduring power of hate to destroy from one generation to the next. If it is not madness to destroy your own children, then I'm sure I don't know what madness is. I read one mother's account as she spoke of her desire for her son to kill himself for the sake of "the cause."

I am a compassionate mother to my children and they are compassionate to me and take care of me. Because I love my son, I encouraged him to die a martyr's death for the sake of (my god). I sacrificed (my son) as part of my obligation. This is an easy thing. . . . The happiness in this world is an incomplete happiness; eternal happiness is life in the world to come, through martyrdom. (My god) be praised, my son has attained this happiness. . . I asked (my god) to give me 10 (of the enemy) for my son, and (my god) granted my request and (my son) made his dream come true, killing 10 (of the enemy civilians) and soldiers. Our god honored him even more, in that there were many (of the enemy) wounded. Then (my son's) brother came to me and told me of (my son's) death. I began to cry, (My god) is the greatest, and prayed and thanked (my god) for the success of the operation.[63]

There have always been gods and religions that have called upon man to murder and hate. In the Old Testament, the religion of Baal called upon parents to sacrifice their children in fire. But our God calls us to life. He calls us to lay down our lives daily and follow His example. This is far more difficult than killing ourselves and others around us.

I've seen enough hatred to fill a lifetime of nightmares. Senator Bob Dole, who was severely wounded in World War II, said, "Each veteran has his own war, which lives on in midnight memories and flashbacks."[64] It isn't a sleep I would wish upon another.

When we awaken to find we have survived when others equally deserving have not, we must somehow find the courage to face the day and move forward. The memories and pain may seem as persistent and inconsolable as the grief of Rachel's tears. But like Paul, I will try to say, "One thing I do; forgetting those things which are behind and reaching forward to those things which are ahead, I press toward the goal for the prize of the upward call of God in Christ Jesus" (Philippians 3:13b-14 NKJV). I don't know if I will succeed, but I must try.

AND THEN COMES RESOLVE

We must ask ourselves as a people, "Do we believe that what we have in blessings and liberty is worth preserving and handing down to a succeeding generation? Do we believe someone else will fight for us, if we ourselves will not sacrifice our comfort?"

The generation of our founding fathers faced a very similar situation as they decided to break from England and fight for independence. They knew it would cost them dearly, yet one after another stepped forward at the cost of their lives, their families, and their fortunes. Can we do any less today against a merciless enemy? If there will be peace on earth, it must be bought with the price of our sacrifice and must begin with determined resolve in the quietness of our hearts.

While we as a nation fight against those who bring evil against us, I believe Jesus calls upon me to lay down the sword of my own heart's desire for revenge. What we must do as a nation to ensure our security and freedom does not mean I should despise those that have set themselves against me. That they must pay dearly for the bitter choices of their leaders will be penalty enough. By laying down the sword of personal hatred, I take away its power to destroy me and my children to come.

I no longer search for reason within the madness. I can find no sanity in those who would turn the faces of children into ashes while we watch their black wreaths of smoke ascend into the sky. I only know there is good, and there is evil—and if we would live, evil must be defeated.

Looking into the eyes of my five children is reason enough to stand up in this hour of freedom's testing. We have every reason to be encouraged. His Word is eternal. As he promised Joshua of old, so He promises to be with us, even in time of war. We are called to serve with courage, and as people of the great "I AM"— with Brave Hearts under Red Skies.

And then comes Hope.

BROKEN LIVES UNDER RED SKIES

HELPING HOMELESS AND ORPHANED CHILDREN

★

I've seen some of the horror of war and the tragedy of the victims it leaves behind. I pray you were deeply moved as you read the stories of children who survived the Holocaust and those, in our own budding nation, who survived captivity in the French and Indian wars.

A dozen years ago, while traveling in India, I saw overwhelming numbers of homeless and orphaned children and decided I couldn't walk away from such a scene.

The war, or "red skies," these children faced was as real as any shooting war. It was a battle for survival, a daily battle for the basic necessities of life: food, water, clothing, shelter, and medical care. So I opened my first orphanage in 1990 in eastern India.

I started small, taking fifteen orphaned children into our care in a rented building. God blessed our humble beginnings and faithful efforts. Today we have hundreds of children growing up to adulthood instead of dying as children. Our ministry, Mission of Joy, currently has four orphanages and feeds thousands of meals to hungry children every week. We provide around-the-clock care and education for children who were considered "untouchable."

In spite of our efforts, we continue to be besieged by children at the gates of our facilities. As such, we are always in need of additional sponsors to help us heal the hurting and reach more who are near the brink of death. The cost to do such mighty things is very modest, if we would share our abundant blessings.

If you would like to participate or learn more about our work among homeless and orphaned children in India, please check out our Web site at www.missionjoy.org. Your may also write me through the e-mail address below. Mission of Joy is a recognized nonprofit organization in the United States.

I couldn't walk away from the sight of so many children in such incredible need when I had the ability to do something. I pray the same is true for you. God bless you.

> Col. Jeff O'Leary (Ret.)
> Founder and Director, Mission of Joy
> www.jeffoleary.com

For information on scheduling Colonel O'Leary to speak for your event, please contact Speak Up Speaker Services toll free at (888) 870-7719 or e-mail speakupinc@aol.com.

ENDNOTES

★

[1]Bob Boardman, *Unforgettable Men in Unforgettable Times*: (Surprise AZ, Selah Publishing Group, 1998), 54.

[2]*Reporting World War II, Part Two: American Journalism 1944-1946* (New York: The Library of America, 1995), 510, 512.

[3]Fifty-three years after this event, Captain Day was recognized for his heroic actions and awarded the Medal of Honor.

[4]Boardman, 198. Note *"Colonel Yahara to US interrogators after the war"* (Originally cited in James H. Hallas, *Killing Ground on Okinawa;* Westport, Conn.: Praeger Publishers, 1996, 17).

[5]George Feifer, *Tennozan: The Battle of Okinawa and the Atomic Bomb* (New York: Ticknor & Fields, 1992), 502.

[6]Feifer, 505.

[7]Feifer, 507.

[8]Woodrow Wilson, *War Messages*, 65th Cong., 1st Sess. Senate Doc. No. 5, Serial No. 7264, Washington, D.C., 1917; 3-8, passim.

[9]John McCrae, *In Flanders Fields and Other Poems, With an Essay in Character by Sir Andrew Macphail* (Toronto: William Briggs; New York: G. P. Putnam's Sons, 1919), 3.

[10]Richard Wheeler, ed., *Sergeant York and the Great War* (Bulverde, Tex.: Mantle Ministries, 1998) , 154-155.

[11]"Sgt. Alvin C. York's Diary," <http://volweb.utk.edu/school/York/diary.html> , downloaded 18 October 2001.

[12]Gerald York, grandson of Alvin York, Presidio of Monterey, Calif., April 1996.

[13]Wheeler, 58-60.

[14]Romans 13.

[15]Wheeler, 68.

[16]Wheeler, 72.

[17]Wheeler, 79-82.

[18]Wheeler, 81-82.

[19]Gladys Williams, Alvin C. York biography, <http://volweb.utk.edu/Schools/York/biography.html>, downloaded 18 October 2001.

[20]Wheeler, 158.

[21]"The Diary of Alvin York," <http://acacia.pair.com/Acacia.Vignettes/The.Diary.of.Alvin.York.html>, downloaded 18 October 2001.

[22]Leonard Roy Frank, ed., *Random House Webster's Quotationary* (New York: Random House: 1999), 948.

[23]Frank, 949.

[24]Frank, 292.

[25]Frank, 950.

[26]Frank, 365.

[27]"Eichmann's Own Story: Part II," *Life,* 5 December 1960.

[28]Frank, 367.

[29]Frank, 904.

[30]Frank, 905.

[31]The Regimental Support Squadron (RSS) provides the regiment with logistical support, or

as we called it, the "beans and bullets."

[32]Ur is the ancient town where Abraham once lived before his migration to the Holy Land. One of our chaplains, James White, was very familiar with the ruins and guided thousands of U.S. soldiers through them.

[33]Former U.S. Marine Corps Commandant Charles Krulak also testifies of this event and the significant role it played in blunting Saddam's plans to use chemical weapons.

[34]These two were the Hammurabi and Medina Republican Guard armored divisions, both of which saved Saddam's regime during the Kurdish and Shiite civil war that shook Iraq after Desert Storm.

[35]*God's Little Devotional Book for Men* (Colorado Springs: Honor Books, 1996), 69.

[36]Ibid.

[37]Japanese fighter aircraft, designated "zeros" by the Allies because of the large zeros on their wings and body that were colored in bright red (like the Japanese flag).

[38]Charles Hembree, *From Pearl Harbor to the Pulpit* (Akron, Ohio: R. Humbard, 1975), 95.

[39]Jacob DeShazer, *Fuchida Remembererd* (Tokyo: Japan Harvest, 1975), 18.

[40]John Toland, *Rising Sun, Vol. 1* (New York: Random House, 1970), 386.

[41]Hembree, 37.

[42]Hembree, 39.

[43]Hembree, 40-41.

[44]Hembree, 43.

[45]Hembree, 99-100.

[46]DeShazer, 19.

[47]Colonel George Washington miraculously survived this war, following a battle in which he later found four bullet holes in his coat. (For a complete account of this episode see the story *Summer Escape: Col. George Washington, Beloved Enemy* in the book *Taking the High Ground* [Colorado Springs: Victor Books, 2001], 27-29*).

[48]Verna M. Hall and Rosalie J. Slater, *The Bible and the Constitution of the United States of America* (San Francisco: Foundation for American Christian Education, 1983), 31.

[49]Washington, George. June 1, 1774, in an entry in his diary. See also: E.C. M'guire, *The Religious Opinions and Character of Washington* (1836), 142. (E.C. M'Guire was the son-in-law of Mr. Robert Lewis, Washington's nephew and private secretary); William J. Johnson, *George Washington—The Christian* (St. Paul, MN: William J. Johnson, Merriam Park, February 23, 1919; Nashville, TN: Abingdon Press, 1919; reprinted Milford, MI: Mott Media, 1976; reprinted Arlington Heights, IL: Christian Liberty Press, 502 West Euclid Avenue, Arlington Heights, Illinois, 60004, 1992), 62; and John Eidsmoe, *Christianity and The Constitution—The Faith of Our Founding Fathers* (Baker Book House, 1987), 136.

[50]Washington, George. July 4, 1775, in his General Orders from the Headquarters at Cambridge. See also: Jared Sparks, ed., *The Writings of George Washington,* 12 vols. (Boston: American Stationer's Company, 1837, NY: F. Andrew's, 1834-1847), Vol. III, 491; William J. Johnson, *George Washington—The Christian* (St. Paul, MN: William J. Johnson, Merriam Park, February 23, 1919; Nashville, TN: Abingdon Press, 1919; reprinted Milford, MI: Mott Media, 1976; reprinted Arlington Heights, IL: Christian Liberty Press, 502 West Euclid Avenue, Arlington Heights, Illinois, 60004, 1992), 69-70; John Clement Fitzpatrick, ed., *The Writings of George Washington*, from the Original Manuscript Sources 1749-1799, 39 vols. (Washington, D.C.: United States Government Printing Office, 1931-1944), Vol. III, 309; William Barclay Allen, ed., *George Washington - A Collection* (Indianapolis: Liberty Classics, Liberty Fund, Inc., 7440 N. Shadeland, Indianapolis, Indiana 46250, 1988; based almost entirely on materials reproduced from The Writings of George Washington from the original manuscript sources, 1745-1799/John Clement Fitzpatrick, editor), 42-43; Norman Cousins, *In God We Trust—The Religious Beliefs and Ideas of the American Founding Fathers* (NY: Harper & Brothers, 1958), 50; Peter Marshall and David Manuel, *The Light and the Glory* (Old Tappan, NJ: Fleming H.

Revell Company, 1977), 289; Saxe Commins, ed., *The Basic Writings of George Washington* (NY: Random House, 1948), 122; *The American Vision - 360 Years Later* (Atlanta, GA: The American Vision, Inc., 1980), 10-11; John Eidsmoe, *Christianity and the Constitution - The Faith of Our Founding Fathers* (Grand Rapids, MI: Baker Book House, A Mott Media Book, 1987, 6th printing 1993), 116; Peter Marshall & David Manuel, *The Glory of America* (Bloomington, MN: Garborg's Heart 'N Home, 1991), 7.5.

[51]Peter Marshall and David Manuel, *The Light and the Glory,* (New Jersey: Fleming H. Revell Co., 1977), 319-326. Used with permission.

[52]Philip Van Doren Stern, ed., *The Life and Writings of Abraham Lincoln,* (New York: Random House, 1940), 752-53.

[53]Joshua Lawrence Chamberlain, "Through Blood and Fire at Gettysburg," *The Gettysburg Magazine*, January 1992, 48.

[54]Alice Trulock, *In the Hands of Providence* (Chapel Hill, N.C.: University of North Carolina Press, 1992), 215.

[55]Willard M.Wallace, *Soul of the Lion: A Biography of General Joshua L. Chamberlain* (New York: Thomas Nelson & Sons, 1960; reprint, Gettysburg, Penn: Stan Clark Military Books, 1991).

[56]Joshua L. Chamberlain, *Through Blood and Fire at Gettysburg: My Experiences with the 20th Maine Regiment on Little Round Top* (Gettysburg, Penn.: Stan Clark Military Books, 1994).

[57]Joshua Lawrence Chamberlain, "Through Blood and Fire at Gettysburg," *The Gettysburg Magazine*, January 1992, 52.

[58]Trulock, 340.

[59]Joshua L. Chamberlain, address, 20th Maine monument dedication, 1889, <http://users.ids.net/~tandem/joshua.htm>, downloaded 22 October 2001.

[60]Robert N. Scott, [ed.], *The War of the Rebellion: A Compilation of the Official Records of the Union and Confederate Armies*, Series I, Volume XXVII, Part I (Reports), (Washington, D.C.: Government Printing Office, 1889), 626.

[61]Joshua Lawrence Chamberlain, "Through Blood and Fire at Gettysburg," *The Gettysburg Magazine*, January 1992, 55.

[62]The 20th Maine was down to 386 men before the battle. This includes the 120 from the 2nd Maine Regiment who "joined" Chamberlain before the battle. See Scott, 615-30.

[63]*The Hideous Physics of the 'Suicide State'* The Washington Times, Friday June 21, 2002, page A-4.

[64]Life, "The Power and the Glory", April 29, 2002, 11.